BETTER BUSINESS DECISIONS FROM DATA

STATISTICAL ANALYSIS FOR
PROFESSIONAL SUCCESS

Peter Kenny

Apress®

Better Business Decisions from Data: Statistical Analysis for Professional Success

Copyright © 2014 by Peter Kenny

This work is subject to copyright. All rights are reserved by the Publisher, whether the whole or part of the material is concerned, specifically the rights of translation, reprinting, reuse of illustrations, recitation, broadcasting, reproduction on microfilms or in any other physical way, and transmission or information storage and retrieval, electronic adaptation, computer software, or by similar or dissimilar methodology now known or hereafter developed. Exempted from this legal reservation are brief excerpts in connection with reviews or scholarly analysis or material supplied specifically for the purpose of being entered and executed on a computer system, for exclusive use by the purchaser of the work. Duplication of this publication or parts thereof is permitted only under the provisions of the Copyright Law of the Publisher's location, in its current version, and permission for use must always be obtained from Springer. Permissions for use may be obtained through RightsLink at the Copyright Clearance Center. Violations are liable to prosecution under the respective Copyright Law.

ISBN-13 (pbk): 978-1-4842-0185-5

ISBN-13 (electronic): 978-1-4842-0184-8

Trademarked names, logos, and images may appear in this book. Rather than use a trademark symbol with every occurrence of a trademarked name, logo, or image we use the names, logos, and images only in an editorial fashion and to the benefit of the trademark owner, with no intention of infringement of the trademark.

The use in this publication of trade names, trademarks, service marks, and similar terms, even if they are not identified as such, is not to be taken as an expression of opinion as to whether or not they are subject to proprietary rights.

While the advice and information in this book are believed to be true and accurate at the date of publication, neither the authors nor the editors nor the publisher can accept any legal responsibility for any errors or omissions that may be made. The publisher makes no warranty, express or implied, with respect to the material contained herein.

> Publisher: Heinz Weinheimer
> Acquisitions Editor: Jeff Olson
> Developmental Editor: Robert Hutchinson
> Editorial Board: Steve Anglin, Mark Beckner, Ewan Buckingham, Gary Cornell, Louise Corrigan, James DeWolf, Jonathan Gennick, Jonathan Hassell, Robert Hutchinson, Michelle Lowman, James Markham, Matthew Moodie, Jeff Olson, Jeffrey Pepper, Douglas Pundick, Ben Renow-Clarke, Dominic Shakeshaft, Gwenan Spearing, Matt Wade, Steve Weiss
> Coordinating Editor: Rita Fernando
> Copy Editor: Tiffany Taylor
> Compositor: SPi Global
> Indexer: SPi Global
> Cover Designer: Anna Ishchenko

Distributed to the book trade worldwide by Springer Science+Business Media New York, 233 Spring Street, 6th Floor, New York, NY 10013. Phone 1-800-SPRINGER, fax (201) 348-4505, e-mail `orders-ny@springer-sbm.com`, or visit `www.springeronline.com`. Apress Media, LLC is a California LLC and the sole member (owner) is Springer Science + Business Media Finance Inc (SSBM Finance Inc). SSBM Finance Inc is a Delaware corporation.

For information on translations, please e-mail `rights@apress.com`, or visit `www.apress.com`.

Apress and friends of ED books may be purchased in bulk for academic, corporate, or promotional use. eBook versions and licenses are also available for most titles. For more information, reference our Special Bulk Sales–eBook Licensing web page at `www.apress.com/bulk-sales`.

Any source code or other supplementary materials referenced by the author in this text is available to readers at `www.apress.com`. For detailed information about how to locate your book's source code, go to `www.apress.com/source-code/`.

Apress Business: The Unbiased Source of Business Information

Apress business books provide essential information and practical advice, each written for practitioners by recognized experts. Busy managers and professionals in all areas of the business world—and at all levels of technical sophistication—look to our books for the actionable ideas and tools they need to solve problems, update and enhance their professional skills, make their work lives easier, and capitalize on opportunity.

Whatever the topic on the business spectrum—entrepreneurship, finance, sales, marketing, management, regulation, information technology, among others—Apress has been praised for providing the objective information and unbiased advice you need to excel in your daily work life. Our authors have no axes to grind; they understand they have one job only—to deliver up-to-date, accurate information simply, concisely, and with deep insight that addresses the real needs of our readers.

It is increasingly hard to find information—whether in the news media, on the Internet, and now all too often in books—that is even-handed and has your best interests at heart. We therefore hope that you enjoy this book, which has been carefully crafted to meet our standards of quality and unbiased coverage.

We are always interested in your feedback or ideas for new titles. Perhaps you'd even like to write a book yourself. Whatever the case, reach out to us at editorial@apress.com and an editor will respond swiftly. Incidentally, at the back of this book, you will find a list of useful related titles. Please visit us at www.apress.com to sign up for newsletters and discounts on future purchases.

The Apress Business Team

Dedicated to Rosa and William, my two grandchildren, who, at some time in the future, may find a few useful tips among these pages.

Contents

Preface ix
About the Author xi
Acknowledgments xiii
Introduction xv

Part I: **Uncertainties** 1
Chapter 1:   The Scarcity of Certainty 3
Chapter 2:   Sources of Uncertainty 7
Chapter 3:   Probability 13

Part II: **Data** 23
Chapter 4:   Sampling 25
Chapter 5:   The Raw Data 33

Part III: **Samples** 45
Chapter 6:   Descriptive Data 47
Chapter 7:   Numerical Data 55

Part IV: **Comparisons** 87
Chapter 8:   Levels of Significance 89
Chapter 9:   General Procedure for Comparisons 91
Chapter 10: Comparisons with Numerical Data 93
Chapter 11: Comparisons with Descriptive Data 103
Chapter 12: Types of Error 115

Part V: **Relationships** 119
Chapter 13: Cause and Effect 121
Chapter 14: Relationships with Numerical Data 125
Chapter 15: Relationships with Descriptive Data 149
Chapter 16: Multivariate Data 155

Part VI: Forecasts 177

Chapter 17: Extrapolation 179
Chapter 18: Forecasting from Known Distributions 183
Chapter 19: Time Series 197
Chapter 20: Control Charts 205
Chapter 21: Reliability 211

Part VII: Big Data 219

Chapter 22: Data Mining 221
Chapter 23: Predictive Analytics 229
Chapter 24: Getting Involved with Big Data 243
Chapter 25: Concerns with Big Data 251
Appendix: References and Further Reading 257

Index 261

Preface

I am not a statistician, so it may seem odd that I have put together a book on statistics. Some explanation is required.

In my work, first as a research scientist and then as a manager of engineering departments, I needed to use basic statistics and to have some appreciation of the more complex statistical methods. With a limited education in statistics, I struggled to find textbooks that gave me what I needed concisely and in a way that I could readily understand. I have sympathy for those who find themselves in a similar situation. I have also worked for nearly twenty years as a private tutor, and the one-to-one contact with students has confirmed the difficulties that can arise in coming to grips with statistics.

In addition, I have sympathy for statisticians. They do an excellent job but they get a bad press. The general view is that they can fiddle around with numbers and prove anything they wish to prove. I feel concerned for the majority of the population who hold this general perception, and I would like to see them achieve a better understanding of statistics. We have figures thrown at us, supposedly proving statements ranging from the trivial to the life-threatening, and often contradictory, and this helps to reinforce the prejudices.

This book is the result of these experiences and concerns. It is the book I have dreamed of, the book I wanted and couldn't find many years ago. It is for those who want an understanding of basic statistics and an appreciation of more advanced methods. It is, as the title indicates, for decision makers—but not only for the decision makers in business and industry but also for each one of us struggling to make sense of the statistics forced on us daily in shops, in newspapers, and on television. The book is also in praise of statisticians and the work they do and seeks to bring a little more understanding and respect for statistics among the general public. It is a book to enjoy, not struggle with, written by someone who really does understand where the difficulties are.

—Peter Kenny
Lichfield, UK
kenny.peter@physics.org

About the Author

Peter Kenny, educated at Birmingham and Oxford Universities, was employed by the National Coal Board (later British Coal), first as a research scientist and then as manager of various engineering departments. At the time of his early retirement, he was British Coal's Reliability Manager. Since then, he has taught mathematics and science subjects at colleges of further education and as a private tutor. He is a Fellow of the Institute of Physics, Member of the Institute of Materials, a Chartered Physicist, and a Chartered Engineer. He has published many technical papers and general-interest articles. He holds the LAMDA Diploma in public speaking, which is also the subject of his book *A Handbook of Public Speaking for Scientists and Engineers*.

Acknowledgments

I would like to thank my wife, Joan, for supporting me throughout this project, particularly at times when it didn't seem worthwhile continuing and when she saw nothing of me for hours on end.

The team at Apress has been excellent, guiding me through the intricacies of present-day publishing. In particular, I am grateful to Jeff Olson, who discovered my manuscript and rescued it from obscurity. Thanks also to Robert Hutchinson, Rita Fernando, Jill Balzano, and Tiffany Taylor.

Introduction

The man who is denied the opportunities of taking decisions of importance begins to regard as important the decisions he is allowed to take. He becomes fussy about filing, keen on seeing that pencils are sharpened, eager to ensure that the windows are open (or shut) and apt to use two or three different-coloured inks.

—C. Northcote Parkinson

Statistics are not popular. One might even say they are disliked. Not by statisticians, of course, but by the millions who have to cope with the steady flow of statistics supporting all kinds of assertions, opinions, and theories. Received wisdom harrumphs, "You can prove anything by statistics"—and then sneers, "Lies, damned lies, and statistics." My sympathies do not lie with these sentiments, which, I believe, have their origins in the misuse of statistics. I believe that statisticians are skilled in their work and act professionally, sincerely desiring their results to be interpreted and used correctly. The misuse arises when statements by those who have limited understanding of the subject are claimed to be justified by statistics.

The misuse is frequently due to misunderstanding. Results of statistical investigations often have to be worded with many qualifications and precise definitions, and this does not ease the understanding of the casual reader. Misguided attempts to summarize or simplify statistical findings are another cause of distortion. And undoubtedly an element of intentional misrepresentation is sometimes involved. Often, the misuse arises from a desperate attempt to justify a viewpoint with what is seen to be a scientific statement. Hence the suggestion that statistics are sometimes used as a drunk uses a lamp post: more for support than illumination.

This book is not for practitioners or would-be practitioners of statistics: it is, as the title implies, for those who have to make decisions on the basis of statistics. Most of us, at one time or another, make use of statistics. The use may be to make a trivial decision, such as buying a tube of toothpaste in the face of claims that nine out of ten dentists recommend it; or it may be to commit a large sum of money to a building project on the basis of an anticipated increase in sales. We are decision makers in our work and in our domestic affairs, and our decisions are frequently based on or influenced by statistical considerations.

Introduction

My aim in writing this book is to help decision makers to appreciate what the statistics are saying and what they are not saying. In order to have this appreciation, it is not necessary to understand in detail how the statistics have been processed. The key is to understand the underlying perspective that is the foundation of the various procedures used and thereby understand the characteristic features of results from statistical investigations. This is the understanding that this book is intended to provide, by means of easy-to-follow explanations of basic methods and overviews of more complicated methods.

The decision makers I have primarily in mind are managers in business and industry. Business decisions are frequently taken on the basis of statistics. Whether to expand, whether to move into new areas, or whether to cut back on investment can make a big difference to the fortunes of a company. The building of houses, new roads, and new facilities of various kinds affects large numbers of people, and getting it wrong can be economically and socially disastrous for years ahead. Those who have to make such decisions are rarely statisticians, but the evidence on which they have to operate, whether in-house or from consultants, is frequently based on statistics. These people—the executives, planners, and project managers in all kinds of business—I aim to address, in the belief that, while the methods of statistics can be complicated, the meaning of statistics is not.

A better appreciation of statistics not only helps the decision makers in assessing what the statisticians have concluded, but also allows a more reliable judgment at the outset of what they should be asked to provide—recognizing what is possible, what the limitations are, and with what levels of uncertainty the answers are likely to be qualified. This is particularly important when consultants are to be involved, their fees being not insignificant.

I also have in mind students—the managers of the future—but not students who are studying statistics, as there are many excellent text books that they will know of and will be using (though some beginners might welcome a friendly introduction to the subject). The students who, I believe, will find this book useful are those who need to have an understanding of statistics without being involved directly in applying statistical methods. Many students of medicine, engineering, social sciences, and business studies, for example, fall into this category.

As I mentioned previously, we are all subjected to a regular deluge of statistics in our domestic affairs, and I therefore believe that interested non-professionals would find the book useful in helping them to adopt a more informed and critical view. Readers of newspapers and viewers of television, and that includes most of us, have a daily dose of statistics. We are told that sixty percent of the population think the government is doing a poor job, that there is more chance of being murdered than of winning a million dollars in the lottery, that there are more chickens in the country than people, and so on. Shoppers are faced with claims regarding price differentials and value for money. Advertisements constantly make claims for products based on statistical evidence: "Ninety percent of women looked younger after using Formula 39," and so on. If this book encourages just a few people to understand statistics a little better and thereby question statistics sensibly, rather than simply dismissing all statistics as rubbish, it will have been worthwhile.

In its most restricted meaning, statistics (plural) are systematically collected related facts expressed numerically or descriptively, such as lists of prices, weights, birthdays or whatever. Statistics (singular) is a science involving the processing of the facts—the raw data—to produce useful conclusions. In total, we have a procedure that starts with facts and moves by mathematical processing through to final statements, which, although factual, involve probability and uncertainty.

We will encounter areas where it is easy to be misled. We will see that we are sometimes misled because the conclusions we are faced with are not giving the whole story. But we shall also see that we can be misled by our own misunderstanding of what we are being told. We are, after all, not statisticians, but we need to understand what the statisticians are saying. Our task is to reach that necessary level of understanding without having to become proficient in the mathematical procedures involved.

The chapters of the book progress in a logical sequence, though it is not the sequence usually adopted in books aimed at the teaching of statistics. It is a sequence which allows the reader readily to find the section appropriate for his or her immediate needs. Most of the chapters are well subdivided, which assists further in this respect.

Part I shows why statistics involves uncertainties. This leads to explanations of the basics of probability. Of particular interest are examples of how misuse of probability leads to numerous errors in the media and even in legal proceedings.

Part II concerns raw data—how data can be obtained and the various methods for sampling it. Data may be descriptive, such as geographical location or eye color, or numerical. The various ways that data can be presented and how different impressions of the meaning of the data can arise are discussed.

Part III examines how data samples are summarized and characterized. A sample can give us information relating to the much larger pool of data from which the sample was obtained. By calculating confidence intervals, we see how the concept of reliability of our conclusions arises.

Part IV investigates comparisons that can be made using the characteristics of our samples. We need to search for similarities and differences, and to recognize whether they are real or imaginary.

Part V moves to the question of whether there are relationships between two or more different features. As the number of features represented in the data increases, the examination of relationships becomes more involved and is usually undertaken with the help of computer packages. For such methods, I have given an overview of what is being done and what can be achieved.

Part VI deals with forecasting. Practical examples are worked through to illustrate the appropriate methods and the variety of situations that can be dealt with.

The final part, Part VII, is devoted to big data. This is the most important development in the application of statistics that has arisen in recent times. Big, in this context, means enormous—so much so that it has affected our basic concepts in statistical thinking.

Where examples of data and collections of data are given, they are realistic insofar as they illustrate what needs to be explained. But there the realism ends. I have used simple numbers—often small discrete numbers—for the sake of clarity. The samples that I have shown are small—too small to be considered adequate. In real investigations, samples need to be as large as can be reasonably obtained, but my use of small samples makes the explanation of the processing easier to follow.

The examples I have included have been kept to a minimum for the sake of brevity. I have taken the view that one example explained clearly, and perhaps at length, is better than half a dozen all of which might confuse in the same way.

To clarify the calculations, I have retained them within the main text rather than relegating them to appendices with formal mathematical presentation. This allows me to add explanatory comments as the calculations proceed and allows the reader to skip the arithmetic while following the procedure.

In describing procedures and calculations, I have adopted the stance that we—that is to say you, the reader, and I—are doing the calculations. It would have been messy to repeatedly refer to some third person, even though I realize that you may be predominantly concerned with having to examine and assess procedures and calculations carried out by someone else.

I have given references by quoting author and year in the main text, the details being listed at the end of the book.

If you have read this far, I hope I have encouraged you to overcome any prejudices you might entertain against the elegant pastime of statistics and read on. Believe it or not, statistics is a fascinating subject. Once you get into the appropriate way of thinking, it can be as addictive as crossword puzzles or Sudoku. As a branch of mathematics, it is unique in requiring only simple arithmetic: the clever bit is getting your head around what is really required.

If you have read this far and happen to be a statistician, it must be because you are curious to see if I have got everything right. Being a statistician, you will appreciate that certainty is difficult if not impossible to achieve, so please let me know of any mistakes you find.

PART I

Uncertainties

In this world nothing can be said to be certain, except death and taxes.
—Benjamin Franklin

We need to understand the reasons why statistics embodies uncertainties. This will give us a feel for what statistics can do and what it cannot do, what we can expect from it and what we should not expect. This will prepare us for critically viewing the statistics and the conclusions from them that we are presented with. Some understanding of basic probability, which is required to appreciate uncertainty, is presented without assuming any previous knowledge on the part of the reader.

CHAPTER 1

The Scarcity of Certainty
What Time Will the Next Earthquake Be?

On the twenty-second of October, 2012, in Italy, six geophysicists and a government civil protection officer were sentenced to six years in prison on charges of manslaughter for underestimating the risk of a serious earthquake in the vicinity of the city of L'Aquila. Following several seismic shocks, the seven had met in committee on March 31, 2009, to consider the risk of a major earthquake. They recorded three main conclusions: that earthquakes are not predictable, that the L'Aquila region has the highest seismic risk in Italy, and that a large earthquake in the short term was unlikely. On April 6, a major earthquake struck with the loss of more than 300 lives.

The court's treatment of the seismologists created concern not only among seismologists working in other countries, but also among experts in other fields who are concerned with risk assessment. All seven filed appeals in March 2013, but it seemed unlikely that there would be a ruling on the case for some years. Whatever that may be, the case highlights the difficulties and the dangers in making decisions that have to be based on data that are statistical. If it is decided that an event is unlikely, but it then occurs, was the decision wrong? The correct answer is no, because unlikely events do happen—but there is a common misperception that the answer is yes.

An unfortunate consequence of this perception is either that it becomes more and more difficult to find anyone who is prepared to make a decision where risk is involved, or else that decisions become based on worst-case scenarios and thereby frequently create unwarranted disruption and expense.

There are instances of this in relation to health and safety legislation. Some school teachers have refused to take children on school field trips in case an accident occurs. Warnings are posted at gas stations instructing customers not to use their mobile phones near the pumps, although there has never been a reported case of a fire having been caused by their use. Homeowners are hesitant whether to clear snow from their sidewalk, for fear inadequate clearance might result in a passerby suffering a fall that could lead to a claim for compensation. A traditional British game, *conkers*, played by schoolchildren, involves two contestants, each of whom has a horse chestnut at the end of a length of string. Taking turns, each player attempts to shatter the other's suspended conker by whirling his or her own conker against it. The playground is scattered with fragments! The game has been played for generations with no public concern, but some schools in the UK now insist that the children must wear gloves and goggles.

Even the trivial decisions we make every day are often based on statistical data and have a degree of uncertainty. We have a meeting to get to, and we decide to catch the 9:20 AM train. We know from past experience that the train is usually on time, and we have never known it not to run. If, on the other hand, we knew that the train were late more often than not, then we would probably decide to catch an earlier one. Of course, we cannot be certain that the train will be on time. We cannot even be certain that the meeting will take place.

There are, of course, decisions we can make that are based on matters we can be certain of, but these are fairly inconsequential routine activities or observations encountered on a regular basis. The decisions are based on well-established facts. The difficult decisions—the important ones—usually involve issues that are uncertain to some degree.

Proof is often adduced as justification for decisions, but even here we have to be careful to recognize that qualifications or exceptions may apply. A court of law demands proof, but there is the qualification that it should be proof beyond a reasonable doubt. Scientists are said to be in the business of proving things by experiment and observation. In reality, scientists are able to do no more than provide theories that explain the way things work and allow predictions to be made. These theories are always considered to be provisional. Should they fail to make correct predictions, they will be modified or replaced. We frequently hear that science has proved this, that, and the other, when it has done no such thing. It has, of course, provided explanations and numerous correct predictions, from which our knowledge has increased and on which our technological advances have been based.

A statement may be true by definition. In mathematics, we define 2 to be the sum of 1 and 1, so that 1 plus 1 is always equal to 2. Other numbers are defined accordingly and, by defining mathematical processes—multiplication, taking the square root, and so forth—in a precise way, we can ensure that our mathematical proofs are indeed proofs. The rules of logic, based again on definition, lead to proofs. A valid syllogism—for example, "All cows eat grass; this animal is a cow; therefore, this animal eats grass"—is beyond dispute, though the truth of the conclusion does, of course, depend on the truth of the initial propositions. Statements that are true by definition do not add to our knowledge—for they are simply expressing it in a different way—but they may add usefully to our understanding.

Common sense is frequently used as a substitute for proof. We recognize a proposition as obvious, and we are then critical when we see investigations sponsored to show it to be correct. A waste of time and money, we conclude. But, as Duncan Watts (2011) demonstrates comprehensively, although common sense is useful in guiding us through our numerous daily activities, it is quite unreliable when we make judgments on more complex matters. Indeed, we can often recognize both a situation and its opposite as being obvious, depending on which we are told is correct. Children are healthier now than they were forty years ago. That seems obvious enough: health care is now better and there is better guidance on diet. But what about the opposite proposition, that children were healthier forty years ago than they are now? Common sense tells us this also is true: children then had more exercise, less time in front of the computer screen, and a simpler healthier diet.

When we use the justification of common sense to simply reinforce our own prejudices, the consequences may be trivial; but when those responsible for important decisions base them on common sense, the consequences can be serious. Government policy, company strategy, and marketing initiatives, for example, affect the well-being of many people and may do so for a long time.

Daniel Kahneman (2013) has produced an extensive study of how we suffer from errors and make bad judgments as a result of what he refers to as *fast thinking*. Our intuition is rarely reliable, and we are easily unconsciously influenced by circumstances. Our feeling for how much we should pay for something is influenced by the asking price. If you are asked whether Ghandi was more than 114 years old when he died, you will suggest a higher age than if the question asked whether he was more than 35 years old when he died.

There is a somewhat different use of the word *obvious*. The conclusion from a piece of reasoning or a calculation may be obvious to you, but the person sitting next to you may not find it so or even understand it. When tutoring students, I avoid the word. What is obvious to one person may not be obvious to another. For that reason, you will not encounter the word in the remainder of this book.

CHAPTER 2

Sources of Uncertainty
Why "Sure Thing!" Rarely Is

The results of any investigation will, of course, be uncertain, if not completely wrong, if the information on which the investigation is based is not correct. However, in statistical investigations there are additional sources of uncertainty, because of the need to extract a neat and useful conclusion from information that may be extensive and variable.

Statistical Data

Statements that appear at first sight to be clear and unambiguous often hide a great deal of uncertainty. In the previous chapter, I used the proposition "All cows eat grass" as an example of an acceptable starting point from which to draw a logical conclusion. Looking closely, you can see that it is a statistical statement. It relates cows to the eating of grass via the word *all*, which is in effect numerical. If I had said "100% of cows eat grass," the statistical nature of the statement would have been more apparent. Uncertainties in the statement arise even before we question the statistical claim of 100%. There is the question of what is included in the definitions of *cows* and *eating grass*. Am I including young cows, sick cows, or cows in all parts of the world? Do I mean eating grass and nothing else, or eating grass if they were given it? And what do I include in the term *grass*?

This may seem to be rather pedantic, but it illustrates that we have to question what, precisely, the things are that a statistical statement claims to relate in some way. A more realistic example could relate to unemployment. In Wabash, three out of four men are unemployed, we may read. How have the boundaries of the district been defined for the survey? Is it Wabash town, or is it the total extent covered by Wabash County? Then there is the question of how we are to understand the term *unemployed*. Does it include the retired, the sick, the imprisoned, the part-time workers, the casual workers, the voluntary workers, or the rich who have no desire or need to work? The way the terms are defined needs to be questioned before the statistics can be considered to have real meaning.

Turning now to the statistical aspects, we appreciate that data are gathered from many different sources. Opinion polls are fruitful and popular. We seem to spend as much time prior to an election listening to the details of polls as we do listening to the election results being declared. Data collected this way cannot be taken at face value and should always be questioned. Do people tell the truth when asked for their opinions or their activities, or even their ages or where they live? Probably not always, but who can really say? Even if they have every intention of being truthful, there is the possibility of misunderstanding the question. More commonly, perhaps, the question forces a difficult judgment or recollection. "Do you replace a light bulb once a week, once a month, or once every three months?" "When did you last speak to a policeman or policewoman?" In addition, many questions require answers that are completely subjective.

Statistics are often taken from "official sources," and this suggests reliability. However, the question remains how the figures were obtained. We would expect that the number of cars on the roads would be known quite accurately, whereas we accept that the number of illegal immigrants in the country is vague. Between these extremes are debatable areas. The number of street muggings could appear to be low if only the reported and successfully prosecuted cases were included, but could appear much greater if attempted muggings, or even estimated unreported muggings, were included.

Statistics from authoritative sources are sometimes simply not true. Charles Seife (2010) gives numerous examples ranging from intentional lies to statements that are impossible to verify. US Senator Joe McCarthy in 1950 claimed to have a list of 205 names of people working in the US State Department who were members of the Communist Party. The claim had serious repercussions, yet he never produced the names, and no evidence was ever found that he had such a list. At the other end of the scale, such as when in 1999 UN Secretary-General Kofi Annan declared a Bosnian boy to be the six billionth person on Earth, the repercussions may be trivial.

When statistics are quoted, a reference to the source is frequently given. This is, of course, good practice, but it does impart an air of authority that may not be warranted. Rarely does the recipient follow up on the reference to check its validity. The originator may not even have checked the reference but simply have grabbed it from somewhere else. Worse is the situation where the originator has been unfairly selective in his or her choice of statistics from the referenced source. Be aware that organizations with a particular agenda may, in their literature, give references to publications from the same organization, or to those closely allied with it (Taverne 2005: 82-86).

Wikipedia is now an important and frequently used source of information. Bear in mind that it is based on contributions from anyone who wishes to contribute. A consequential degree of regulation results, but the information Wikipedia contains at any moment in time is not necessarily correct.

So far we have been considering statistical data, which is in a sense secondhand. It is derived from what others, who have no way of determining the truth of what they quote, tell us. But there are other situations where objective measurements are made and data are provided by those who have made the measurements. Factories supplying foodstuffs have weighing machines for controlling the amount of jam or corn flakes that goes into each container. The weighing machines are inspected periodically to ensure accuracy. Though accurate, the machines will be imprecise to some degree. That is to say, when the machine registers one kilogram the true weight will be one kilogram plus or minus a small possible error. The smaller the possible error, the greater the precision, but there still remains a degree of uncertainty.

A company supplying car parts has to ensure that a bracket, say, is 10 cm long plus or minus 0.5 mm. The latitude permitted is referred to as the *tolerance*. Within the company, regular measurements of the lengths of brackets are made as they are produced. These measurements, to an accuracy of perhaps 0.1 mm or less, provide a data sample, which when properly processed provides the company with warnings that the tolerance is being or in danger of being exceeded. Such situations result in statistical data that is reliable to a degree dependent on measuring equipment, and with this knowledge the degree of reliability can be quantified.

Results of investigations in the various science and technology disciplines are published in reputable and often long-established journals. A process of refereeing the articles submitted to the journals provides good assurance that the results quoted are valid and that any provisos are made clear. References to such journals are a good sign.

Processing the Data

Raw data, which as you have seen already have a degree of uncertainty, are processed by mathematical procedures to allow you to draw conclusions. Recalling what I have said about the truth of mathematics, you might think that the processing will introduce no additional uncertainty. If raw data are factual, we might expect that our conclusions would be factual. However, as you shall see, processing introduces further uncertainty. But you will also see that the conclusions are factual. They are factual statements expressing the probability of something being true, or expressing the uncertainty involved in stating that something is true. For example, we might have a conclusion saying that hair restorer A is more effective than hair restorer B with a 90% certainty, or saying that the weight of a randomly chosen bag of sugar is half a kilogram within one hundredth of a kilogram either way, with a 99% certainty. Both statements are factually correct, but neither gives us a precise conclusion regarding the performance of a particular treatment of hair restorer or the weight of a specific bag of sugar.

When such statements are made without the necessary qualifications of uncertainty, they appear to provide proof. "Hair restorer A is more effective than hair restorer B" and "This bag of sugar weighs half a kilogram" are the kinds of statements we usually encounter. With regard to the bag of sugar, the statement is near enough correct, and it would be considered extremely pedantic to insist on a precise statement. But with regard to the hair restorer, the situation is much more serious. The statement, when looked at carefully, is seen to convey almost no useful information, yet it is likely to encourage customers to spend their money on the product.

The uncertainties that arise in statistical processing do not reflect any inadequacy of the mathematical procedures. They arise in the summarizing of the data and in the use of samples to predict the characteristics of the populations from which the samples were drawn.

Raw data is summarized because there is generally too much to allow easy recognition of the important features. Simply picking out bits and pieces to illustrate underlying principles can lead to incorrect conclusions but may sometimes be done to justify prejudiced views. Summarizing—averaging, for example—is carried out according to accepted procedures. Nevertheless, any procedure that reduces the data necessarily results in loss of information and therefore some uncertainty.

The second source of uncertainty lies in the difference between a sample and a population, and in the attempt to characterize a population using the features of a sample. It must be recognized that the words are being used as statisticians use them. A population in the statistical sense is not a group of people living in a particular area (though it could be, in a study involving actual people living in some area of interest).

A *sample* is more easily explained first. It is a set of data of the same kind obtained by some consistent process. We could ask shoppers coming out of a supermarket how many items they purchased. The list of the number of items that we obtained would be the sample. The size of the sample would be the number of shoppers we asked, which would correspond to the number of data in our sample. In this example, the *population* would be the replies from the larger number of shoppers or potential shoppers that might have been asked, including of course the ones who were actually asked.

Sometimes the sample embraces the entire population. If we produce, by a novel process, 100 pewter tankards and measure and weigh each one to examine the consistency of the process, our sample corresponds to the population. The monthly profits made by a company over a period of time comprise the entire population of results relating to that particular company and can be treated as such to derive performance figures for the company. If, however, the accumulated data were considered to be representative of similar companies, then they would be treated as a sample drawn from a larger population.

My wife's birthday book shows the birthdays of relatives and friends that she wishes to recall. The number of birthdays in each month of the year is as follows.

Jan	Feb	Mar	Apr	May	Jun	Jul	Aug	Sep	Oct	Nov	Dec
1	3	6	7	5	3	2	4	7	7	9	7

The data can be considered a sample or a population, depending on what we wish to do. Considering the whole of the world population or a hypothetical large collection of people, the data is a sample. It is not a very reliable sample because it suggests that many more people are born in November than in January. However, in terms of the people actually included, the data are the population; and it is true to say that the probability of selecting a person at random from the book and finding his or her birthday to be in November would be 9/61 (=0.15) rather than a probability of 1/12 (=0.08) that we would expect in a much larger sample.

In each of these examples—the shoppers, the pewter mugs, and so on—the population is finite. In many situations, however, the population is hypothetical and considered to be infinite. If we make repeated measurements of the diameter of the Moon, in order to improve the accuracy of our result, we can consider that the measurements are a sample drawn from a population consisting of an infinite number of possible measurements. If we carry out an experiment to study the effectiveness of a new rat poison, using a sample of rats, we would consider the results applicable to a hypothetical infinite population of rats.

Because the sample is assumed to be representative of the population from which it is drawn, it is said to be a *random sample*. *Random* means that of all the possibilities, each is equally likely to be chosen. Thus if we deal 6 cards from a well-shuffled pack of cards, the selection of 6 cards is a random sample from the population of 52 cards. The randomness that is achieved in practice depends on the method of sampling, and it can be difficult in many real situations to ensure that the sample is random. Even when it is random, it is simply

Chapter 2 | Sources of Uncertainty

one of a very large number of possible random samples that might have been selected. Because the subsequent processing is restricted to the data in the sample that happens to have been selected, the results of the processing, when used to reveal characteristics of the population, will carry uncertainties.

A 6-card sample is very likely to be random; but returning to the supermarket shoppers, you can see the difficulty of obtaining a random sample. Do we stop men and women, or just women? If both, do we take account of there being more women shoppers than men? And should we spread our enquiries through the day? Perhaps different days of the week would give different results. And what about time of year? And so on. We could restrict the scope of our sample to, say, women shoppers on Friday afternoons in summer, but this of course restricts our population similarly, and restricts the scope of the results that we will obtain from our statistical analysis. Any attempts to apply the results more generally—to women shoppers on any afternoon, summer or winter, say—will introduce further uncertainties.

It should be noted that the information we can obtain, and the uncertainty associated with it, depend entirely on the size of the sample and not on the size of the population from which it is drawn. A poll of 1,000 potential voters will yield the same information whether it relates to a population of 1 million or 10 million potential voters. The absolute size of the sample, rather than the relative size of the sample, is the key value to note.

CHAPTER 3

Probability
How Bad Statistics Can Put You in Jail

To appreciate statistical analysis it is necessary to have some understanding of probability. Surprisingly, perhaps, not very much is required. Knowing how several different probabilities work together in combination and how the probability of occurrence of an event is affected by an overriding condition are all that are needed for most purposes.

Probability Defined

Because of the uncertainties discussed in the preceding chapter, statistical results are quoted together with an indication of the probability of the results being correct. Thus it is necessary to have an understanding of basic probability, which fortunately is not difficult to achieve. *Probability* is defined as the ratio of all equally likely favorable outcomes to all possible equally likely outcomes. It is usually expressed as a fraction or a decimal and must lie between zero denoting impossibility and unity denoting certainty. Thus if we throw a die, there are 6 possible equally likely outcomes. The probability of throwing a 2 is 1/6 as there is only one favorable outcome. The probability of throwing an odd number is 3/6 (i.e., a half), as there are three favorable likely outcomes. The probability of throwing a 7 is zero (i.e., impossible), and the probability of throwing a number less than 10 is one (i.e., certain).

When interpreting probability results it is important to recognize that, simply because an event has a low probability of occurring, we must not conclude that we will never encounter it. After all, something has to occur, and most things that occur have only a small probability of occurring, because there are always many more things that could occur.

To take a fairly inconsequential example, if we deal a pack of cards to give 4 hands each of 13 cards, we would be surprised to find that each hand consisted of a complete suit. The probability of this happening is about 1 in 5×10^{28} (5 followed by 28 zeros). However, each time we deal the cards, the probability of the particular hands we find we have dealt, whatever the distribution of the cards, is exactly the same: about one in 5×10^{28}. So, an event with this low probability of happening happens every time we deal a pack of cards.

Each day of our lives, we encounter a series of events—a letter from the bank, a cut finger, a favorite song on the radio, and so on—each of which has a probability of happening. Taken together and considering only independent events, the probability of each day's sequence of events is extremely unlikely to have happened—yet it did!

It would be out of place and unnecessary to give an extensive account of probability theory, but it is important appreciate the basic rules used to manipulate probabilities in drawing conclusions. The next two sections are concerned with these rules.

Combining Probabilities

Combining several probabilities is a simple process but it needs care to do it correctly. If we know the probability of each of two events, we can calculate the probability of both events occurring. Suppose we toss a coin and throw a die. The probability of getting a head is 1/2 and the probability of getting a 2 on the die is 1/6. The probability of both events, a head and a 2, is obtained by multiplying the two probabilities together. The answer is 1/2 x 1/6 = 1/12 or one in twelve, as can be seen from the listing of all the possibilities.

Coin	H	<u>H</u>	H	H	H	H	T	T	T	T	T	T
Die	1	<u>2</u>	3	4	5	6	1	2	3	4	5	6

The procedure can be extended to any number of events, the individual probabilities being multiplied together. However it is important to note that this is a valid process only if the events are independent—that is, their occurrences are not linked in some way.

The need for independence can be illustrated by a different example. The probability of me being late for work on any particular day is 1/100, say. The probability of my colleague being late is 1/80. Multiplication of the probabilities gives 1/8,000 as the probability of us both being late on the same day. This is clearly wrong. Many of the circumstances that make him late also make me late. If the weather is foggy or icy, we are both likely to be late. We may even travel on the same train, so a late train makes us both late.

An example of a serious error caused by the unjustified multiplication of probabilities was publicized some years ago. Two children in the same family died, apparently suffering crib deaths. The mother, Sally Clark, a British solicitor, was charged with murder in 1999. An expert witness for the prosecution suggested that the chance of one crib death in a family as affluent as the one in question was one in 8,500. By squaring this probability (i.e., by multiplying 1/8,500 by 1/8,500), he obtained an estimate of 1 in 73 million for the chance of two crib deaths occurring in the family. The figure was not challenged by the defense, and the mother was found guilty and jailed. She won her second appeal in 2003. Clearly, it is possible that the likelihood of crib deaths could run in families for genetic reasons, and the two crib deaths could not be assumed to be independent events. The multiplication of the two (equal) probabilities was unjustified. As a result of the Sally Clark case, other similar cases were reviewed and two other mothers convicted of murder had their convictions overturned.

In 2003 in the Netherlands, a nurse, Lucia de Berk, was sentenced to life imprisonment for the murder of four patients and the attempted murder of three others. Part of the evidence was a statistical calculation provided by a law psychologist. It was claimed that the chance of a nurse working at the three hospitals being present at so many unexplained deaths and resuscitations was one in 342 million, the result being arrived at by a multiplication of probabilities. In the following years, many reputable statisticians criticized the simplistic calculation, and a petition to reopen the case was started. Eventually, in 2010, after lengthy legal processes, a retrial delivered a not-guilty verdict. There were, of course, many considerations other than the statistical calculation, but it is evident from the proceedings that the calculation carried weight in the original conviction.

The rule of multiplication of probabilities for independent events is often referred to as the *"and" rule*, because it expresses the probability of event A, and event B, and event C, and so on. A second rule—the *"or" rule*—is used to combine probabilities when we wish to know the probability of event A, or event B, or event C, etc. Here, we add the probabilities. As with the previous rule, this rule also carries an important condition: that the events must be mutually exclusive. That means that only one of the events is possible at any one time. To illustrate, if we throw a die, the probability of a 2 is 1/6 and the probability of a 3 is 1/6. The probability of a 2 or a 3 is 1/6 + 1/6 = 1/3. The two events are mutually exclusive in that it is impossible in throwing the die to get both a 2 and a 3 at the same time. If we extend the example to clarify further, the probability of getting a 1, or a 2, or a 3, or a 4, or a 5, or a 6, is 1/6 + 1/6 + 1/6 + 1/6 + 1/6 + 1/6 = 1 (i.e., a certainty).

Because the sum of the probabilities of all possible mutually exclusive outcomes equals unity (a certainty), it follows that that the probability of something not happening is equal to one minus the probability of it happening.

Chapter 3 | Probability

To illustrate the misuse of the "or" rule we can return to our tossing of a coin and throwing of a die together. The separate probabilities of a head and a 2 are respectively 1/2 and 1/6. If we added these together we would conclude that the probability of getting a head or a 2 is 1/2 + 1/6 = 2/3, which is quite wrong. Getting a head and getting a 2 are not mutually exclusive events since both can occur. A proper analysis of this situation shows that:

Probability of heads and a 2	= 1/12
Probability of either, but not both	= 6/12 = 1/2
Probability of neither	= 5/12
Probability of both, or either, or neither	= 1/12 + 6/12 + 5/12 = 1

The final statement is a correct use of the "or" rule, since "both", "either", and "neither" constitute a set of mutually exclusive events. These results can be checked by viewing the full list of possibilities shown above.

The results are also shown in Figure 3-1 in the form of a tree diagram. The difference between the "and" rule and the "or" rule is made clear. Following a sequence of events horizontally across the diagram involves a coin event followed by a die event. The two "and" probabilities are multiplied together. The "or" alternatives are seen in the vertical listing of the final combined probabilities. This tree diagram is a rather trivial example, but you will encounter tree diagrams again in examples of more practical situations. It is worth pointing out here that although a tree diagram can be replaced by a quicker calculation, it is nevertheless an excellent means of clarifying or checking the logic behind the calculation.

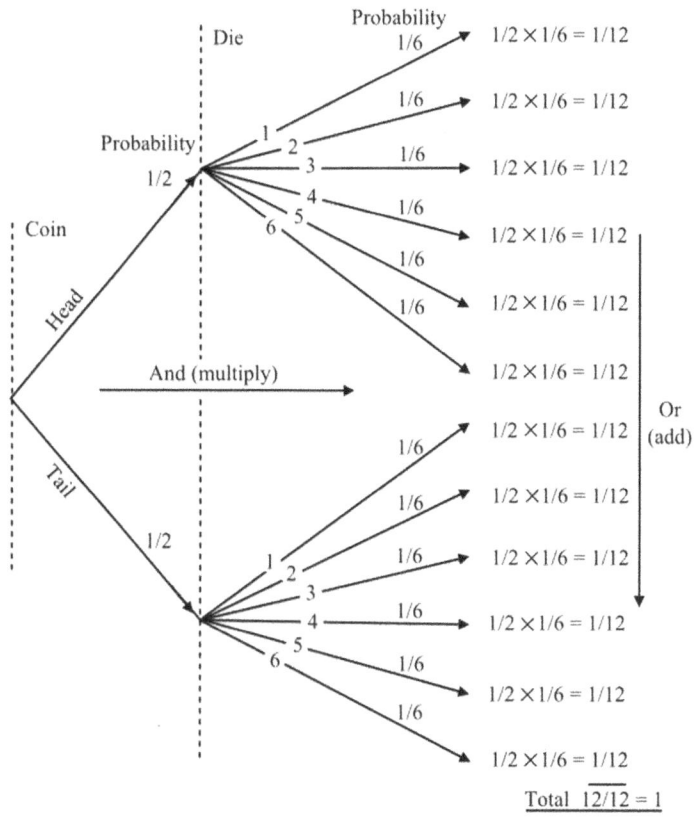

Figure 3-1. Tree diagram of the various outcomes of tossing a coin and throwing a die

Note that when probabilities are multiplied together, the result is smaller than either of the two original probabilities. Thus, application of the "and" rule always leads to a decrease in probability. This is as we would expect: the probability of predicting the winner and the second in a horse race is less than the probability of predicting just one of the results. On the other hand, adding probabilities together increases the probability. Thus, application of the "or" rule increases the probability. Predicting the winner or the second in a horse race is more likely than predicting just one of the results.

Combinations of probabilities appear extensively in studies of reliability of systems, as you will see later in more detail. When systems consist of many components, the overall probability of failure depends on the individual probabilities of failure of the components and the way in which they combine. Suppose we have a simple smoke alarm consisting of a sensor connected to a siren. Failure of the system occurs if the sensor or the alarm fails, or both fail (the "or" rule). If we install a duplicate system, failure occurs only if the first system fails and the second system fails (the "and" rule).

Since such analyses are concerned with failures that have to be avoided as much as possible, the values of probability that are quoted are often very small. We are all more at home with probabilities in the range of tenths or perhaps hundredths; but when probabilities of 0.0001 (one in ten thousand) or 0.000001 (one in a million) are presented, we have difficulty not only in recognizing their significance but also in taking them seriously. A chance of a disastrous fire might be one in a million, and some safety procedure we introduce might reduce it to one in two million. This would halve the chance of a fire—a very significant reduction, but a comparison of the two values, 0.000001 and 0.000002, does not carry the same impact.

Conditional Probability

Probability calculations can become complicated when the required probability is conditional on some other event happening. You need not worry about these complications, but you do need to appreciate how false conclusions can be drawn in such situations. The conclusions, whether accidental or intentional, are particularly dangerous because they appear at first sight to be perfectly valid.

To see what is meant by conditional probability, think of two dice being rolled one after the other. What is the probability that the total score is 5? There are four ways of getting a score of 5—1+4, 2+3, 3+2, and 4+1—out of a possible 36 combinations of the two scores. So the probability is 4/36 or 1/9. If we introduce a condition—for example, that the first die is showing a 2—the probability of getting a total of 5 becomes 1/6 because the second die must show a 3 and there is a 1 in 6 chance of this happening.

Now consider a situation in which we have a bag of coins, of which 100 are forgeries, as illustrated in Figure 3-2.

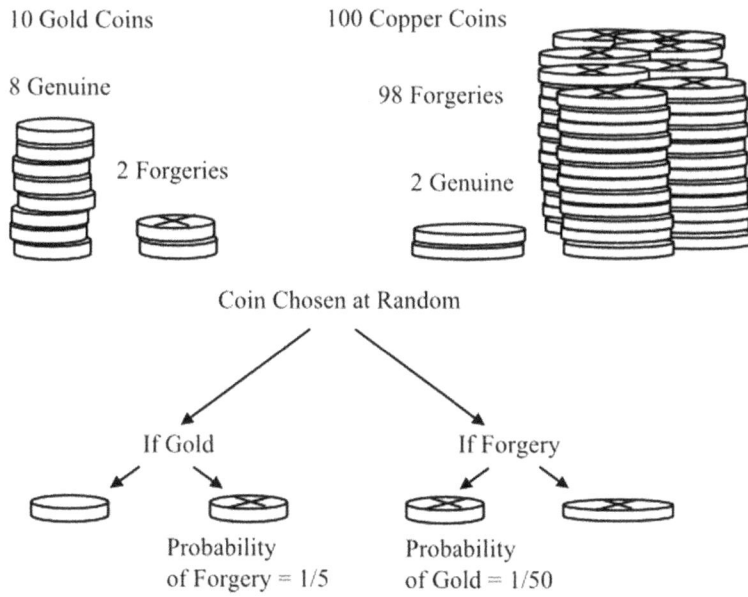

Figure 3-2. Conditional probability illustrated by counterfeit coins

Ten of the coins are gold, and two of these are forgeries. We draw one coin from the bag and see that it is gold (the condition). The probability that it is a forgery is 2 out of 10, or 1/5. Alternatively, when we draw the coin out of the bag we may find it to be a forgery (the condition). The probability that it is gold is 2 out of 100 (i.e., 1/50). This illustrates the fact that the probability of event A, given event B, is generally not the same as the probability of event B, given event A. The two conditional probabilities are generally different and can be very different.

The so-called *prosecutor's fallacy* arises from the use of the wrong conditional probability. Suppose a suspect is found to have matching DNA characteristics of the unknown perpetrator of a crime. Only one person in 10,000 would be expected to have a similar match. The prosecution argues, therefore, that there is only one chance in 10,000 that the suspect is innocent. But the 1/10,000 probability is the probability of a DNA match given the condition that the suspect is innocent. This is not the appropriate probability to use. The relevant probability is the probability that the suspect is innocent given the condition that there is a DNA match. We cannot evaluate this probability without knowing how many other possible suspects there might be who are equally likely to be guilty. (This would be like trying to solve the bag of coins example without knowledge of the total number of forgeries.) But the figure could be very much greater than 1/10,000. In a population of

100,000, say, there would be on average 10 people with the DNA match and, assuming that two of these, say, are also suspect, our suspect has a probability of 2/3 of being innocent.

As one might expect, there is also the *defender's fallacy*. It arises from the supposition of a large population of equally suspected people. Following on from the previous example, if the population was taken to be 1,000,000 there would be 100 with the appropriate DNA match; so, the defender would argue, our suspect has a 99/100 probability of being innocent. Raising the supposed population to 10 million increases the probability of innocence to 999/1000. The fallacy lies in the assumption that everyone in the population is equally suspect.

Haigh (2003) and Seife (2010) give useful accounts of how the misuse of probability can result in errors in legal decisions. Many of the examples are taken from actual cases.

It is not only in legal arguments that errors of this sort arise. They are commonly encountered in political debates and in advertising. Have a look at the following examples.

"Of those dying of lung cancer each year, 75% are smokers. This shows that smokers have a 75% chance of dying of lung cancer." No it doesn't! We need to know the probability of someone dying of lung cancer, given that he or she is a smoker, not the probability of the person having been a smoker, given that he or she dies of lung cancer. The following data helps to show the fallacy.

	Smokers	Nonsmokers	Total
Number dying of lung cancer	75	25	100
Number dying of other causes	225	175	400
Total	300	200	500

Of the 300 smokers who died, 75 (i.e., 25%) died of lung cancer. This is very different from the quoted 75% of deaths from lung cancer associated with smoking. Take note that these are invented figures and must not be used to draw any medical conclusions!

"Of dental patients who were found to have had no fillings in ten years, 90% had brushed regularly with Toothglo." But what we would really like to know is what percentage of those who brushed regularly with Toothglo had had no fillings in ten years.

"Eighty percent of winning horses in yesterday's races were tipped by our racing correspondent." Maybe, but what percentage of his tips predicted the winning horse?

SWITCHED ON

The atmosphere was becoming tense. Rod Craig, representative of Jenson's Switches, was in the manager's office at Boilfast, a manufacturer of electric kettles. Boilfast fitted most of its kettles with switches supplied by Jenson's, and it was the switches that were being discussed.

The manager of Boilfast, Tom Richards, was concerned about the number of kettles he was having to repair under guarantee because of a problem with the on-off switch.

He quoted some figures from a sheet of paper he was holding.

"Over the past two years, of the number of kettles returned because of a faulty on-off switch, sixty-seven percent were fitted with your switches. And I don't think that is acceptable."

Rod could hardly do anything but apologize and assure the manager, who was now leaning forward in a somewhat threatening manner, that he would refer the matter back to his technical department.

On the way back to Jenson's, Rod had chance to think through the situation. His company supplied most of the switches that Boilfast fitted to its kettles, so Boilfast was a customer they would not want to lose. But how meaningful was the complaint? Rod began to see the light and, by the time he arrived in his office, he had a smile on his face.

He picked up the phone and dialed.

"Tom, the issue is not the one you described."

"No?"

"You are saying that of the kettles returned because of a faulty switch, 67% were fitted with our switches. The real issue is, given that the kettle has our switch fitted, what percent are returned because of a faulty switch? Perhaps you should look at your figures more closely."

Tom was thrown off balance and felt slightly confused.

"I'll get back to you," he said.

He did look at the figures. Of the number of kettles with Jenson's switches returned for any reason, 22% had a faulty switch. This was similar to the figures relating to kettles fitted with switches from other suppliers, the corresponding percentage being 19%. Because the majority of Boilfast kettles were fitted with Jenson's switches, the predominance of their switch failures that was troubling Tom was readily explained.

PART II

Data

The temptation to form premature theories upon insufficient data is the bane of our profession.

—Arthur Conan Doyle

We now look at how data is obtained. This is the critical first stage in making use of data as the reliability of the conclusions of any statistical investigation depends on the data being obtained in an appropriate and fair manner. The features and format of the data, and how we can classify the data, are then discussed.

CHAPTER 4

Sampling
Did Nine out of Ten Really Say That?

An essential feature of a sample is that it is representative of the population from which it is drawn. Unfortunately, it is impossible to predict that this will be so, or even check that it is so when the sample has been obtained. A judgment has to be made as to the adequacy of the sampling procedure in relation to the individual circumstances. This has given rise to many different methods of sampling to cover a wide range of situations.

Problems with Sampling

When the data obtained represents the entire population, the question of how relevant the sample is does not arise: the sample is the population. Thus the monthly profits of a company over a twelve-month period represent the complete picture for the specifically defined twelve-month period. If, however, the sample is drawn from a population larger than the sample, the question of how representative the sample of the population is becomes critical. If the twelve-month sample mentioned above was claimed to be representative of other twelve-month periods—in other words, if it were considered to be a sample from a population of numerous twelve-month periods—the evidence for its wider relevance would need to be examined.

For those carrying out statistical investigations, the adoption of appropriate sampling methods is a priority. The credibility of everything that follows in an investigation hinges on whether the samples are representative of the populations to which the conclusions of the investigation will be applied. If we are not carrying out the investigations but simply looking at results of investigations that others are responsible for, we have a considerable advantage.

We have the benefit of hindsight and can assess what populations the samples best represent, and whether these are the appropriate populations or close enough to what we require for our purposes.

Even with proper sampling, arrangement problems can arise. Some of the data may be incorrect. A meter may be misread, or the meter may be faulty. Tallies can be miscounted. A respondent may accidentally or intentionally give a false answer. The question may be worded in a way that invites a particular answer. Charles Seife (2010: 117) gives an amusing example of how the wording of a question is likely to determine the reply. "Do you think it is acceptable to smoke while praying?" is likely to get the answer "No"; whereas "Do you think it is acceptable to pray while smoking?" is likely to get the answer "Yes."

Worse still is the slanted reporting of the results of a survey when the questions may have already biased the answers received. In 2011, the media reported that a children's charity had commissioned a survey which included the question, "Are children becoming more feral?" The conclusion from the commissioning charity was that almost 50% of the public felt that children were behaving like animals. A further question asked at what age it was too late to reform children. Although 44% said never too late, and 28% said between 11 and 16 years, it was reported that a quarter of all adults think children are beyond help at the age of 10.

Blastland and Dilnot (2007) give an account of questionable information arising from surveys. It is worthwhile reading for anyone examining the results of an investigation based on sampling. Examples range from the number of immigrants entering the UK every day to the decline in the hedgehog population. The latter is particularly intriguing. The Mammals on the Road Survey, as it is called, is carried out from June to August each year. The numbers of squashed hedgehogs on selected roads are counted. The numbers are decreasing each year, from which it is deduced that the hedgehog population is declining. However, there are many reasons why the sample of dead hedgehogs may not represent the total population of hedgehogs. Traffic density on the selected roads may be changing. Hedgehogs may be evolving and becoming more wary of traffic. Climate change may be altering the time of year when hedgehogs are likely to be on the roads, and so on. Of course, one has to recognize that it is not easy to devise a better method without involving greater expense.

It must be remembered that sampling costs money. There always has to be a compromise between having large samples to maximize the reliability of the results and small samples to minimize costs. As mentioned previously, the reliability of the results depends directly on the size of the sample and does not depend on the size of the population from which the sample is drawn. It does not follow therefore that samples have to be large because the target populations are large, though it may be more difficult to ensure that a small sample is representative of a population when the population is large.

Some of the data required from a survey may be missing, and the reason why they are missing may relate to how representative the sample is. For example, older respondents may refuse to state their age, and simply deleting their contribution to the sample will bias the sample in favor of younger respondents. Samples should include a record of any data that has been deleted. David Hand (2008) provides a useful discussion of missing data and other potential problems in sampled data, and he describes ways of dealing with them.

Repeated Measurements

In scientific investigations, certain properties that have fixed values have to be ascertained. For example, the density of pure copper or the rate of decay of a radioactive material may have to be determined as accurately as possible. The laboratory faced with such tasks will repeat the measurements several times, and each time a slightly different value may be obtained.

The set of values constitutes a sample and, since there are in principle an infinite number of such possible values, it is a sample drawn from an infinite population. The sample and the method by which the data is obtained define the population.

Compare this situation with an apparently similar one that is in reality somewhat different. Suppose our scientists are interested in determining accurately the circumference of the Earth around the Equator. Such measurements have been made over many centuries by different investigators. If we were to bring together all the values obtained in the past, we could not say that we had a sample from the same population. Each of the values would have its associated method of measurement and its level of precision and would be representative of an infinite population of such values, all obtained in the same way. But each of the populations would be different. Nevertheless, because all the values are targeted at the same property, such as the circumference of the Earth, it ought to be possible to make use of the collection of data, and indeed it is by weighting the values, as you shall see in Chapter 7.

Simple Random Sampling

For *simple random sampling*, each datum from the population must have an equal chance of being selected, and the selection of each must be independent of the selection of any other. This is more difficult to achieve than might appear at first sight.

The first difficulty arises because people are not good at adopting a random procedure. If faced with a tray of apples and asked to select ten at random, people generally make selections that are likely to be biased. Some may select "average-looking" apples, ignoring the very small or very large. Others may attempt to get a full range of sizes from the smallest to the largest. Some will be more concerned with the range of color, others with shape.

A similar difficulty can arise because of the nonrandom times of sampling. An inspector visits a production line in a factory, at supposedly random times, to select an item for quality-control inspection. But production starts at 8:00 a.m., and he is not available until 9:30 a.m. Also, he takes a coffee break between 11:00 and 11:15.

Rather than using the judgments of individuals to establish the randomness of the sampling, it is preferable to make use of random numbers. These are generated by computer and are listed in statistics books. (Strictly speaking, computer-generated numbers are "pseudo-random," but this is not a problem.) A sequence of random numbers can be used to determine which apples to select or which products to take from the production line.

When surveys are required and people have to be questioned, the difficulties are greater. The population may be widely spread geographically. If the study relates to adult twins, for example, and the results are intended to be applicable to all such twins in the United Kingdom, say, then the population is spread throughout the United Kingdom and the sample has to be randomly selected from this widespread population. Even if available finances allowed the sampling of adult twins to extend so widely, there is still the problem of ensuring randomness. If the twins were located by telephone, those without a phone, on holiday, or away from home for some other reason, for example, would be excluded. And, of course, there are always those people who refuse to take part in surveys and those who never tell the truth in surveys.

Questioning people in the street is easier to do in fine weather. But those who are out in the pouring rain or freezing temperatures, who are unlikely to be questioned and unlikely anyway to be prepared to stop and answer, may have quite different views from fine-weather strollers.

It is because of such difficulties that other sampling methods have been devised. Not all the problems can be overcome: if someone is determined to be untruthful, no sampling method is going to rectify the situation.

Systematic Sampling

For *systematic sampling* a number is chosen—say, 10. The sample is then selected by taking every tenth member from the list or from the arrangement of items. The first member is chosen at random. If necessary, the end of the list is assumed to be joined to the beginning to allow the counting to continue in a circular fashion until the required sample size is reached.

It is important to consider whether the choice of the arbitrary number creates any bias because of patterns in the listing. If the list is of people arranged in family groups, for example, then a number as large as 10 would make it unlikely that two members of the same family would be chosen. If the list was arranged in pairs—man–wife, say—then any even number would bias the results in favor of the wives.

Stratified Random Sampling

If the population under study consists of non-overlapping groups, and the sizes of the groups relative to the size of the population are known, then *stratified random sampling* can be used. The groups or subpopulations are referred to as *strata*.

Suppose a survey needs to be carried out to get the views of a town's adult population on the plans for a new shopping mall. People of different ages could well be expected to have different views, so age could be used to define the strata. A stratum would be a particular age range: for example, 20–29 years. Suppose this age group makes up 25% of the town's adult population. The sample is then defined as requiring 25% to be within this age range. The other age ranges are used similarly to fix the composition of the sample. This is referred to as *proportional allocation*.

It could be decided that in addition to age affecting the views of the respondents, the geographical location of their homes might have an effect. A second level of stratification might be introduced, dividing the town into a number of districts. If proportional allocation is again applied, it may put unbearable demands on the size of the sample. It may be found that some of the subgroups—for example, the over-60-year-olds in one of the town districts—are represented in the sample by only a handful of individuals. *Disproportional allocation* could be applied, increasing the number in the sample for these groups but not for the others.

Stratified random sampling is a popular procedure used in surveys, but it is not easy to set up in the most efficient way. It may turn out that the choice of strata was not the most appropriate. In the example above, it might have been better to define annual household income as the strata. Not until the sample results have been processed will some of the shortcomings come to light. In order to achieve a better sampling design, a pilot survey is often undertaken, or results of previous similar surveys are examined.

There is a mathematical procedure for calculating the optimum allocation for a single level of stratification, called the *Neyman allocation*, but this requires prior knowledge of the variability of the various groups within the strata. Again, a pilot study would be required to provide the information.

Cluster Sampling

Cluster sampling is used when the population under study is widespread in space or time. For example, it might be necessary to survey fire engine drivers over the whole country, or hospital admissions 24 hours a day, 7 days a week.

To limit sampling costs, the geographical or time extents are divided into compact zones or clusters. For the fire engine drivers, the country could be divided into geographical zones, such as counties. A random sample of the clusters, the primary sampling units, is selected. In multistage cluster sampling, further clustering takes place. The fire stations within the selected counties would be identified. Random sampling would then be applied to select the fire stations for study in each selected county. Clearly, the validity of the results hinges critically on how well the random selection of the clusters represents the population.

Quota Sampling

Interviewers employed in surveys are frequently given quotas to fulfill. They may be required to interview three middle-aged professionals, six young housewives, two retired pensioners, and so on. This is *quota sampling*. The quotas are determined from the known constitution of the population, as in stratified sampling.

The advantages of quota sampling are that the required procedure is easily taught, and the correct quotas are obtained even for very small samples which can then be pooled. However, no element of randomization is involved and bias can easily arise as the interviewer can choose who to approach and who to avoid.

Sequential Sampling

In *sequential sampling*, the size of the sample is not defined at the outset. Instead, random sampling is continued until a required criterion is met. This is particularly useful when the cost of obtaining each response is high. After each response the data is analyzed and a decision made whether to obtain a further response.

Databases

The rapid growth of the use of computer systems in business and industry has produced vast databases containing data of all kinds. Banking, insurance, health, and retailing organizations, for example, have data relating to patterns of behavior linking customers, purchasing habits, preferences, products, and so on. Much of the data has been collected because it is easy to do so when the operations of the organizations are computerized. Thus databases are a source of large samples that can be used for further analysis. I shall discuss databases further when I describe data mining and big data in Part VII.

Resampling Methods

If we have a sample from a population, we can consider the question of what other samples we could have obtained might have looked like. Clearly, they could have consisted of a selection of the values we see in our existing sample and they could well have duplicated some of the values. This is the thinking behind *resampling*. We can produce further samples by randomly selecting values from our existing sample.

Suppose we have a sample consisting of the following values:

1 2 3 4 5 6.

If we now select groups of six randomly from these values, we might get

1 3 3 4 5 6,
1 3 4 5 5 5,
etc.

Numerous additional samples can be generated in this way, and from the samples it is possible to gain information about the population from which the original sample was drawn.

Particular techniques of this type include the *jackknife*, where one or more values are removed from the original sample each time, and the *bootstrap*, where a random selection of the values provides each new sample. They are computer-intensive, requiring large numbers of randomly generated samples.

Data Sequences

If the sample is random, it is not expected that the data viewed in the order they were obtained would show any patterns. Data that is collected over a period of time could show a trend, increasing or decreasing with time, and this would raise suspicions. Similarly, a sample of members of the public answering yes or no to a question should show a random distribution of the two answers. It would be suspicious if most of the yes answers were early in the listing and most of the no answers were later. Equally, of course, it would be suspicious if the two answers alternated in perfect sequence.

A statistical test called the *one-sample runs test* can be used to check the randomness of a sequence of yes and no answers. The following sequence

YYY N Y NN Y N YYY NN Y NN YYY

has 20 data, 12 of which are Y and 8 of which are N. There are 11 runs, such as YYY, followed by N, followed by Y, ... etc. The number of runs can be referred to published tables to establish whether the sequence is unlikely to be random. Note that it cannot be confirmed that the sequence is random.

Numerical data can be coded in order to carry out the one-sample runs test. The following sequence

5 3 8 4 6 7 4 3 5 8 9 5 4 2 5 6 4 8 6 7

has 20 data, with an average (mean) value of 5.5. The sequence can be rewritten with H representing higher than the mean and L representing lower than the mean. This gives the sequence

LL H L HH LLL HH LLLL H L HHH

which has 10 runs.

The test is of limited use, not only because it cannot confirm that a sequence is random but because runs arise more commonly than our intuition would suggest (Havil, 2008: 88-102). In a sequence of 100 tosses of a coin, the chance of a run of 5 or more is 0.97; and in a sequence of 200 tosses, there is a better than even chance of observing a run of 8.

CHAPTER 5

The Raw Data
Hard to Digest Until Processed

Raw data is the expression used to describe the original data before any analysis is undertaken. It is not a very palatable phrase. Something like "original data" or "new data" would have been more inviting, but I have to stick to convention. The purpose of this chapter is to explain the different kinds of data and present a number of definitions to be used in the chapters that follow. In addition, I will demonstrate how figures can mislead or confuse even before the statistical analysis has started.

Descriptive or Numerical

Data may be descriptive or numerical. *Descriptive data*, which is also called *categorical*, can be placed in categories and counted. Recording the way people vote in an election, for example, requires the categories—namely, the political parties—to be defined, and each datum adds one more to the appropriate category. The process of counting produces numerical values which summarize the data and can be used in subsequent processing. Thus we can express voting results as proportions of voters for each of the political parties.

If descriptive data can be placed in order but without any way of comparing the sizes of the gaps between the categories, the data is said to be *ordinal*. Thus we can place *small*, *medium*, and *large* in order, but the difference between *small* and *medium* may not be the same as the difference between *medium* and *large*. The placing in order in this way is referred to as *ranking*. Not only can the numbers in each category be totaled to give numerical values, but it also may be possible to attribute ordered numbers to each category. Thus *small*, *medium*, and *large* could be expressed respectively as 1, 2, and 3 on a scale indicating increasing size, to allow further processing.

Chapter 5 | The Raw Data

Descriptive data that cannot be placed in order is called *nominal*. Examples include color of eyes and place of birth. Collections of such data consist of numbers of occurrences of the particular attribute. If just two categories are being considered and they are mutually exclusive (for example, yes/no data), the data is referred to as *binomial*.

Numerical data may be *continuous* or *discrete*. Continuous data can be quoted to any degree of accuracy on an unbroken scale. Thus 24.31 km, 427.4 km, and 5017 km are examples of distances expressed as continuous numerical data. Discrete data can have only particular values on a scale that has gaps. Thus the number of children in a family can have values of 0, 1, 2, 3, 4, ..., with no in-between values. Notice that there is still a meaningful order of the values, as with continuous data.

Strictly speaking, continuous data becomes discrete once it is rounded, because it is quoted to a finite number of digits. Thus 24.31 is a discrete value located between 24.30 and 24.32. However, this is a somewhat pedantic observation and unlikely to cause problems. Of more importance is recognition of the fact that discrete data can often be processed as if the data were continuous, as you will see in Chapter 11.

Within a set of data there are usually several recorded features: numerical, descriptive, or both. Each feature—for example, cost or color—is referred to as a *variable*. The term *random variable* is often used to stress the fact that the values that the variables have are a random selection from the potentially available values.

A *distribution* is the set of values of the variable represented in a sample or a population, together with the frequency or relative frequency with which each value occurs. Thus, a listing of shoe sizes for a group of 50 men might show the following:

Shoe size: 8, 9, 8, 7, 9, 9, 8, 6, 10, 9, 10, 7, 9, 6, 11, 9, 8, 8, 7, 9, 9, 6, 10, 9, 8, 9, 10, 8, 7, 9, 6, 7, 8, 10, 7, 10, 9, 9, 10, 8, 7, 8, 9, 7, 10, 9, 8, 7, 8, 9

The values, 50 in total, can be counted and grouped as follows:

Shoe Size	Number of Men (Frequency)
6	4
7	9
8	12
9	16
10	8
11	1

The distribution can be shown diagrammatically in the form of a bar chart, as in Figure 5-1. The values can be seen to cluster around the central values. Starting in Chapter 7, I will discuss such distributions in more detail. In particular, you will meet the so-called *normal distribution*, which is of this form and which plays a major part in statistical analysis.

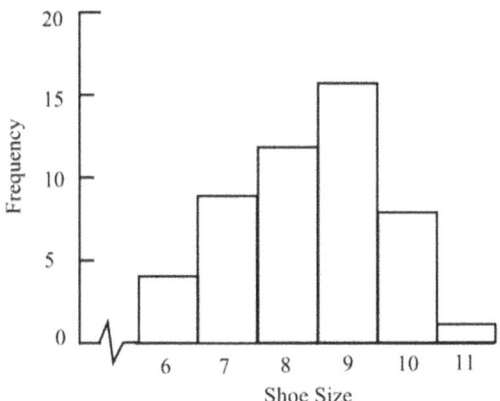

Figure 5-1. Bar chart showing the distribution of shoe sizes in a sample of 50 men

Some distributions are quite irregular in appearance when shown as bar charts. Others, including the normal distribution, not only are regular but also can be described exactly by mathematical formulae. Some of these will be encountered in Chapters 7, 11, and 18.

Format of Numbers

We are all familiar with the numbers we meet in our daily lives. Generally, these are neither too small nor too large for us to easily visualize them. However, very large or very small numbers can be a source of confusion.

Because large numbers written in full are very long, scientific reports adopt a shorthand method called *standard index form*. Multiplication factors of 10 are indicated by a superscript. So a million is 10^6, meaning $10 \times 10 \times 10 \times 10 \times 10 \times 10$. The number 2,365,000 can be written as 2.365×10^6. It is useful to note that the superscript, 6 in this case, indicates the number of moves of the decimal point to the right that are required to restore the number to the usual format.

Owing in part to computer literacy, the prefixes that are used in scientific work are creeping into common usage even in metrically challenged countries such as the United States. These prefixes are the set of *decadic* (decimal-based) multiples applied to the so-called *SI units* (abbreviated from *Le Systéme internationale d'unités*). Thus *kilo*, or simply *k*, is taken to mean 1000—so we

Chapter 5 | The Raw Data

see *$3k*, meaning $3000. *Mega* means a million and has the abbreviation M in scientific work; but in financial documents we see the abbreviation MM, such that $8MM is taken to mean $8,000,000. To add to the confusion, MM is the Roman numeral for 2000. Further up the scale we have *giga* (G) for 1000 millions (10^9), but in financial writing we see $1B, $1BN, or $1bn. *Giga* became increasingly popularized after consumer hard disk storage capacity crossed into the *gigabyte* (GB) range in the 1990s. The next prefixes up, *tera* (T) for a million millions (10^{12}) and *peta* (P), which is a thousand times larger again (10^{15}), are used in relation to big data, which I will discuss in Part VII.

The superscripts in 10^6 and so on are referred to as *orders of magnitude*. Each added factor of ten indicates the next order of magnitude. To say that two numbers are of the same order of magnitude means they are within a factor of ten of each other.

Very small numbers are encountered less frequently than very large ones. We seem to have no special traditional names for the small numbers except the awkward fraction words like hundredth, thousandth, etc. The standard index form described above extends to the very small, the superscripts being negative and indicating division by a number of tens rather than multiplication. Thus, 10^{-3} means 1 divided by 1000—that is, 10^{-3} means "one thousandth." The number 0.00000378 may be written as 3.78×10^{-6}, meaning 3.78 divided by 10 six times. As with the large numbers, the superscript, –6 in this case, indicates the number of moves of the decimal point that are required to restore the number to the usual format—except that the moves are now to the left, as indicated by the negative sign.

As with the large numbers, prefixes indicate how many tens the number shown has to be divided by. Some of these are in common use. One hundredth (0.01 or 10^{-2}) is indicated by *centi* (c). One thousandth (0.001 or 10^{-3}) is indicated by *milli* (m), and one millionth (0.000001 or 10^{-6}) by *micro* (the Greek letter μ, pronounced "mu"). The prefix *nano* (n) is encountered in the fashionable word *nanotechnology*, which is the relatively new branch of science dealing with molecular sizes. *Nano* indicates one thousand-millionth (0.000000001 or 10^{-9}), one nanometer (1 nm) being about the size of a molecule. Other SI prefixes used in the scientific community but not yet broadly encountered are *pico* (p) for one million-millionth (10^{-12}), *femto* (f) for one thousand-million-millionth (10^{-15}), and *atto* (a) for one million-million-millionth (10^{-18}).

Figure 5-2 brings together the various prefixes mentioned, together with a few even more exotic ones.

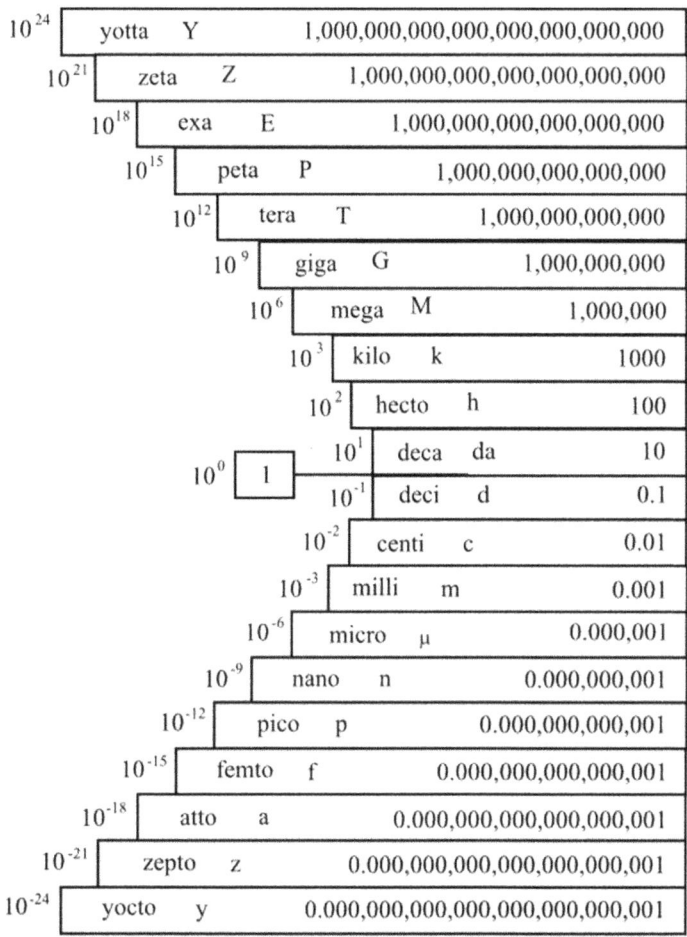

Figure 5-2. Prefixes used to denote decadic multiples or fractions of units

Negative numbers are well understood, but beware of possible confusion when comparing two negative numbers. If sales decrease by 200 units in January and by 300 in February, the change is said to be greater in February than in January. However, −300 is mathematically less than −200.

Multiplying or dividing two negative numbers gives a positive number. For example, if I buy and sell some shares at the same price, and the share price then changes, my profit is the excess number bought multiplied by the increase. Written as a formula, it is

$$\text{Profit} = (B-S) \times P$$

where B is the number bought, S is the number sold, and P is the increase in price. Four situations might be as follows:

Number Bought	Number Sold	B–S	Increase in Price	Profit
B	S		P	
100	90	10	$1	$10
100	90	10	–$1	–$10
100	110	–10	$1	–$10
100	110	–10	–$1	$10

The profit is negative if either the number sold is greater than the number bought or the price decreases. However, if both of these occur, as shown in the bottom line, the profit is positive.

In financial reports, negative values are avoided whenever possible. I have often wondered why this is so. It seems so odd in bookkeeping that, when balancing books, two columns (debit and credit) have to be added separately and then compared and the smaller subtracted from the larger. The result, always positive, is then added to the column with the smaller total to effect a balance, thus completely avoiding any recording of a negative value. Bookkeeping has a long history, and today's rules and procedures date back to medieval times. Perhaps the negative sign in mathematics was then less commonly used. Alternatively, it may be because when adding a list of figures that includes negatives, the negative sign, being at the left side, may not be noticed until it is too late. When a final value, which happens to be negative, has to be quoted, it is placed in brackets. This too is odd, as brackets have a particular and different meaning in mathematics. At one time, such negative values were generally shown in red, and sometimes still are—hence the expression "in the red," meaning overdrawn at the bank.

Rounding

Rounding is usually to the nearest value of the retained last digit. Thus, 4372 would be rounded to 4370 to the nearest ten 4400 to the nearest hundred or 4000 to the nearest thousand. When the digit to be removed is 5, it is common practice to round up, so 65 would become 70 to the nearest ten. It should be noted, however, that this can lead to a bias. In a list of numbers, each having a random final digit to be removed by rounding, more will be rounded up than down. If the numbers are subsequently added together, the total will be greater than the total of the original values. Inconsistencies can arise. If we calculate 10% of $5.25, we get $0.53 rounded up to the nearest penny. But 90%, calculated in the same way, gives $4.73, making the total slightly greater than the original amount. There are alternative methods of dealing with numbers ending with the digit 5 if the particular circumstances make it necessary. For example, in a long list of numbers, those ending in 5 can be rounded up and down alternately.

Raw statistical data that express continuously variable attributes will have been rounded, perhaps because the method of obtaining the values is limited in precision. Weighing precision, for example, is limited by the accuracy of the scales used. Or rounding may have been employed because the minor variations in the values are not considered to have any significance, either in the statistical processing that follows or in the conclusions that are expected following the processing.

Although rounding to the nearest retained last digit is usual, there are situations where always rounding up or always rounding down is adopted. The tax authorities in the UK and Singapore, for example, give the benefit to taxpayers of rounding down income and allowances and rounding up deductions.

Note that some values that appear to be discrete have in fact been rounded. A person's age could be expressed to the nearest day, hour, minute or even closer, but in a statistical list it may be given as an integral year. Furthermore, the rounding is not usually to the nearest year, but to the age last birthday. This makes no difference in many instances, of course, but if we were, for example, considering children between the ages of 8 and 14, we could find that our sample included children from just 8 years old to 15 years old less one day.

Rounding always creates discrete values, of course, but the small intervals relative to the size of the values render the values continuous in effect.

As a general principle, rounding should be carried out at the end of a calculation and not part way through, if errors are to be avoided. Successive roundings can give rise to cumulative errors. If we start, for example, with the number 67 and subject it to a number of arithmetic operations, we must wait until the final operation before rounding the answer to the required digit. Suppose we divide it by 5 and then multiply the answer by 7. We get 93.8, which we round to the nearest whole number, 94. If, alternatively, we round to the nearest whole number after the first operation, the sequence runs as follows: 67 divided by 5 is 13.4, which we round to 13; multiplying by 7 gives 91, which is incorrect.

Difficulties can arise if figures that have already been rounded are taken from sources and processed further. If, to take an extreme example, we read that 20 million cars are registered as being in use on the roads, but we see elsewhere that records show only 18 million currently licensed, we might view the difference and deduce that 2 million, or 10%, are unlicensed. In reality, the figure could be almost as low as half this if the original data—19.51 million registered and 18.49 million licensed—had been rounded to the nearest million.

When figures that appear to be rounded are required for further analysis, the maximum and minimum possible values that they may represent should be examined. Unless the worst case combination of the values is inconsequential, it is wise to seek the original data.

I wonder about rounding whenever I hear a time check on the radio. When the announcer says, "It is now sixteen minutes past two"—does he mean "exactly 16 minutes past 2:00"? Or does he mean "correct to the nearest minute"—in which case it could be anything between 15.5 minutes past to 16.5 past? Or he may mean that his digital clock is showing 16 minutes past and the actual time is somewhere between 16 and 17 minutes past. Not that it usually matters, of course.

Percentages

Any number can be represented by a fraction, a decimal, or a percentage. Thus ½ = 0.5 = 50%. To obtain a decimal from a fraction, divide the top by the bottom. To turn either into a percentage, multiply by 100. Expressing numbers as percentages in this way is useful when the numbers are less than 1. For numbers greater than 1, there is no advantage but it is done for effect. The number 2 is 200%. Notice the difference between sales increasing *by* 200% compared with last year and sales increasing *to* 200% compared with last year. In the first situation, sales have trebled; in the second, they have doubled.

Increases or decreases in sales, income, tax, and so on can be quoted as percentages or as actual values. The impression given can change enormously depending on which is chosen. A small increase of a small value can be a large percentage. A family with one child has a 100% increase in the number of children when the second child is born. A family with 5 children has only a 20% increase when the next one is born. Similarly, a large increase of a large value can be a small percentage. An annual salary increase of $1,000 for somebody earning half a million dollars is only 0.2%, whereas for a full-time worker making the federal minimum wage, it is 7%.

If you read that manufacturing has reduced from 25% of economic output to 12% in the last 20 years, you may well conclude that the amount of manufacturing has reduced. This is not necessarily so. It could actually have increased in absolute terms, its percentage reduction being due to a large increase in another sector of the economy. When data are presented as percentage changes, it is worth examining how the data would look in the form of actual changes.

Ages are usually quoted to the nearest year, but children appreciate that one year is a large proportion of their ages. You hear, "I am nine and a half, but next week I shall be nine and three quarters." Quoting the age of a ten-year-old to the nearest quarter of a year seems pedantic, yet it is less precise, as a percentage, than reporting the ages of pensioners to the nearest year.

Richard Wiseman (2007: 128) gives an interesting example of how people perceive values differently when seen as percentages. In the first scenario, a shopper is buying a calculator costing $20. Immediately before the purchase takes place, the shop assistant says that tomorrow there is a sale and the calculator will cost only $5. The shopper has to decide whether to proceed with the purchase or return to the shop tomorrow. In the second scenario, the shopper is buying a computer costing $999. This time, the assistant explains that tomorrow the cost will be only $984. On putting these scenarios to people, researchers have found that about 70% say they would put off buying the calculator until tomorrow but would go ahead with the purchase of the computer immediately. Yet the saving from delaying is the same in each situation—namely, $15.

This choice between percentage changes and actual changes impinges not only on the presentation of data, but on many issues that affect daily life. Should a tax reduction be a percentage or a fixed value for all? Should a pay rise be a percentage across the board or the same amount for everyone? These questions create lots of debate but little agreement. In reality, a compromise somewhere between the two usually results.

Note that a percentage is always calculated on the basis of the original value. So if my income increases by 10% this year but decreases by 10% next year, I end up with a lower income, because the second calculation is based on a higher income, and the 10% reduction represents more than the earlier increase of 10% did. In a similar way if I purchase stock that has been reduced by 20% and pay $1000, my saving is not $200 but rather more, because the reduction was calculated as a percentage of the original price.

A company having reduced the usage of paper, with the evidence that 12 boxes which were previously used in 4 days now last 6 days, may claim a 50% reduction. At a glance, it may look like 50%, because 6 days is 50% more than 4 days. However, the original usage was 3 boxes per day, and it is now 2 boxes per day—i.e., a reduction of 1 in 3, or 33%.

Sometimes there is ambiguity regarding which is the original value, and this can allow some bias in quoting the result. Suppose my car does 25 miles per gallon of fuel and yours does 30 miles per gallon. You would be correct in saying that your fuel consumption is 20% ((30 − 25) × 100/25) better than mine, the wording implying that it is your consumption that is being calculated, using my consumption as the base value. However, I would be equally correct in saying that my fuel consumption is only 16.7% ((30 − 25) × 100/30) worse than yours, calculating my consumption with yours as the base value.

Also deceptive is the way percentage rates of increase or decrease change as the time period considered increases. If the monthly interest rate on my credit card balance is 2%, I need to know what this is equivalent to when expressed as an annual rate. A debt of P will have risen to P × (1 + 2/100) at the end of the first month. At the end of the second month, this sum has to be multiplied by (1 + 2/100) to get the new total. By the end of the year, the original balance will have been multiplied by this factor 12 times. The final figure is 1.268 × P: an increase of nearly 27% compared with the quick-glance impression of 24%. Many will recognize this as a compound interest calculation and will be familiar with a formula that allows a quicker way of arriving at the result. Those not familiar with the calculation will nevertheless recognize with some pleasure that their bank accounts show this feature in producing increasing interest each year, even without additional deposits being made.

Confusion can arise when a percentage of a percentage is calculated. If the standard rate of tax is 20%, say, and the chancellor decides to increase it by 5%, the new rate will not be 25% but 21%. If he wished to be really unpopular and increase the rate to 25%, he could say that the rate would be increased by 5 percentage points, rather than by 5 percent.

Simple Index Numbers

Index numbers are used to render a trend in a sequence of values more easily appreciated. Thus we might have, say, the number of washing machines sold by a shop each year, as follows:

	Year 1	Year 2	Year 3	Year 4	Year 5	Year 6
Sales	224	246	249	258	260	269
Index	100	110	111	115	116	120

Year 1 has been adopted as the base, so the index is shown as 100. The succeeding indices are obtained by expressing each sales value as a percentage of the base value. Thus, for Year 2, (246/224) × 100 = 110.

The impression given to the reader depends very greatly on what has been chosen as the base value. If we look again at the above values but now take Year 2 as the base value, we get the following sequence:

	Year 1	Year 2	Year 3	Year 4	Year 5	Year 6
Sales	224	246	249	258	260	269
Index		100	101	105	106	109

The increasing sales now look less impressive.

A fair picture will emerge, provided the chosen base is typical in the appropriate sense. We would really need to know whether the sales for Year 1 were unusually low or whether they represented an increase on previous years.

A *chain index* can be calculated using each previous value as the base instead of the initial value. Thus for the above sales figures, we would have the following:

	Year 1	Year 2	Year 3	Year 4	Year 5	Year 6
Sales	224	246	249	258	260	269
Index		110	101	104	101	103

In such sequences, favorable indices tend to be followed by unfavorable ones, and vice versa. The sequence has the advantage of better illustrating a rate of change. A steady rise in sales or a steady fall in sales would be shown by a sequence of similar values. A sequence of rising values would indicate an increasing rate of increase in sales, whereas a sequence of falling values would indicate an increasing rate of decreasing sales.

Samples

The tendency of the casual mind is to pick out or stumble upon a sample which supports or defies its prejudices, and then to make it the representative of a whole class.

—Walter Lippmann

The raw data may provide all the information that is required and therefore undergo no subsequent processing. In most situations, however, this will not be so. The data may be too extensive to be readily appreciated and may require summarizing. It is essential that the summarizing be done in a suitable manner so that it represents the original data in a fair way. Processing may then be required to estimate the characteristics of the population from which the data were drawn.

CHAPTER 6

Descriptive Data
Not Every Picture Is Worth a Thousand Words

There is not much that can be done to characterize a sample of descriptive data in comparison with the options available for numerical data. The latter has had the advantages of centuries of development of mathematics. Where possible, and usually by simply counting, descriptive data is rendered numerical. In addition, the frequent use of diagrams provides neat summaries of the data, though there are many ways in which diagrams can mislead.

Diagrammatic Representation

Nominal data consists of numbers that can be placed in categories and totaled, the categories having no numerical relationship to each other. Thus an employer might group the staff according to the mode of transport used to get to work, and use the total in each group to draw conclusions about the required size of the car park or bicycle shed.

In Figure 6-1(a), the populations of each of four towns are shown in the form of a bar chart. Because there is no numerical relation between the categories (towns), the bars could have been lined up in any order.

The bar chart format is useful in allowing the relative numbers in each category to be visualized: the eye is quite sensitive in spotting small differences between the heights of the bars while at the same time assimilating large differences. Bar charts are sometimes presented in a way that exaggerates the differences between the large and the small bars, as shown in Figure 6-1(b). The origin has been suppressed, giving the impression that the population of Northton is very much greater than that of the others. Suppression of the origin in this fashion is generally not acceptable and should arouse suspicion regarding the intentions behind the presentation of the statistics. A bar chart of this sort was used in advertising Quaker Oats, suggesting that eating the breakfast cereal reduced the level of cholesterol (Seife, 2010: 35-36). The diagram was withdrawn after complaints were received.

In situations where it is considered necessary to exaggerate—for instance, we might wish to ensure that it is clear that Easton has a larger population than Weston—the vertical axis, and possibly the bars, should show breaks as in Figure 6-1(c).

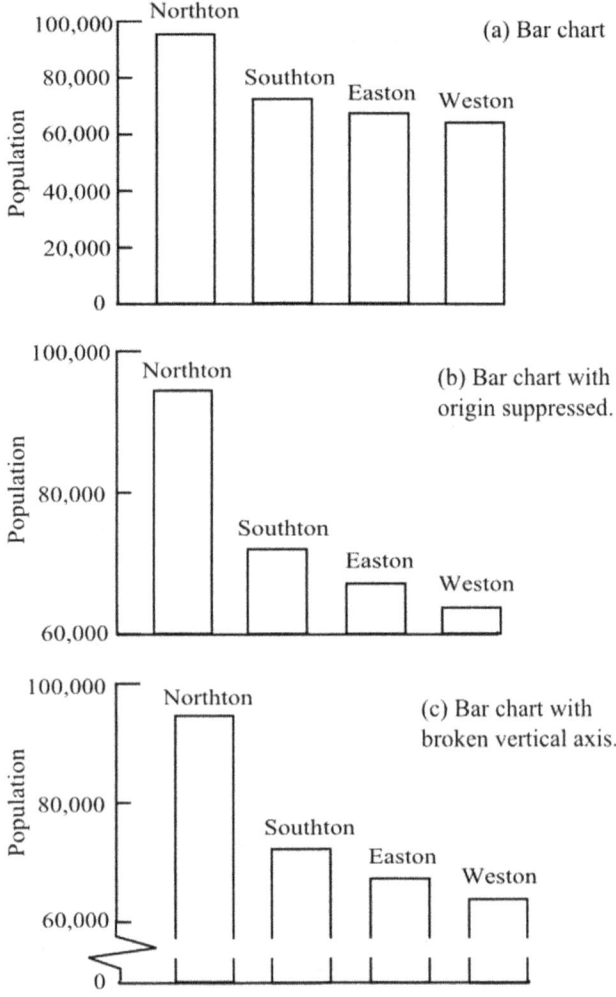

Figure 6-1. Three representations of the same bar chart, showing the visual effects of suppressing the origin and breaking the vertical axis

Better Business Decisions from Data 49

When it is important to draw attention to the relative proportions of each of the categories, a pie chart is preferable to a bar chart. Figure 6-2(a) shows the results of an election. The impression given visually is the relative support for each political party rather than the actual number of votes received. However, it is not easy to see whether the Yellow Party or the Blue Party won the election without looking at the numbers. A bar chart, Figure 6-2(b), shows more clearly who won the election, but the impression of proportion of votes is lost.

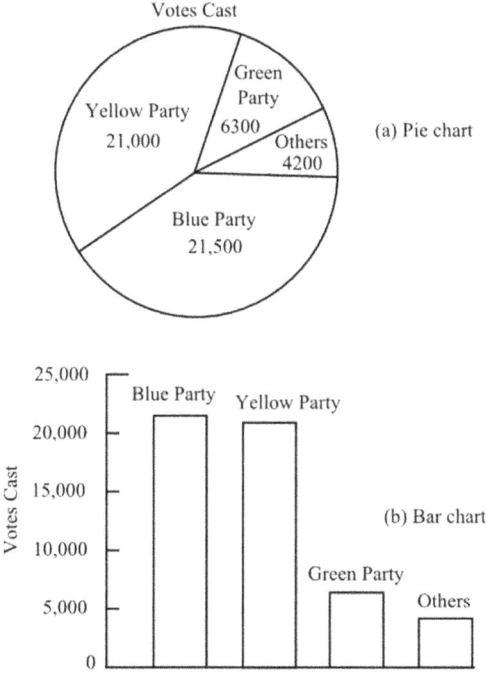

Figure 6-2. A pie chart and a bar chart representing the same data

Diagrams that consist of two or more pie charts can be visually misleading. In Figure 6-3(a), the number of households in two districts are shown and divided into three categories: those that have dogs, those that have cats, and those that have neither. The area of each sector of the pie chart represents the number in each category, and the total area of each pie chart represents the total number of households in each district. Upper Dale, with 3000 households, has a chart with 50% greater area than that for Lower Dale, which has 2000 households. To achieve the correct area proportion, the chart for Upper Dale has a diameter only 22% greater than the Lower Dale chart. This gives a visual bias to the distribution of pets in Lower Dale. The stacked bar chart in Figure 6-3(b) gives a fairer visual impression of the relative numbers of dogs and cats.

Chapter 6 | Descriptive Data

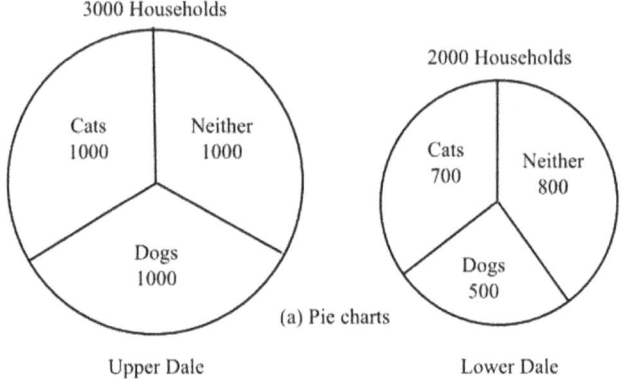

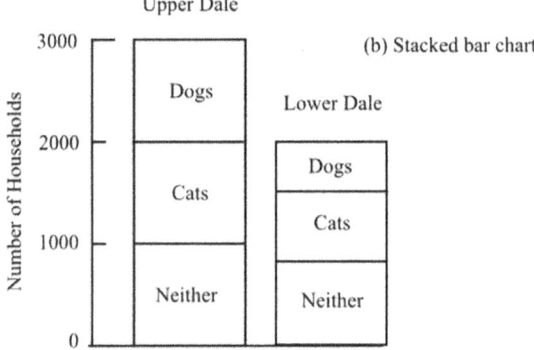

Figure 6-3. A pair of pie charts and a stacked bar chart representing the same data

Pictograms can be even more misleading. Figure 6-4(a) shows a comparison of the number of cats in Upper Dale and Lower Dale. The vertical scale indicates the number of cats, so only the vertical height of the image of the cat is significant. However, because the taller cat is also wider, the difference between the numbers of cats appears visually to be greater than it really is. The style of pictogram shown in Figure 6-4(b) is preferable in showing no bias. Here a small image of the cat is used to represent 100 cats in each of the districts.

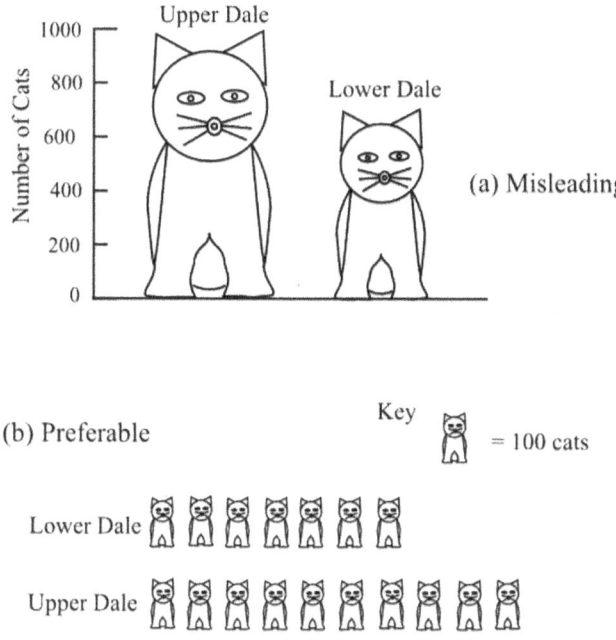

Figure 6-4. The use of pictograms in charts may be more or less visually misleading, as exemplified in (a) and (b), respectively

The use of three-dimensional images in pictograms can be extremely misleading. Figure 6-5 shows the output of two factories. Visually, it appears that there is not a great difference between the two. However, as the actual cubic meters for each confirm, Factory A has an output almost twice that of Factory B. The illusion occurs because although the volumes of the two cubes represent the outputs correctly, the length of the side of the cube for Factory A is only 25% greater than that for Factory B. Thus: 50 × 50 × 50 = 125,000, and 40 × 40 × 40 = 64,000.

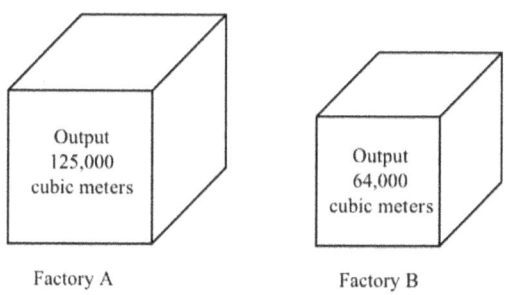

Figure 6-5. A misleading visual comparison of the outputs of two factories

Chapter 6 | Descriptive Data

When categories overlap, the data is often represented by a *Venn diagram*. Consider the following data. In a group of 100 students, 30 are not studying a language, 50 are studying French, and 30 are studying German. Thus 10 are studying both French and German. Figure 6-6 shows the data diagrammatically. Enclosed regions represent the different categories, but the actual sizes of the areas enclosed are not intended to represent the numbers within the categories. The intention is purely to illustrate the overlaps. It is therefore important when viewing Venn diagrams to be aware of the actual numbers and avoid visual clues from the sizes of the regions.

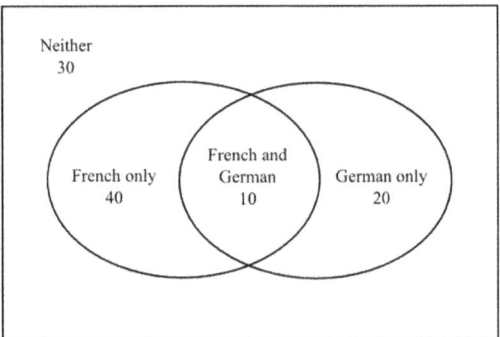

Figure 6-6. Venn diagram showing the numbers of students studying French and German

Venn diagrams are useful in visualizing conditional probability (Chapter 3). Suppose we choose a student randomly from those shown in Figure 6-6 but specify the condition that the student studies French. The only students of interest to us are those in the left ellipse, 50 in total. If we ask what the probability is that the student studies German, we see from the overlap region that 10 students would meet the requirement. So the probability is 10/50 = 0.2. If, on the other hand, we specify the condition that the student studies German and ask for the probability that the student studies French, we are concerned only with the right ellipse. The probability is thus 10/30 = 0.33.

For *ordinal data*, although pie charts can be used, bar charts have the advantage of allowing the categories to be lined up in logical order. Figure 6-7 shows the number of medals won by a sports club in the form of a bar chart.

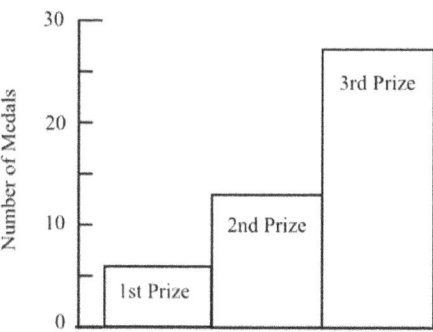

Figure 6-7. Bar chart showing the numbers of medals won by a sports club

Proportion

Nominal data can be rendered numerical insofar as the numbers in each group can be expressed as *proportions* or percentages of the total. Thus the data in Figure 6-2 yield the following proportions:

	Blue Party	Yellow Party	Green Party	Others	Total
Votes	21,500	21,000	6300	4200	53,000
Proportion	0.406	0.396	0.119	0.079	1
Percentage	40.6	39.6	11.9	7.9	100

Use of proportions or percentages is often adopted to disguise the fact that the numbers involved are very small. It may sound impressive to be told that 12% of the staff of a local company are still working full time at the age of 70 years, but less so when you learn that the number represents just one person.

Ordinal data can be represented as proportions or percentages, as with nominal data. Thus, sales of shirts could be reported as 30% small size, 50% medium, and 20% large.

CHAPTER 7

Numerical Data
Are Your Statistics Normal?

When a sample consists of numerical data, it has many features that can be quantified. These features can be used to summarize the data, to provide information about the population from which the sample was obtained, and to indicate the reliability of such information. Also, the calculated properties of the sample can be used subsequently if the sample becomes part of a further investigation.

A well-known feature of a sample of numerical data is the average value. Indeed, we get a daily dose of averages from the media and from general conversation. But an average value, though having its proper uses, can be extremely misleading when quoted in isolation. A proper consideration of a data sample requires information about how the data is spread over a range of values.

Diagrammatic Representation

Chapter 5 introduced the idea of a distribution and used a sample of sizes of shoes worn by a group of men to plot the distribution as a bar chart (Figure 5-1). Notice that the area covered by the bar chart represents the total number of data, since each bar has a height representing the number of data in the particular group. If the bar chart is shown with the vertical axis representing relative frequency—that is, frequency divided by the total, as in Figure 7-1(a)—the appearance is exactly the same, but the total area covered by the bar chart is now unity and the relative frequency is equivalent to probability. Thus we could deduce from the diagram that the probability of selecting from the group a man who wears a size 8 shoe is 0.24. The diagram may be referred to as a *probability distribution*. Generally speaking, we use *relative frequency* as the label for the vertical axis when the data is observed or measured data. When the diagram is theoretical or being used to determine probabilities, we label the axis *probability*.

Diagrams such as Figure 7-1(a), which display relative frequency and have a numerical sequence along the horizontal axis, are often called *histograms*. This is to distinguish them from the type of bar chart shown, for example, in Figure 6-1, where frequency is indicated on the vertical axis and where the horizontal axis has no numerical property. The practice is popular and has some advantage, but the term *histogram* applies strictly to diagrams in which the bars are not all of equal width. This is explained further in the "Grouped Data" section.

Figure 7-1(b) shows the data of Figure 7-1(a) as a relative frequency polygon, the term *polygon* indicating the joining of points with straight lines.

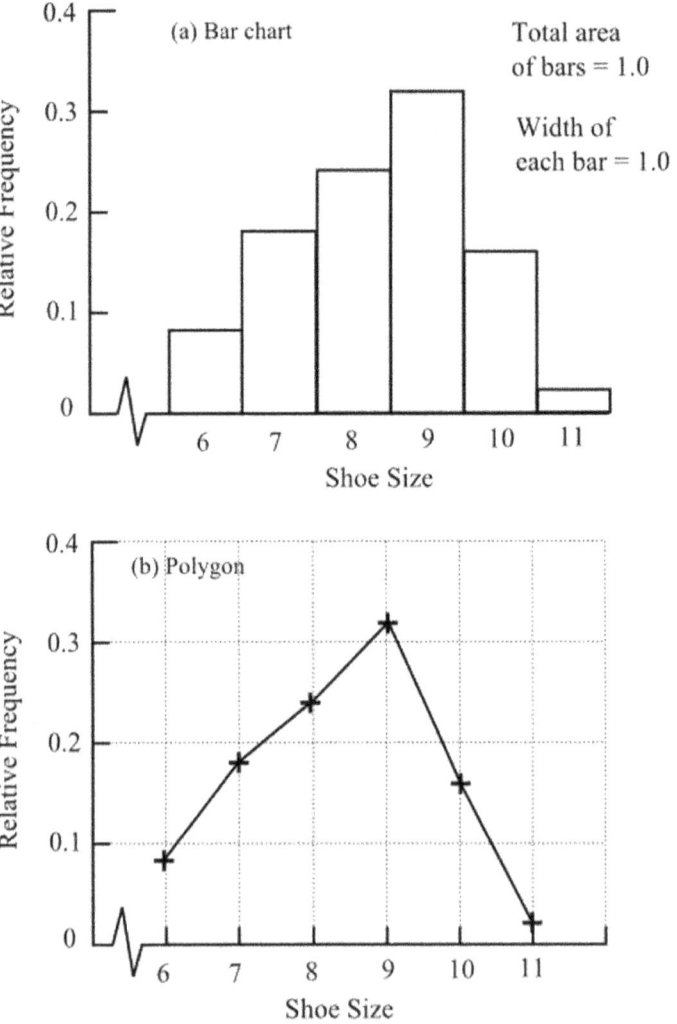

Figure 7-1. Relative frequency shown as (a) a bar chart and (b) a polygon

Such data can be presented as cumulative values. The shoe size data are extended below to include the cumulative frequency, cumulative relative frequency and cumulative percentage.

Shoe Size	Frequency	Cumulative Frequency	Relative Frequency	Cumulative Relative Frequency	Cumulative Percentage
6	4	4	0.08	0.08	8
7	9	13	0.18	0.26	26
8	12	25	0.24	0.50	50
9	16	41	0.32	0.82	82
10	8	49	0.16	0.98	98
11	1	50	0.02	1.00	100

Figure 7-2 shows the cumulative frequency in the form of (a) a bar chart and (b) a polygon.

Chapter 7 | Numerical Data

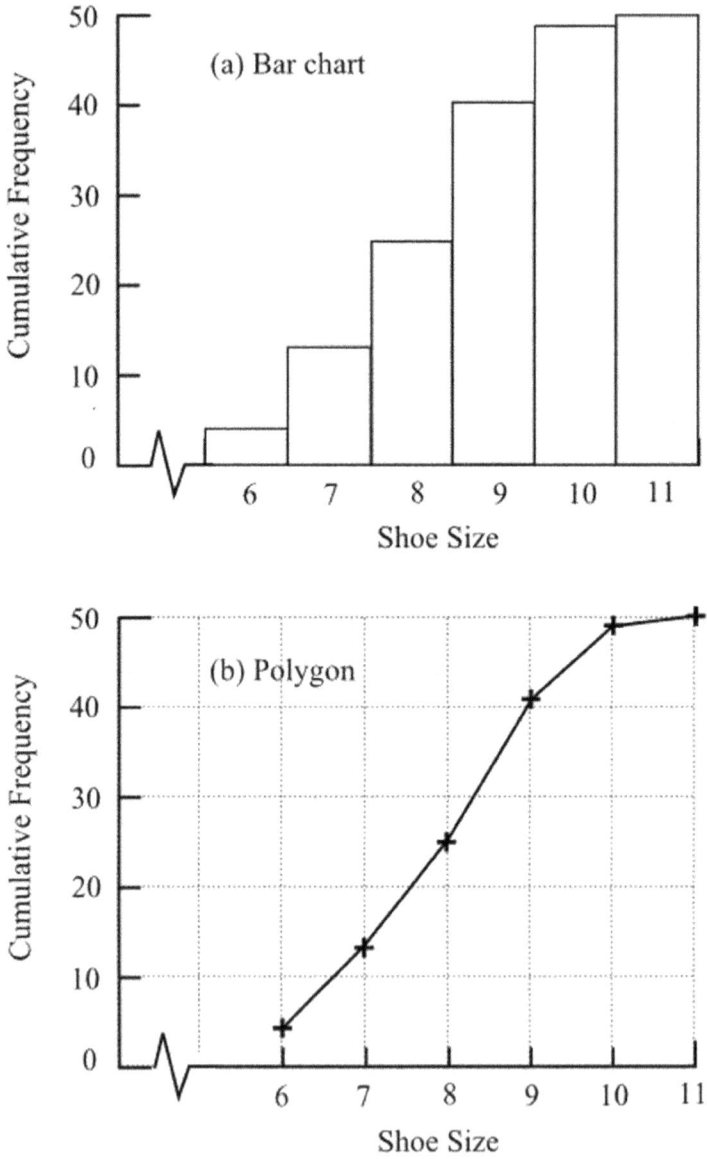

Figure 7-2. Cumulative frequency shown as (a) a bar chart and (b) a polygon

The above data are discrete, but if the data are continuous a cumulative frequency graph can contain more information than its corresponding frequency bar chart. To see this, suppose instead of noting the size of shoe worn by each of our volunteers, we had measured the length of his foot. The data, measured in cm and arranged in order of size, might have been as follows:

Group 1	22.1, 22.3, 22.9, 23.7
Group 2	24.2, 24.4, 24.6, 24.6, 25.1, 25.4, 25.5, 25.8, 25.9
Group 3	26.0, 26.3, 26.4, 26.6, 26.7, 26.9, 27.0, 27.3, 27.5, 27.8, 27.8, 27.9
Group 4	28.1, 28.1, 28.2, 28.2, 28.4, 28.5, 28.5, 28.7, 28.8, 28.8, 28.9, 29.1, 29.3, 29.6, 29.8, 29.9
Group 5	30.0, 30.2, 30.5, 30.6, 30.7, 31.0, 31.4, 31.8
Group 6	32.1

When plotted as a bar chart the data have to be grouped. The groups could be, for example, as shown above, 22.0 to 23.9, 24.0 to 25.9, 26.0 to 27.9, and so on. Figure 7-3(a) shows the resulting bar chart. Within each group, the individual values become equivalent to each other, each simply contributing to the total number of values within the group. From the bar chart there is no way of knowing what the individual values are within each group. In contrast, the cumulative frequency graph can be plotted using each value, as shown in Figure 7-3(b). A smooth curve is generally drawn when the data is continuous, and the curve is frequently referred to as an *ogive*. When the vertical axis is cumulative relative frequency or cumulative probability, the shape of the curve remains the same, but the graph may be referred to as a *cumulative distribution function* or simply as a *distribution function*.

Chapter 7 | Numerical Data

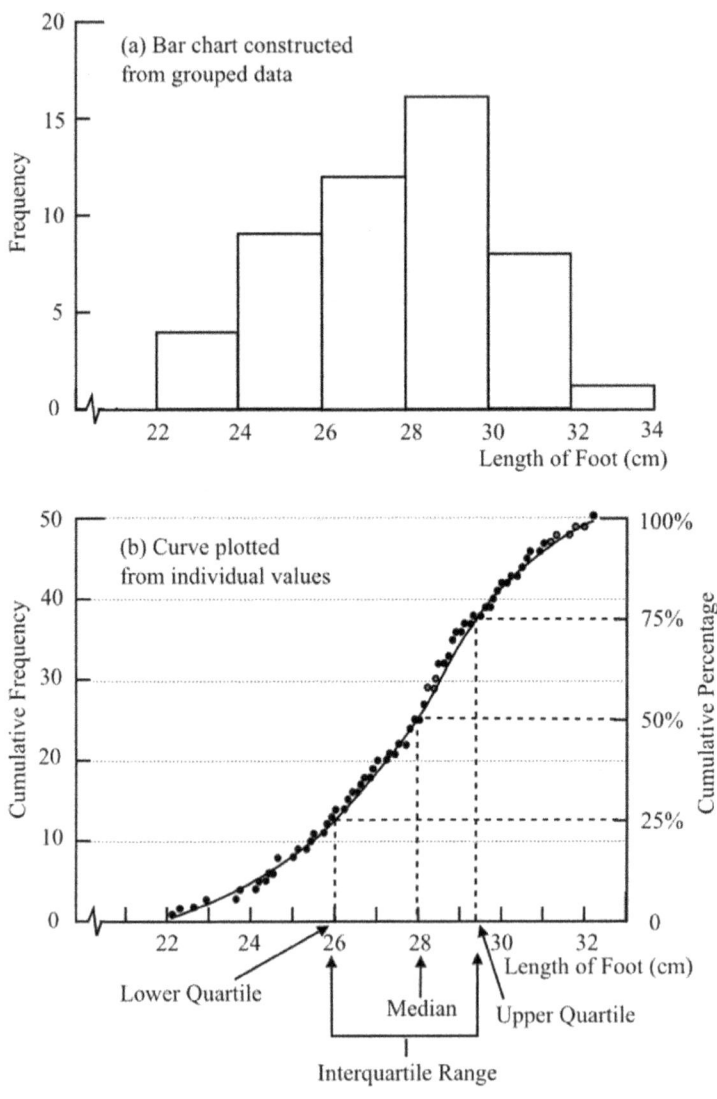

Figure 7-3. Frequency and cumulative frequency shown as (a) a bar chart constructed from grouped data and (b) a curve plotted from individual values

Sets of data often show a tendency to cluster around a central value, as in Figure 7-3(a). As we would expect, there are relatively few of the small or large sizes. Most are close to the average size for the group. When the data is centrally clustered, the cumulative frequency graph has a characteristic S-shape as seen in Figures 7-3(b). The graph additionally provides a convenient way of determining the *median*, or middle value, as Figure 7-3(b) illustrates.

The *quartiles*, at one quarter and three quarters of the values, are frequently quoted in statistical conclusions and are also shown. The interquartile range embraces the middle half of the data.

If we have a bar chart with the peak at the low end of the data, the distribution is said to be *positively skewed*. Family incomes would be expected to be of this kind, a peak occurring well below the midpoint value (Figure 7-4(a)). When the peak of the distribution is towards the high end of the data, the distribution is *negatively skewed*. If we looked at ages of people at death, we would expect to see the distribution negatively skewed, with most people dying in old age (Figure 7-4(b)).

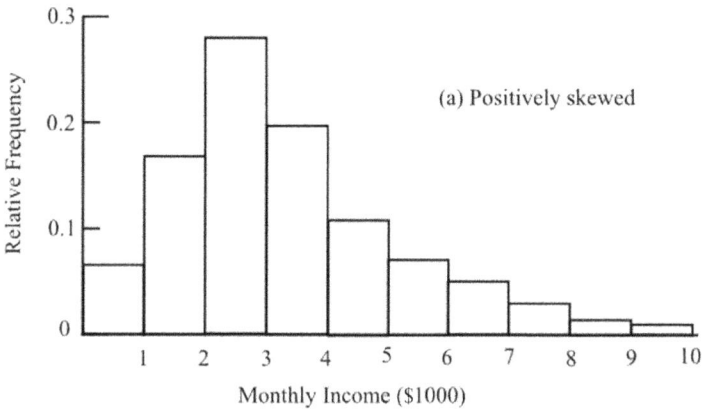

Figure 7-4. (a) Positively and (b) negatively skewed distributions

Normally Distributed Data

Fortunately, in the statistical term *normally distributed* the word *normal* does carry the conventional meaning of "usually encountered" or "of everyday occurrence." Nevertheless, it is not easy to summarize in a few words what is meant by the important concept of *normally distributed data*.

Normally distributed data are centrally clustered and symmetrical—i.e., not skewed positively or negatively. They are, however, special in the way the distribution varies across the range of values encompassed.

Heights and weights of people are normally distributed. Suppose we measure the heights of a small sample of men, say 20. We could represent the data in the form of a bar chart with a group width of 8 cm, as shown in Figure 7-5(a). Central clustering around a mean value is clearly shown but the data are presented very coarsely with wide steps in relation to the total width. If we decide to reduce the group width to 4 cm in an attempt to improve the presentation we might end up with Figure 7-5(b). Because we now have so few data in each group, the bar chart begins to lose its shape.

If we now consider having larger samples, we can reduce the group width and still have a sufficient number in each group to represent the distribution of heights in a reliable way. Figure 7-5(c) shows what we might get with a sample size of 10,000 and a group width of 2 cm. The bar chart now has a smoother outline. Extending the process to larger sample sizes and narrower group widths eventually gives a smooth curve, superimposed on the bar chart in Figure 7-5(c), which is the normal distribution. The curve, also known as the *Gaussian curve*, has a characteristic bell shape. It has an exact though complicated mathematical formula that defines it precisely. It is not, of course, derived from bar charts in the way I may have implied: the description via bar charts is useful in providing a simple and correct view of the meaning of the normal distribution.

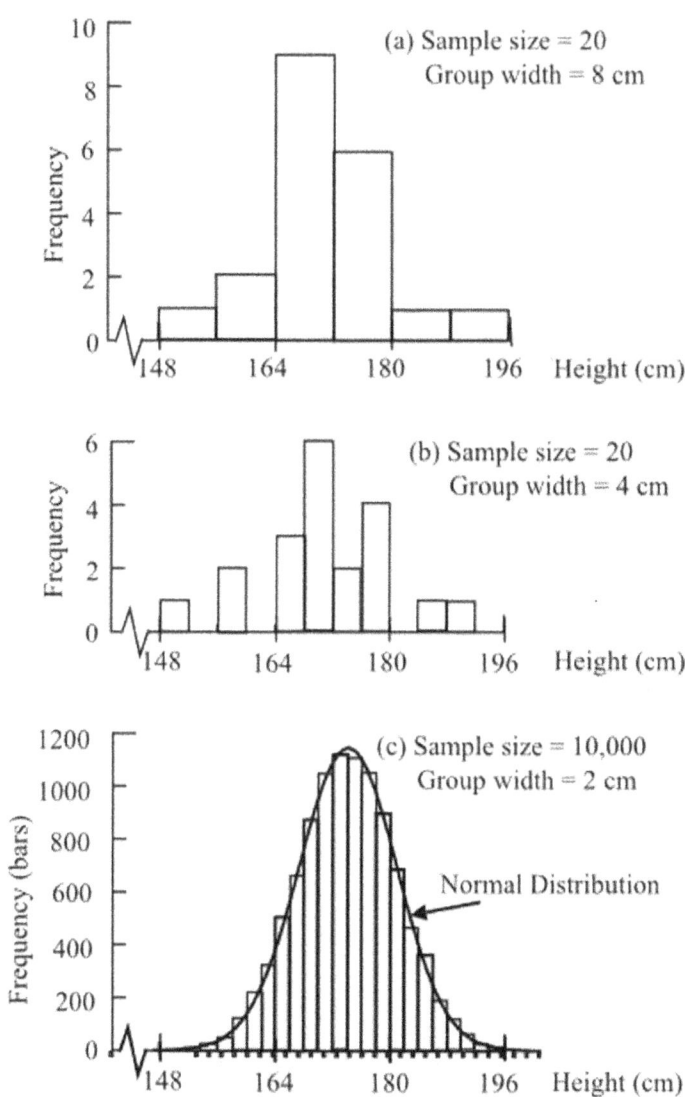

Figure 7-5. Distributions of heights of men

Just as in the bar charts, where the number of data within each group is indicated by the area of the corresponding vertical bar, any vertical strip defined under the normal distribution curve represents the relative number of data lying between the horizontal limits of the strip. The proportion of data within the strip relative to the total number of data is thus equal to the proportion of the area within the strip relative to the total area under the curve. Furthermore, this proportion is equal to the probability of a man, chosen at random from the total, having a height lying between the limits of the strip.

Progressing from the bar chart in Figure 7-5(a) to the continuous curve in Figure 7-5(c) necessitates a change in the labeling of the vertical axis. For the bar chart, the label is frequency. Provided the bar width is constant across the whole of the diagram, the scale on the axis will always allow us to read off the frequency. However, once we replace the set of bars with a smooth curve, we can no longer read off frequency: the frequency will depend on the width of strip that we choose. The axis is labeled *frequency density*.

Clearly, each set of data will have its own scale in terms of the numerical values on the horizontal axis and the frequency on the vertical axis. But the shape of the curve will be the same, provided the data follow a normal distribution. In order to utilize the normal distribution in analyzing data, a standard normal distribution, shown in Figure 7-6, is defined with a peak value located at zero on the horizontal axis. Thus the curve extends symmetrically in the positive and negative directions. The horizontal scale is explained in the "Spread of Data" section of this chapter. The vertical scale is adjusted so that the total area under the curve is 1. The area of any vertical strip then expresses directly the probability of occurrence of values within the strip. Any set of data fitting a normal distribution can be reduced to the standard normal distribution by a change of scale, taken up later in the context of analyzing data.

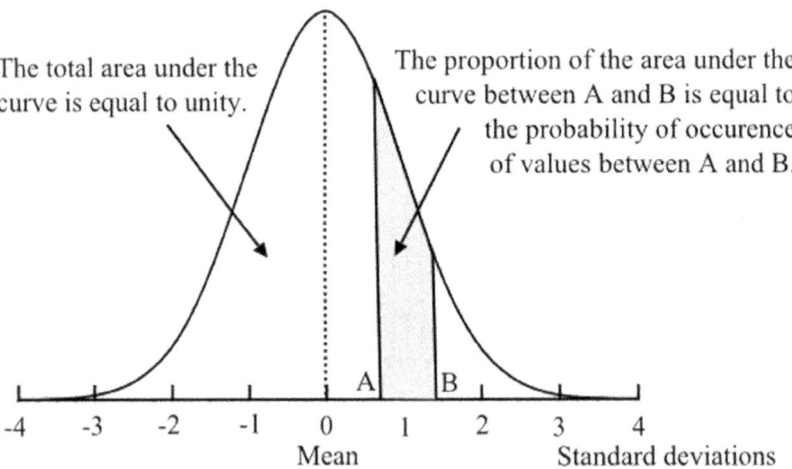

Figure 7-6. The standard normal distribution

This characteristic curve results whenever the variation of the data is due to numerous random effects. The effects may be intrinsic to the property being measured, as in the example of the heights of the men sampled, but in other situations the effects may be due to errors in the method of measurement. Repeated measurements of the height of Mount Everest would be expected to give a normal distribution of data clustering around a central value. The normal distribution is found to arise in many situations of data collection and is used extensively in subsequent statistical analysis. There are, of course, other special distributions that are encountered, and I will describe some of these in later chapters.

Examples of data that conform to the normal distribution fall into several categories. The first category is where there exists a true value and the sample consists of estimates or measurements of the value, which inevitably are inaccurate to some degree. The inaccuracies arise from random errors in the observation or measurement methods. Repeated measurements of the density of pure copper, various chemical and physical constants, or estimates of the volume of water in the oceans of the world would fall into this category.

The second category is where an attempt has been made to produce items consistent in such properties as size and weight. Because of random fluctuations in materials or manufacturing processes each item is slightly different. Measurements on a number of the items would be expected to follow a normal distribution.

The third category consists of data that are correct (within some error of measurement, of course) but in reality quite different. That is to say, the observed differences are due not to small errors of measurement or manufacturing, as in the previous two categories but reflect their differences by nature. Nevertheless the values exhibit a tendency to cluster around a central value—the likelihood of departure greater or smaller than the central value being less the greater the departure. Examples of such data are the heights and weights of people, examination marks, and intelligence quotients. A comparison between this category and the previous category raises an interesting point. It is as if natural processes attempt to produce everything the same, as we do in our factories, but don't quite succeed because of random errors, just as we don't quite succeed. Viewed this way, categories two and three are in a sense the same.

The fourth category consists of data that theoretically conform to distributions other than the normal distribution but that, under certain circumstances, can be well represented by the normal distribution. Usually it is when samples are large that we find the closest approximations to the normal distribution.

The ability of the normal distribution to represent data that does not conform exactly to the theoretical requirements of the distribution helps to give it its primary role in statistics. In reality, of course, no set of data is likely to conform exactly. The theoretical distribution tapers to infinity in both directions, indicating that there is always a probability, albeit very small, of observing a value of any size. In reality, this cannot be so, not only because of practical limits on the maximum value but also because the low-value tail is limited by the value of zero. Negative values would be meaningless in most situations.

Distribution Type

A data sample may, simply by inspection, be judged to be of a particular type of distribution or approximately so. Data may be seen to be approximately normally distributed, clustering around a central value with few extreme values. Other sets of data may appear, for example, to be uniformly distributed with no evidence of central clustering.

It is possible to make a comparison between the data and an assumed distribution in a way that provides a measure of the likelihood of the data belonging to the distribution. Such a comparison is called a *goodness-of-fit test*.

The data are laid out in sequence, and calculations are made of the corresponding values that are obtained on the basis of the assumed distribution. For example, we may have data showing how many employees are late for work on different days of the week, and we wish to test the hypothesis that the number late for work is independent of the day of the week. If the hypothesis is correct, the distribution of data should be uniform: that is, the numbers for different days should be the same within the likely random fluctuations. We therefore lay out the expected data, each value being the average (mean) of the actual data:

Day	Late Arrivals	Expected Late Arrivals	Difference	Difference Squared	Difference Squared Divided by Expected
		e	d	d^2	d^2/e
Monday	25	24	1	1	1/24
Tuesday	16	24	−8	64	64/24
Wednesday	18	24	−6	36	36/24
Thursday	28	24	4	16	16/24
Friday	33	24	9	81	81/24
Total	120				198/24 = 8.25
Mean = 24		Degrees of Freedom = 4			

The differences between the two sets are calculated. From the squares of these differences, a statistic called *chi-squared*, χ^2 (Greek letter chi), is determined. In this example, chi-squared = 8.25. You will appreciate that a value of zero would be obtained if the data agreed exactly with the expected data. So the larger the value is, the more likely the distribution is not uniform. The value obtained is referred to tables of the chi-squared distribution to obtain the probability of there being a dependence on the day of the week as opposed to the actual number of late arrivals being subject to a random fluctuation. The following is an extract from tables of the chi-squared distribution:

Degrees of Freedom	10% Significance	5% Significance	1% Significance	0.1% Significance
1	2.71	5.02	6.64	10.80
2	4.61	5.99	9.21	13.80
3	6.25	7.82	11.30	16.30
4	7.78	9.49	13.30	18.50
5	9.24	11.10	15.10	20.50

In this example we find from the tables that, with 4 degrees of freedom (see above), 8.25 lies between the values for 10% and 5% significance. Thus we have a greater than one in twenty (5%) chance of being wrong if we claim that the number of late arrivals does depend on the day of the week. The claim would be unreliable. Figure 7-7 shows the distribution of the data and, for comparison, the supposed uniform distribution.

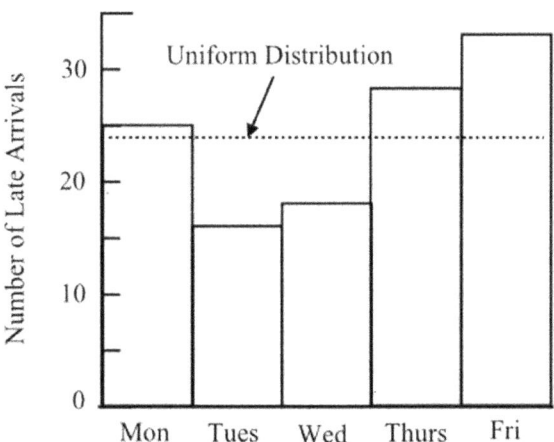

Figure 7-7. Comparison of an observed distribution and a supposed uniform distribution

For a non-uniform expected distribution, the required expected values would have to be obtained from tables. To test whether data conformed to a normal distribution, for example, values would be obtained from tables of the normal distribution. The calculation would then proceed as above, the differences between the actual values and the expected normally distributed values being squared and summed.

I need to explain the term *degrees of freedom*, which I stated above is a feature of the data and which is required to obtain the level of significance from the published tables. In a sense, the *freedom* referred to is the freedom to be different—and this, I suggest, is a useful way of appreciating what is meant by degrees of freedom. If we have data consisting of just one value, there is no difference involved and no variation or measure of uncertainty. If we have two values, there is one measure of difference, that being the difference between the two values. Thus we have a measure of variation based on a single difference, and we refer to this as one degree of freedom.

With three values—a, b, and c—there are two measures of variation: a–b and b–c. Note that a–c is not a further measure of variation, because its value is fixed by the other two differences. Thus we have two degrees of freedom. With four values, we have three degrees of freedom, and so on.

The degrees of freedom in the above example are shown as four. There are actually five differences involved—i.e., the difference between each of the five daily values and the number 24. However, the value 24 was obtained from the five daily values by ensuring that the totals of the actual and expected values were the same. This restriction removes one degree of freedom, leaving four. When distributions other than a uniform distribution are selected for comparison, there may be additional reductions in the degrees of freedom. This arises when additional features of the assumed distribution have to be calculated from the original data.

Various statistical tests are in standard use to establish the reliability of estimated values from the data, or the likelihood of there being differences or similarities between sets of data. In these tests, use is made of published tables, and the tables generally require the appropriate degrees of freedom of the data to be entered.

The chi-squared test can also show evidence of surprisingly good agreement with a supposed distribution. Too-good agreement should be viewed with some suspicion. Is the data genuine? Has some of the data been removed?

There are other goodness-of-fit tests. The *likelihood-ratio test* produces a statistic, G^2, which is similar to χ^2. The *Kolmogorov-Smirnov test* is similarly based on the differences between the observed data and the data expected from the assumed distribution.

Averages

The word *average* in common usage refers, from a mathematics point of view, to the *mean value*—the sum of all the data in a collection divided by the number of data. The mean value expresses a central value around which the other values are arranged. It is a useful summary of the data, especially when, evident from the nature of the data, there is a central clustering effect. As we said previously, the heights or weights of people would be expected to cluster around the mean value, there being relatively few people with extreme, large or small, height or weight. The description of the normal distribution in the section "Normally Distributed Data," recognized the symmetry about the peak value, which is the mean value.

Using a mean value where there is no clustering would be misleading and rather pointless in some situations. But not always: the scores when a die is repeatedly thrown show no central clustering, each of the possible six scores occurring roughly equally, but the average score is useful in allowing an estimate of the total score expected after a given number of throws. Thus, the mean value is $(1+2+3+4+5+6)/6 = 3.5$—so ten throws, say, would be expected to give a total of about 35.

Statisticians use the word *expectation* to mean the *expected mean value* as opposed to the *achieved mean value*. So if we throw a die a number of times, the expectation is 3.5. The actual achieved mean value is likely to be close to 3.5 but could be any number between 1 and 6.

There are two other averages frequently used in statistical presentations: the median and the mode. The *median*, described in the "Diagrammatic Representation" section and shown in Figure 7-3, is the middle value of the data ordered by size, such that half the data are less than and half are greater than the median. The *mode* is the most common value—i.e., the value that occurs most frequently in the data. There could be more than one mode in the sample, whereas the mean and median have unique values.

The decision as to which average to use depends on the nature of the data. The use of an inappropriate average can distort the impression gained. If we were looking at the average number of children per family, a calculation of the mean would probably give a non-integer value, 2.23 say. Although no family has 2.23 children, the value could be extremely useful because, given a total number of families, it would allow us to calculate the best estimate of the total number of children. The median would probably lie between 2 and 3, telling us that half the families had 2 or fewer children and half had 3 or more, which is not very informative. The mode, with a value of 2 probably, would at least tell us that the families were more likely to have 2 children than any other number.

If we were looking at family incomes, we would have different considerations. The mean income could be, say, $50,000 per annum. However, there will be in the data a few very high earners with incomes three or four times the mean. Most families will lie well below the mean. Thus there is an upward bias effect that can be misleading. If we work out the median we might find that the value is $40,000, showing that half the families have incomes less than this. If we wish to see what the mode is, we find that because income has continuous values (no finer than a penny, of course), there are insufficient families, or perhaps none, with the same value of income. This could be overcome by rounding off the data or, better, by grouping the data. This might give us an answer that the most common family income is in the range $35,000 to $40,000.

As data fit the normal distribution more exactly, the mean, median, and mode come closer together. As the distribution becomes positively skewed, the mode moves below the mean; as it becomes negatively skewed, it moves above the mean. The median usually lies between the mode and the mean.

Choice of the inappropriate average can give erroneous impressions of the meaning of the data and is often done with the intention of misleading. The situation is made worse when the type of average that has been used is not specified. The moral is to be wary of averages of unspecified type and—even when it is stated that the mean, median, or mode has been quoted—to explore the consequences of viewing the results in terms of the other averages.

Spread of Data

Average values are extremely useful but give no indication of the spread of the values from which they were derived. It is not possible to make any judgment about how valid it will be to base decisions on the average values. Some indication of the spread of the data should accompany any quoted average.

The maximum and minimum values, and the difference between them, the latter being referred to as the *range*, are easily quoted but of limited use. They give no information as to how the individual values are distributed within the sample. Of course, if one were interested in knowing the weight of the heaviest parcel to be transported or the smallest size of skates to be provided at a skating rink, then the information could be useful.

Of more general use are the *quartiles*, described in the first section of this chapter and Figure 7-3. The lower quartile, or 25 percentile, is defined such that one quarter of the data lies below it and three quarters above. The upper quartile, or 75 percentile, occupies a corresponding position with a quarter of the data above it and three quarters below. The interquartile range is the difference between the two quartiles and thus embraces the middle 50% of the data. Sometimes other percentiles are quoted: the 90 percentile, for example, embraces the lower 90% of the data.

The most useful measure of the spread of data is the *standard deviation*. This is calculated using all the data in the sample. The deviation of each data value from the mean value contributes to the standard deviation, but each deviation is effectively weighted, by squaring the value, to give greater contribution to the larger deviations. The squares of all the deviations are totaled and the mean calculated. The square root of this mean value is the standard deviation.

As an example, suppose we have the following rather unlikely, but easy on the eye, values:

2   3   4   4   5   5   6   6   7   8

The mean value is 50/10 = 5.

The deviation of each value from the mean is

−3   −2   −1   −1   0   0   1   1   2   3

and the squares of the deviations are

9   4   1   1   0   0   1   1   4   9

The mean of the squares of the deviations is 30/10 = 3, and the standard deviation is the square root of 3—viz., 1.73.

The standard deviation has particular meaning in relation to the normal distribution. It is half the width of the normal curve at a particular height. Its position is such that the area under the curve between one standard deviation below the mean and one standard deviation above the mean is 0.683 of the total area under the curve. It follows that 68.3% of the data lies within one standard deviation of the mean value. Two standard deviations either side of the mean value include 95.4% of the data, and three standard deviations include 99.7% of the data. These figures provide a very useful quick way of visualizing the spread of data when the mean and standard deviation are quoted. In the example above, one standard deviation each side of the mean is from 3.27 to 6.73, and 60% (6 of the 10 values) of our data lie within this band.

The preceding discussion sets up the completion of the description of the standard normal distribution introduced in the "Normally Distributed Data" section and shown in Figure 7-8. The mean value, which is the central peak value, is located at a value of zero on the horizontal axis, the area under the curve is equal to 1, and now the scale along the horizontal axis is in units of standard deviations. The vertical scale is probability density but it is not of direct interest, having been selected in order to render the area under the curve equal to unity, given that the horizontal scale is in units of standard deviations.

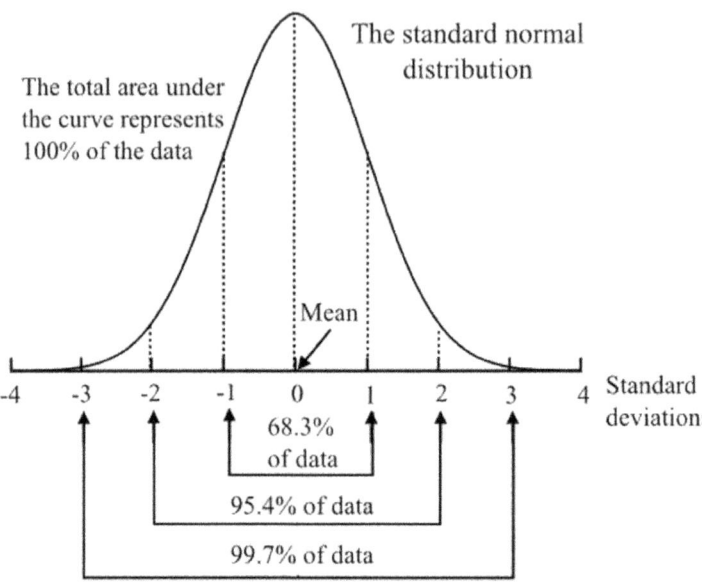

Figure 7-8. The percentage of data within a number of standard deviations from the mean

The square of the standard deviation is called the *variance*. It is used extensively in statistical analysis by reason of its special properties, discussed later. It has no readily visualized meaning: indeed, its units are rather odd. If our standard deviation happens to be in dollars, the variance is in dollars squared—or, if you prefer, square dollars (whatever they are!).

Even when the data does not conform well to the normal distribution, the standard deviation still provides a useful measure of the spread of the data. To illustrate this point, consider data that we might accumulate by throwing a die. Because all numbers from 1 to 6 have equal chance of appearing, we would expect to get nearly the same number of each of the scores. The data would conform to a uniform distribution, and the bar chart would be flat-topped, not looking anything like the normal distribution. The mean score is 3.5, and the standard deviation is calculated to be 1.87. So we would predict that about two thirds of the scores would lie between 1.63 and 5.37. In fact, two thirds of the scores are from 2 to 5, which is roughly in agreement.

Statistical tables are available that give values for the area under the standard normal distribution curve at various distances from the mean. The total area under the curve is defined as 1, so the partial areas appear as fractions between 0 and 1 and represent directly the probability of occurrence of the required range. The tables are not particularly easy to use. Because the curve is symmetrical, the tables give values for only half of the distribution—the positive, right-hand, half. The economy is justified in view of the extent of the tables demanded by the level of precision required, but it does mean that considerable care has to be taken when probabilities represented by areas extending to both sides of the mean are required.

Figure 7-9 shows the values of the standard normal distribution in a simpler, but abridged, form that is more convenient for obtaining approximate values and for checking that declared values are not grossly in error. The values are given to only two digits, to economize on space; and they are given as percentages, which are more readily appreciated than the conventionally used decimal fractions. Furthermore, the probability between any two limits can be read immediately, whereas the published tables require separate values to be extracted for the two limits and the difference to be then calculated.

Chapter 7 | Numerical Data

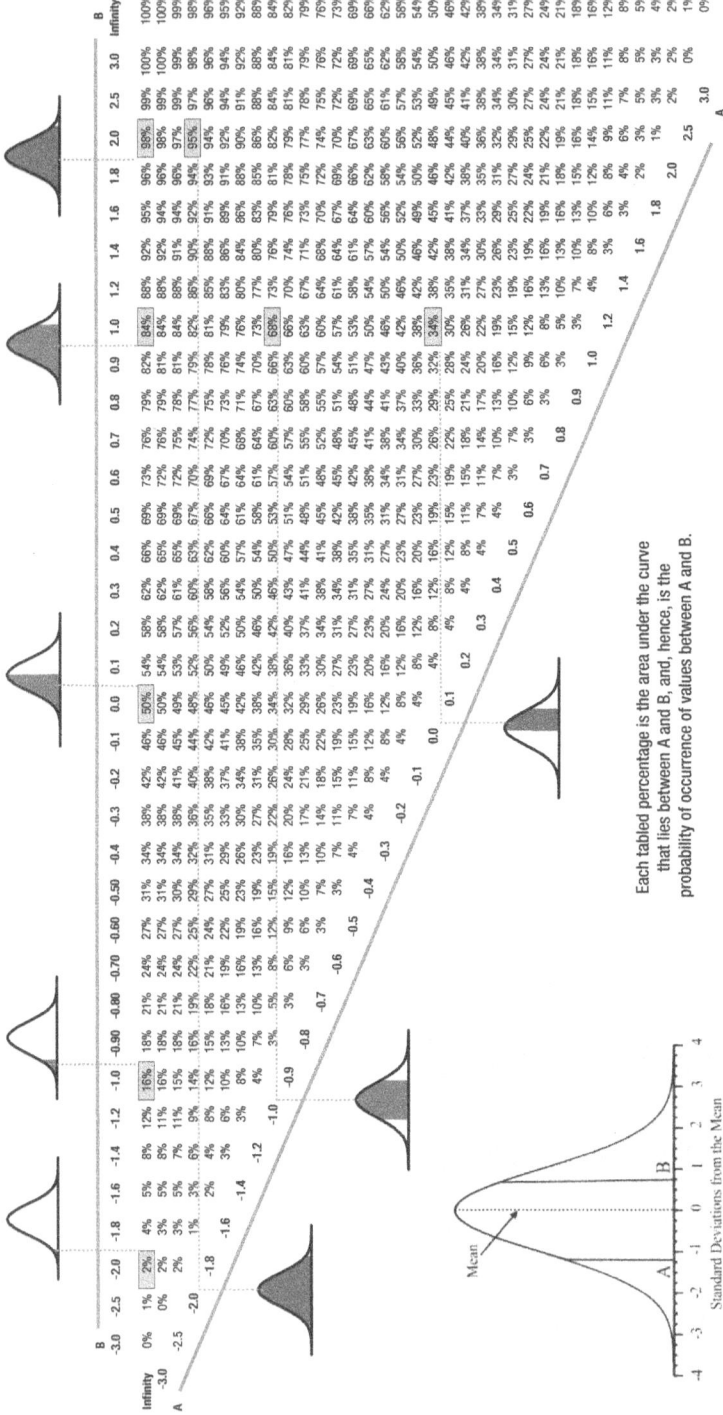

Figure 7-9. Tabulated probabilities of occurrence of normally distributed values between lower and upper limits

It needs to be emphasized that the probability of occurrence is represented by an area. We are asking for the probability of occurrence between two values. We cannot ask for the probability of a unique value being observed. In the earlier example of the heights of people, we cannot ask for the probability of an adult being exactly 160 cm tall. This would be a single vertical line on the normal distribution graph and would enclose no area. The answer is that there is no probability of an adult being exactly 160 cm tall. If this seems odd at first sight, note that the word "exactly" is used. We could ask for the probability of an adult being between 159.5 and 160.5 cm tall, between 159.9 and 160.1 cm tall, or between any other closer limits. These narrow strips would have areas representing the required probabilities. The areas would be small, so the resulting probabilities would be small. This is perfectly reasonable inasmuch as the probability is indeed small of finding someone of a very precisely defined height.

The probability of occurrence can be expressed as a proportion. Thus, if the probability of occurrence of an adult of height between 159.5 cm and 160.5 cm is 0.1, one can say that that the proportion of adults between 159.5 cm and 160.5 cm tall is 0.1, or one tenth, or one in ten.

Grouped Data

Data are often not available in detail but are grouped at the outset. Information, for example, may be gathered from a number of people of different ages, but the ages may not be recorded or even obtained individually but simply classified within bands. The bands have to be carefully defined and equally carefully understood.

We might have bands each of ten years in extent. If we define a band from 20 years to 30 years and the next one as 30 years to 40 years, we do not know in which group to locate someone who is 30. To avoid this problem, we have to define the bands as 20 years to 29 years and 30 years to 39 years. If the data is not discrete, a different procedure has to be adopted. Heights of people vary continuously, so we cannot have, for example, a group 130 cm to 139 cm and then one from 140 cm to 149 cm. There is nowhere to locate 139.5 cm. The groups have to be "equal to or greater than 130 cm and less than 140 cm" followed by "equal to or greater than 140 cm and less than 150 cm." These designations are quite a mouthful and are instead usually shown using mathematical notation as ≥ 130 to <140 followed by ≥ 140 to <150.

If a single representative value is quoted for the group, it is usually the midpoint of the group width. Take note, however, that if the values have been rounded off, the midpoint may not be where it seems. If the group is 10 to 19 and the values have been rounded to the nearest whole number, the group actually ranges from 9.5 to 19.5. The midpoint is then 14.5. But if the group is ≥ 10 to <20, the midpoint is 15.

Sometimes the groups are not of equal width. This may be because of unevenness in the sampling or simply because there is a real shortage of data within certain bands. Ages of people, for example, are more thinly spread between 80 and 100 years than between 20 and 40 years. Notice that when this happens, the area of each block on a bar chart must still represent the total number of data values within the specified band. The following data can be plotted as a relative frequency bar chart, shown in Figure 7-10(a):

Age Range (Years)	20 to 29	30 to 39	40 to 49	50 to 59	60 to 69	70 to 79	80 to 89	90 to 99	Total
Frequency	10	13	12	8	4	1	0	2	50
Relative Frequency	0.20	0.26	0.24	0.16	0.08	0.02	0.00	0.04	1.00

The groups are of equal width. Each person is represented by an area of 0.02 so that the total area is 1.00 for the 50 people. The tail end of the distribution is uneven; to avoid this, the data can be pooled in a wider group, as shown in Figure 7-10(b). The final group has just three members, so the height is 0.02 in order to make the area of the final block equal to 0.06 units. Notice that we cannot now label the axis as relative frequency because the final group (70 to 99 years) has an actual relative frequency of 0.06. The correct designation is relative frequency density, as shown.

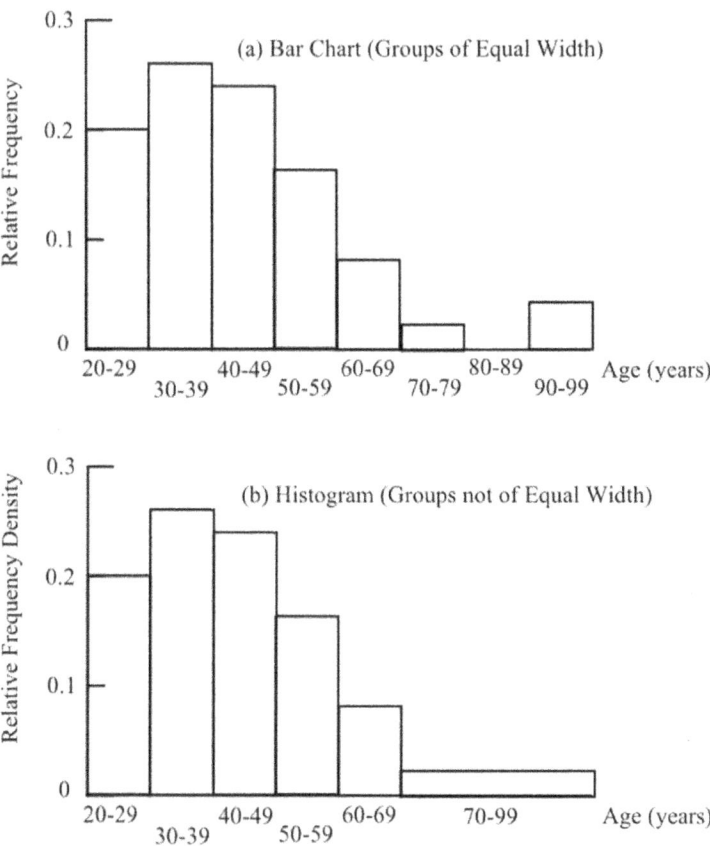

Figure 7-10. The difference between (a) a bar chart and (b) a histogram

I can now explain the difference between a bar chart and a histogram. A *bar chart* represents discrete data or discrete groups of data, and the groups are all of the same width. The vertical axis represents frequency or relative frequency, and the latter is equivalent to probability. In a *histogram*, which also represents discrete groups of data, the groups are not all of the same width. The vertical axis represents frequency density or relative frequency density, the latter being equivalent to probability density. The vertical axis on a histogram does not represent probability: it is the area of the block that represents the probability of the data being within the limits of the group. The histogram is thus analogous to continuous data curves, which, as explained in relation to the normal distribution, are also labeled probability density and indicate probability by the area under the curve.

Pooling and Weighting

Several sets of data can be brought together to provide a *pooled mean value*. The pooled value is more representative because it is based on more observations.

When pooling results, a *weighted mean* is often more appropriate in order to allow some values to have a greater influence on the final result. Sometimes this is essential to avoid the result being in error. For example, if I buy ten apples for 20¢ each in one shop and 4 apples for 24¢ each in another shop, the mean cost per apple is clearly not 22¢. The appropriate indicator is the weighted mean, which is the total money paid divided by the total number of apples purchased— i.e., (20 × 10 + 24 × 4) / (10 + 4) = 21.1¢.

The need for weighting is not always so apparent. The tires on the front wheels of my car wear out much faster than those on the rear wheels. I get 45,000 miles from the rear tires but only 15,000 miles from the front ones. So, on average, I get 30,000 miles—that is, (45,000 + 15,000) / 2—from my tires. This is not correct. In 45,000 miles, I will wear out one pair of rear tires and three pairs of front tires, four pairs in all, so a tire lasts on average (45,000 × 1 + 15,000 × 3) / 4, which is 22,500 miles.

Sometimes the need for weighting seems very surprising. Suppose you catch a bus on a regular basis. The buses are scheduled to arrive every 10 minutes, so this is the mean time between buses; but some will be early and some late. If you arrive at the bus stop at random times, what will be your mean waiting time? It seems at first sight that the answer is five minutes, but this is not correct. You are more likely to arrive in one of the longer gaps between buses than in one of the shorter ones, so your waiting time will be slightly longer than five minutes.

A simple example will illustrate this. Think of two buses: one arrives 12 minutes after the previous one, and the second one arrives after a further 8 minutes, so the mean arrival time is 10 minutes. When you arrive in the 12-minute gap, your mean waiting time is 6 minutes; and when you arrive in the 8-minute gap, your mean waiting time is 4 minutes. The longer waiting time is encountered more often than the shorter waiting time, the ratio being 12 to 8, so the overall mean waiting time has to be obtained by weighting:

$$(6 \times 12 + 4 \times 8)/20 = 5.2 \text{ minutes.}$$

Weighting in such examples is necessary and can be applied unambiguously, but the weighting may sometimes be a matter of judgment. If several similar investigations have been carried out previously, it may be decided that some of them, though of value, are not as reliable as others because of the techniques used. So the less reliable results are pooled with the others but given a lower weighting. In the following calculation, three estimates of the height of Mount Everest—h_1, h_2, and h_3—are pooled, but h_3 is given only half the weight of the other two:

$$\text{Pooled estimate} = (2h_1 + 2h_2 + h_3)/5.$$

Chapter 5 described simple index numbers as, in effect, percentages referred to a selected base value. Many index numbers that are frequently encountered are derived from more complex calculations because the values are averages of several items. Thus the UK Retail Price Index is based on prices of various commodities on a specific date, the prices of the commodities being averaged. Different commodities are purchased in different quantities, so the average price has to be obtained by weighting the average in relation to the quantities purchased. Clearly a loaf of bread costing £1 and a liter of wine costing £6 cannot simply be averaged. If two bottles of wine are purchased for every 35 loaves of bread, we take the price of two bottles of wine, £12, add it to the price of 35 loaves of bread, £35, and divide the result by 37, the total number of items. Thus the weighted average price is $(35 \times 1 + 2 \times 6)/37 = £1.27$. Of course, even the initial prices, £1 and £6, would have to be obtained by averaging, taking account of the different types, different brands, and different shops.

The Retail Price Index involves defining the list of commodities to be included and strict procedures for recording the prices at defined outlets at defined times. The commodities are grouped according to type, so an index can be calculated for various groups of commodities. For example, the overall index is constructed from group indices representing household goods, food, housing, and other groups. The household goods index is constructed from section indices representing household consumables, furniture, and other sections. The household consumables section index is constructed from item indices representing envelopes, toilet paper, and other items. The item index for envelopes is constructed from those of specified type purchased in specified shops in specified locations. In total about 700 items are represented in the Retail Price Index.

When the actual quantities purchased are used to determine the weights to be applied in the averaging, the choice still remains as to whether the quantities should be those purchased in the base year or those bought in the current year. The index that results from using the base year quantities is called a *Laspeyres index*. The index incorporating the current year quantities is a *Paasche index* and clearly involves more time and expense in its determination.

As an example, suppose we have data for our base year as follows:

        Bread £1 per loaf   Relative quantity 35 loaves

        Wine £6 per bottle   Relative quantity 2 bottles.

The data for a subsequent year, for which we require the index, are

    Bread £1.20 per loaf   Relative quantity 35 loaves

    Wine £8 per bottle   Relative quantity 1 bottle.

The Laspeyres index, using base year quantities, is calculated thus:

    £1×35 = £35   £1.20×35 = £42

    £6×2 = £12   £8×2 = £16

    Total   £47   Total   £58

    Index = (58 / 47) × 100 = 123.

The Paasche index, using current year quantities, is calculated thus:

    £1×35 = £35   £1.20×35 = £42

    £6×1 = £6   £8×1 = £8

    Total   £41   Total   £50

    Index = (50 / 41) × 100 = 122.

The two indices are quite similar unless the quantities vary appreciably from year to year. A disadvantage of the Paasche index is that indices for different years cannot be compared with each other but only with the base year. The Laspeyres index allows comparison between any two years. The UK Retail Price Index is a Laspeyres-type index, but its derivation is modified in a number of ways. Other well-known index numbers are those illustrating the prices of shares, such as the FTSE 100 and the Dow Jones, and various housing price indices.

Be wary of pooled data that can apparently show a quite different result. The pooling may have been carried out to disguise an embarrassing set of data. Consider the following example.

A company has two new salesmen, Smith and Brown. In their first week Smith makes 5 sales from 40 contacts, giving him an average of one sale per 8 contacts. Brown makes one sale from 10 contacts. So Smith has the best average. The situation is illustrated in Figure 7-11. In the second week, Smith makes 3 sales from 10 contacts, giving him an average of one sale per 3.33 contacts. Brown makes 10 sales from 40 contacts, giving him an average of one sale per 4 contacts. So Smith again has the better average.

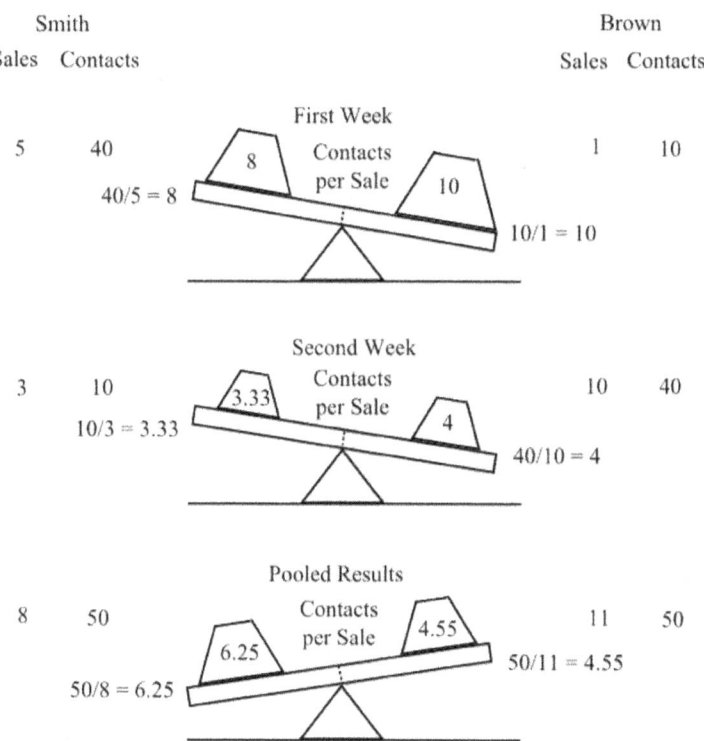

Figure 7-11. Simpson's paradox

But what happens if we pool the results of the two weeks? Smith has a total of 8 sales from 50 contacts, whereas Brown has a total of 11 sales from 50 contacts. So Brown has the better average. Who is the better salesman? Some might argue that Smith is better because he made the greater contribution to the company's performance in both weeks. Others could say that Brown is better because his better performance is revealed when a greater amount of data is available. The most realistic conclusion is that there is not sufficient evidence to distinguish between them. The difference between their own performances in the two weeks is greater than the difference between their own and their colleague's performance. Also, there may be one or more variables affecting the conditions during the two weeks, of which no account has been taken.

This kind of situation is known as *Simpson's paradox* and is usually met with surprise. Apart from its curiosity value, it does illustrate very well the fact that statistical results should not be accepted blindly but should always be judged alongside other evidence and practical considerations.

Chapter 7 | Numerical Data

FOOD FOR THOUGHT

The consultant's report lay on the desk. Liz Fisher, Head of Food Processing at Moroney Cookie Company, picked it up and started to read. The company had decided to introduce a new low-sugar cookie, and Liz's team had produced two recipes, both of which were judged to be marketable.

Graham Consultants had been employed to test the two new cookies on the public before a decision was made as to which one would go into production.

The report described how two shops, already selling Moroney cookies, had each agreed to set up two stalls on a busy afternoon. One stall, handling recipe A, offered each willing customer a sample cookie and then invited the customer to purchase a packet at a reduced price. The second stall did the same with cookies of recipe B. The customers did not know that the two stalls were offering different cookies. The number of customers sampling the cookies and the number of customers purchasing a packet were recorded.

The report concluded that recipe A was more popular than recipe B at both shops, though the difference was not great.

Liz thought the figures looked rather odd. She was not happy with the findings:

Store 1

    Recipe A   22 purchases from 24 sampled   92%

    Recipe B   89 purchases from 106 sampled   84%

Store 2

    Recipe A   50 purchases from 71 sampled   70%

    Recipe B   18 purchases from 26 sampled   64%

Suspecting that the situation was not satisfactory, she decided to pool the results from the two stores and got the following result.

    Recipe A   72 purchases from 95 sampled   76%

    Recipe B   107 purchases from 132 sampled   81%

The situation was now reversed: recipe B was more popular than recipe A! Liz saw that this was an instance of Simpson's paradox. One or more additional variables were influencing the results. The experimental arrangements at the two stores were not comparable.

She knew that the report had to be rejected and Graham's would have to investigate the source of the problem. The experiment would have to be repeated with improved controls.

She picked up the phone ….

Estimated Population Properties

The population, to recap, is the complete, perhaps hypothetical, and perhaps infinite, set of data from which the sample was randomly drawn. It is necessary to realize that the information gained from the sample may not be representative of the population characteristics without some modification, although the modifications are generally quite minor. It has been mentioned already that that the sample sometimes consists of the entire population, which simplifies matters.

The best estimate of the *population mean*, μ, is the *sample mean*, χ_m. Statisticians use the word *expectation* rather than *mean* when speaking of an expected mean rather than a calculated mean. Thus one refers to "the mean of a sample" and "the expectation of the population" from which the sample was drawn.

The best estimate of the *standard deviation of the population*, σ, is the sample standard deviation, s, slightly modified. The modification is required because sample standard deviations slightly underestimate the population standard deviation, particularly when the sample is small. The sample standard deviation has to be multiplied by the square root of the ratio of n to n-1, to give the estimate of the population standard deviation, σ, where n is the number of values in the sample. Thus,

$$\sigma = s\sqrt{\left(\frac{n}{n-1}\right)},$$

and the estimated population variance is

$$\sigma^2 = s^2\, n/(n-1).$$

If the sample is small the alteration of the sample standard deviation may be appreciable, but for large samples the ratio n/(n-1) is close to unity and has a small effect only.

If two samples are pooled to provide a larger single sample, the estimated mean value for the population is obtained in the usual way of obtaining a weighted mean. Thus,

$$\mu_t = (n_1\, \chi_{m1} + n_2\, \chi_{m2})/(n_1 + n_2),$$

where the suffixes 1 and 2 refer to the two samples. The estimated pooled variance is

$$\sigma^2 = \{(n_1 - 1)\, s_1^2 + (n_2 - 1)\, s_2^2\}/(n_1 + n_2 - 2),$$

and the estimated pooled standard deviation is the square root of this.

The best estimate of the population proportion is the sample proportion, and pooling is dealt with in exactly the same way as for the estimated population mean.

Confidence Intervals

The preceding section said that the sample mean provides the best estimate of the population mean (the expectation). Thus if we survey people attending a particular film at the local cinema and find that in a sample of 40 people the mean age is 32 years, then this provides the best estimate of the mean age of the people who did attend or might have attended under the same circumstances. Clearly this may easily be in error, and a useful procedure is to attach *confidence limits*. These are calculated from the population variance, but before you see how it is useful to see how they are presented and what they mean. The result might be quoted as, for example,

$$\text{Mean age} = 32 \pm 5 \ (95\% \text{ confidence}),$$

meaning that the true population mean will be found to lie between 27 years and 37 years in 95% of such investigations.

Note that it does not mean that there is a 95% probability of the true population mean lying in the interval 27 to 37. The true value is either within a given interval or not. The issue is subtle and may be illustrated as follows. Suppose the true population mean is 26. The sample we obtained estimated the mean to be between 27 and 37, which is not correct. However, we were unlucky, as nineteen other similar samples would, on average, have included 26 in the range of uncertainty. It can be seen that this is different from saying that the true value of 26 has a 95% chance of being between 27 and 37. It has no chance of being so. However, it is clearly a fairly infrequent occurrence to have established a range that does not trap the true value, and it is easy to see how the meaning of confidence limits is often wrongly stated.

Let us now see how the confidence limits are obtained. From the previous description of the normal distribution in the second section of this chapter, we know that a single value drawn from a population has approximately a two-thirds chance of being within one standard deviation of the mean. The single value is the best estimate of the mean, but it would clearly be a very poor one. With just one value—one person in the cinema, for example—we cannot calculate a standard deviation, so we do not even know how poor our estimate is.

In reality, we take a sample and calculate the mean value. This is now our best estimate of the population mean. We have a sample mean of 32 years in our cinema example, obtained from, we suppose, a sample size of 40. We can calculate a standard deviation from the sample and obtain a value of 16 years, say. This allows us to calculate the best estimate of the standard deviation of the population, which is found to be 16.2, after making the minor correction described in the preceding section.

The estimate of the population mean is more reliable than the one from a single data value, but how much more? It turns out that when means of samples are obtained, they themselves are distributed normally but with a smaller standard deviation than that of the population. In fact, the standard deviation of samples of equal size is equal to the standard deviation of the population divided by the square root of the number of data in each sample. So the larger the sample, the more likely the sample mean will be close to the population mean. This is what one would expect. The standard deviation of sample means becomes

$$\frac{16.2}{\sqrt{(40)}} = 2.56.$$

Reference to tables of the standard normal distribution shows that there is a probability of 95% that a value lies within 1.96 standard deviations either side of the mean value. In our example,

$$1.96 \times 2.56 = 5.02.$$

Hence, we have the conclusion that that the estimated mean age of those attending or potentially attending the cinema is 32 ± 5 (95% confidence).

It is worth adding that the means of samples are found to be distributed normally, or nearly so, even when the original data departs considerably from a normal distribution.

It is useful to note that the value of 1.96 is always associated with the 95% confidence limits, so there is no need to consult tables of the standard normal distribution on each occasion. Similarly, for other confidence limits, appropriate values that can always be used are summarized as follows:

$$\mu = \chi_m \pm 1.96 \times \sigma / \sqrt{n} \text{ (95% confidence)}$$

$$\mu = \chi_m \pm 2.33 \times \sigma / \sqrt{n} \text{ (98% confidence)}$$

$$\mu = \chi_m \pm 2.58 \times \sigma / \sqrt{n} \text{ (99% confidence)}$$

$$\mu = \chi_m \pm 3.29 \times \sigma / \sqrt{n} \text{ (99.9% confidence)}$$

where

X_m = sample mean

σ = estimated standard deviation of the population

n = sample size

So far in this section we have assumed that our sample is large. If our sample is small, less than about 30, we do not use the normal distribution. Instead, we have to refer to tables of a distribution called Student's-t. This distribution varies as the number of data changes, so we cannot fix the number of standard deviations for a given level of confidence as we did above. As the number of data in the sample increases, the t-distribution comes closer to the normal distribution—hence the need for the t-distribution only for small samples. (*Student* was the pen name of William Gosset, who devised the test for small samples; the test was not so named because of its use by students of statistics.)

Below are tabulated values from the t-distribution for a number of different sample sizes. The values shown replace the numerical factors in the confidence limits statements above, obtained from the normal distribution. The latter factors are repeated in the bottom line of the tabulation for ease of comparison. The tendency of the t-distribution values to approach the normal distribution values can be appreciated.

Sample Size (n)	95% Confidence	98% Confidence	99% Confidence	99.9% Confidence
5	2.57	3.37	4.03	6.87
10	2.23	2.76	3.17	4.59
20	2.09	2.53	2.85	3.85
30	2.04	2.46	2.75	3.65
60	2.00	2.39	2.62	3.46
Normal Distribution	1.96	2.33	2.58	3.29

It can also be seen that smaller samples result in a widening of the confidence limits. This widening is additional to the widening that arises as a result of the smaller value of n in the estimation of the population standard deviation.

PART IV

Comparisons

Reason respects differences, and imagination the similitudes of things.
—Percy Bysshe Shelley

We are now in a position to consider situations in which comparisons are made between the features of samples and populations, in order to decide whether they are different or could simply represent likely variations of the same underlying data.

CHAPTER 8

Levels of Significance
What Odds Are You Giving?

When we obtain two or more samples, we may expect them to be from the same population. Thus we may sample goods produced on two production lines in the same factory, or we could be comparing the same product from two different suppliers. If we find samples to be from the same population, we can pool them to create a larger sample and summarize the data more succinctly. If we find the samples to be from different populations, we are in a position to draw important conclusions. We might change our supplier, for example.

In making comparisons, statisticians propose at the outset that there is a difference or there is not a difference. These proposals are referred to as *hypotheses*. Hypothesis testing describes the process involved. The correctness of a hypothesis cannot be determined with certainty. There is always a degree of uncertainty, which is expressed in terms of a *level of significance*.

The *null hypothesis*, H_0, is the hypothesis whose correctness is being tested. H_1 is the alternative hypothesis, which is accepted if the null hypothesis cannot be accepted.

Thus we might have a null hypothesis that the average income in Midtown is no different from that in the rest of the county. The alternative hypothesis is that the average income in Midtown is different from that in the rest of the county. Acceptance of the null hypothesis would be expressed by stating that the average income in Midtown is found to be not significantly different from that in the rest of the county. A level of significance is attached to the conclusion. A level of 5%, say, means there is a 1 in 20 chance of the conclusion being wrong.

Chapter 8 | Levels of Significance

There is a similarity between the significance level and the confidence limit described in the final section of the preceding chapter. There we used percentages close to 100% to express the level of confidence in our conclusions. Here, our significance levels are close to zero, expressing the probability that our finding of a difference is likely to be wrong. You will see later that the similarity extends to the manner in which the confidence limits and the significance levels are calculated.

The null hypothesis is usually worded in such a way that if it is accepted, then there is no change to the situation, the use of the word "*null*" implying this approach. If the null hypothesis in the Midtown example had been accepted, we would have discovered nothing special about Midtown and the situation would have been in effect unchanged.

This may seem a rather pedantic convention. After all, why not have adopted a null hypothesis stating that the average income in Midtown *is* different from that in the rest of the county? The calculation procedure would remain the same and the result obtained would be identical. However, as shall be seen in Chapter 12, the convention does result in improved clarity when we consider the errors that are possible within our degrees of uncertainty.

Tests may be stated to be *one-tailed* or *two-tailed*. The test just described is a two-tailed test in that we are asking whether Midtown incomes differ from the others, either by being less or greater than those in the rest of the county. If we test to see whether the Midtown incomes are different in being lower than the rest, or test to see whether they are different in being greater, we would have in each case a one-tailed test. The *tail* referred to is the tail of the distribution extending away from the mean—i.e., to larger values of standard deviation from the mean and therefore more unlikely to be observed.

A level of greater than 5% is generally never considered to be significant, as the probability of it being simply an odd result is too great. For many purposes, even 5% is not considered good enough and a level of 1% may be required. The probability of the result being wrong is then 1 in 100, and the result may be termed very significant. Of course, for life-or-death situations in medical activities or health and safety applications, even this level may be inadequate and significance levels of 0.1% or better may be called for.

When results are quoted with their levels of significance, the number of data in the sample or samples may also be quoted. There may also be references to *degrees of freedom*, which were explained in Chapter 7.

In the following four chapters, I will describe various ways of testing hypotheses. The emphasis will be on giving you an understanding of what the statistician is saying and the language she is using. I will not get involved in any complicated mathematics but will outline and illustrate the steps involved. In any case, the mathematical processing is generally carried out by calculator or computer programs rather than by hand. When reference is made to a small or a large sample, the dividing line is around 30 data.

CHAPTER 9

General Procedure for Comparisons
Eight Easy Steps from Null to Significance

After you decide what is to be compared with what, you should clearly define the null hypothesis. It is very easy to later become confused between the null hypothesis and the alternative hypothesis.

The next step is to choose the acceptable level of statistical significance. It is important to fix and declare this significance level at the outset so that your choice will not be influenced by the result you obtain.

Next choose the statistical test you will use. The following three chapters will describe the appropriateness of various tests in relation to the available data and the conclusions sought. Each statistical test employs published tables from which the levels of significance can be obtained. The tables are produced from calculations that are often complex. In practice, the availability of computer programs has removed much of the need to refer to tables; the complete sequence of calculation, from the raw data to the statement of the significance level, is hidden from view. Nevertheless, it is wise to appreciate the steps that are followed within the procedure.

Chapter 9 | General Procedure for Comparisons

The number of available tests is very large, and new ones are being developed. It would be impossible to include them all. Many of the well-established tests are in common use, and I will describe them.

Statistical tests vary in their power, the *power* of a test being a measure of the likelihood of obtaining a result that is not spurious. Clearly, the test should be chosen in order to maximize the power. Tests that make no assumptions about the distribution that the data fits are less powerful than those that assume a particular distribution.

Every collection of data is unique; it would clearly be impossible to provide a table of values for each situation. The data therefore is processed to produce a standard value of what is termed a *test statistic*. In effect, data is scaled to allow a direct comparison with the standard distribution. The idea of scaling the data in order to compare it with a standard distribution was introduced in the section on standard normal distribution in Chapter 7.

The test statistic is referred to the appropriate table together with the number of degrees of freedom, or the number or numbers of data involved in the calculation of the statistic. In some situations you need to distinguish between a one-tailed test and a two-tailed test in referring to the table.

In summary, the procedure for comparing samples of data and their statistical properties is as follows:

1. Decide on the comparison to be made.
2. State the null hypothesis.
3. Decide on the required level of significance.
4. Choose the statistical test.
5. Calculate the test statistic and the degrees of freedom.
6. Note, if necessary, whether to use one-tailed or two-tailed values.
7. Refer to the tables.
8. Read off the level of significance.

So far we have dealt with descriptive data before numerical data, progressing from the simpler to the more complex. Now, however, we will consider numerical data first. This is because comparisons of numerical data have procedures that are usually better known. Furthermore, some descriptive data can be recast in numerical form and dealt with in ways that I will have already described.

CHAPTER 10

Comparisons with Numerical Data

Are Today's Chocolate Bars Smaller Than Yesterday's?

Once a numerical sample or population has been characterized in a quantifiable way, as shown in Chapter 7, it can be compared with others to seek differences or similarities. This chapter explains what can be learned from single values, pairs of values, pairs of samples, and sets of samples. In each case, the null hypothesis, that no difference is evidenced, is set up; and, by calculating the appropriate test statistic, it is established whether the null hypothesis should be accepted or not.

Single Value

The null hypothesis is that a single value could have come from a given population. An example might be to investigate whether a bar of chocolate weighing 121g could have come from a production line producing bars with a mean weight of 120g and a standard deviation of 0.5g. The situation would be considered to involve a normal distribution of chocolate bar weights.

Chapter 10 | Comparisons with Numerical Data

We have already seen that the area under the curve of the normal distribution represents the probability of occurrence of the values within the bounds of the area. If we are interested in a 5% level of significance, say, we would be asking whether or not a value as large as 121g would be found within the 5% tail of the normal distribution which has a mean of 120.0g and a standard deviation of 0.5g.

The difference between 121g and 120g is scaled to fit the standard normal distribution by calculating the so-called Z-score, where

$$Z = \text{(Single Value} - \text{Population Mean)/(Standard Deviation)}$$
$$= (121-120)/ 0.5$$
$$= 2.0 .$$

This gives the amount the value being investigated differs from the population mean, in units of standard deviations. Referring to Figure 7-9, the probability of a value being at least 2.0 standard deviations from the mean is 2%. (Read off A = 2.0, B = infinity, which gives 2%.) Complete tables of the normal distribution give the result more accurately as 0.0228 (2.28%). The value is below the 5% level of significance, and so we conclude that the null hypothesis is incorrect and it is unlikely that the chocolate bar came from the production line. Put another way, there is only a 2.28% chance of our being wrong if we say that the chocolate bar did not come from the production line.

The example is a one-tailed test, because we are quoting the probability of a value as high as 121g being observed. In a two-tailed test, we would be inquiring as to the probability of a value being 1g distant from the mean, either above or below. We would thus work with a 2.5% probability in the upper tail and a 2.5% probability in the lower tail to fix the limits corresponding to a 5% probability of the value not being likely to have been selected from the population.

The relation between probability of occurrence and departure from the mean value is shown as follows for the commonly used levels of significance and for one-tailed and two-tailed tests:

Significance	5%	2%	1%	0.1%
One Tail	1.65	2.05	2.33	3.09
Two Tail	1.96	2.33	2.58	3.29

Use of these preferred values of significance level avoids the need to consult the full table of values for the normal distribution. It is useful to note that the values for two-tailed tests are the same values that we used in setting up confidence limits in Chapter 7. This is not too surprising, because, for example, a 95% probability that a value is within a symmetrical central band is equivalent to a 2.5% probability of it being above the band and a 2.5% of it being below.

Mean of a Sample

The null hypothesis is that a sample mean value could have come from a given population. An example, continuing with our chocolate bars, would be that a production line has been serviced and, after servicing, a sample of 100 bars is found to have a mean of 119.9g, compared with a previously determined population mean of 120.0g. To establish whether the production line is now operating satisfactorily, we set up the null hypothesis that the population from which the sample was drawn has a mean of 120.0g. We suppose that the sample had the expected standard deviation of 0.5g, as before.

The procedure is similar to that in the previous example, a Z-score being obtained and referred to tables of the normal distribution. However, because our sample mean is more representative than the single value was in the previous section, we reduce the standard deviation of the sample to get the standard deviation of the mean. This is done by dividing the variance of the sample by the number of data values in the sample and then taking the square root. This gives us the standard deviation of the mean, which is usually called the *standard error* of the mean. Put another way, we have divided the standard deviation of the sample by the square root of the number of data values to get the standard deviation of the mean. Thus, the standard deviation of the mean is 0.5g divided by the square root of 100—i.e., 0.5/10 = 0.05g. This has the effect of reducing the uncertainty of the result. This reduction in standard deviation was used in a similar way in calculating confidence limits in Chapter 7.

The Z-score is

(119.9 − 120.0)/0.05 = − 2.0.

This value exceeds the required value for 5% significance, almost reaching the 2% level, as can be seen from the values shown in the previous section. We conclude that the null hypothesis should be rejected, there being evidence that the production line is not operating as required. (The negative value obtained for the Z-score simply shows that the value being tested is below the population mean; you will recall that the mean of a standard normal distribution is located at zero.)

It is better to use a large sample because of the reducing effect on the Z-score. However, because the reduction is by the square root of the sample size, a situation of diminishing returns sets in. With a sample size of 16, the Z-score is reduced by a factor of 4 compared with the Z-score for a single value. If we wish to reduce it by a factor of 8, we need a sample of size 64. The effort and cost of obtaining samples thus rises rapidly as we attempt to reduce the uncertainty in the results.

If the size of the sample is small, a slightly different procedure is adopted. The Z-score is modified slightly but then referred not to tables of the normal distribution, but to tables of the t-distribution (Chapter 7). The t-distribution approaches the normal distribution, giving the same results for large samples.

Difference between Variances

The null hypothesis is that two samples having different variances could have been drawn from the same population. This amounts to examining whether the two samples differ significantly, because if they could not have come from the same population, they must have been drawn from different populations.

The ratio of the two variances, F, is calculated by dividing the larger variance, s_1^2 by the smaller, s_2^2, to give a value greater than 1,

$$F = s_1^2/s_2^2 .$$

If n_1 and n_2 are the numbers of data in the two samples, the degrees of freedom are $n_1 - 1$ and $n_2 - 1$. The value of F and the degrees of freedom are referred to tables of Snedecor's F-values. The tables are fairly extensive because of the need to cater to each level of significance and the number of data in each of the two samples. Extracts from the tables are shown in the "Multiple Samples" section and in Chapter 16, where further uses of the F-test are illustrated.

If the two variances are not significantly different, they may be pooled and the weighted mean value used as a more reliable estimate of the population variance. Thus, as shown in Chapter 7, the pooled estimated population variance is given by

$$\sigma^2 = \{(n_1 - 1) s_1^2 + (n_2 - 1) s_2^2 \}/(n_1 + n_2 - 2) .$$

Difference between Means

The null hypothesis is that two samples having different means could have been drawn from the same population. Notice that the previous test, the variance ratio test, should be first carried out. If the F-test shows the two samples to be significantly different, it might be pointless to ask if the means show the samples to be different. Of course, the F-test is subject to a degree of unreliability, so it becomes a matter of judgment how to proceed.

On the assumption that we continue to examine the two mean values, a Z-score is calculated, expressing the difference between the means in terms of the number of standard deviations. This is similar to what we did in the "Mean of a Sample" section when we compared the mean of a single sample with a population mean. However, we now have two samples, each of which is an estimate of the supposed underlying population. We will use the difference between the two means, as we did before, but the required standard deviation now refers to a new distribution—that is, the distribution of the differences between two samples. The standard deviation to be used here is the standard deviation of the difference. Each of the mean values has its associated variance, expressing its uncertainty. So the sum of the two variances expresses the uncertainty in the difference between the means.

At this stage an example will make clear how to proceed. Assume we have details of sales of a particular product by two sales staff over a period of time, and we wish to make a comparison:

Staff	Number of Days	Mean Sales per Day	Standard Deviation
	n	x_m	s
1	30	16	6
2	35	12	5

The variance of the difference of the means is $\sigma^2 / n_1 + \sigma^2 / n_2$ where σ^2 is the population variance, which has to be estimated as we do not know its value. The estimate of the population variance, using the sample standard deviations, is

$$\sigma^2 = \{(n_1 - 1) s_1^2 + (n_2 - 1) s_2^2\}/(n_1 + n_2 - 2).$$

This is the equation you met in Chapter 7 and in the preceding section for pooling two samples to estimate the population variance. Using the values in the table above gives 30.06, so the variance of the difference of the means is 30.06/30 + 30.06/35—that is, 1.86. The standard deviation of the distribution of the difference of the means is the square root of this, which is 1.36.

The Z-score, the difference between the two means in terms of standard deviations, is therefore (16 − 12)/1.36, which is 2.94. It can be seen from the values for the normal distribution shown in the "Single Value" section of this chapter that this is significant at the 1% level, so we would conclude that the null hypothesis is rejected and the two members of staff differ in performance.

Notice that use is made here of the additive nature of variance: we cannot simply add the two values of standard deviation to get the standard deviation of the difference between the means.

Means of Paired Data

Paired data frequently arise in before-and-after situations. Thus we could have test results for a group of students before and after a week of revision. For example:

Student	A	B	C	D	E	Mean	Variance
Before	20	60	40	50	30	40	
After	30	55	50	65	50	50	
Increase	10	−5	10	15	20	10	87.5

If there had been no effect of the revision sessions, we would expect these increases to be small, with an average close to zero. We can therefore ask whether this distribution of increases differs significantly from the values that might be obtained from a population with a mean value of zero. Our null hypothesis is therefore that the sample of increases could have been drawn from a population of values with a mean of zero.

The calculation can now follow a procedure similar to that used in the previous section, where we compared two sample means. The variance of the difference of the means reduces to the variance of the mean of the increases, and the estimate of the population variance reduces to the variance of the increases.

The values from the table above give the following:

Estimated population variance		= 87.5
Variance of difference of means	= (87.5)/5	= 17.5
Standard deviation of difference of means	= $\sqrt{17.5}$	= 4.18
Z-score	= (10 − 0)/4.18	= 2.39

The sample is small; so, rather than quote a Z-score, the result should be referred to as a value of Student's-t, and tables of t-values should then be used to determine the level of significance. Samples are commonly small in paired data because exact pairing becomes more difficult when the required sample size gets larger. In this example, the t-value of 2.39 is somewhat short of the value required to indicate a 5% level of significance for a sample size of 5. (See the selection of t-values in Chapter 7.) It would be concluded therefore that the null hypothesis is accepted and there is insufficient evidence to show that the revision sessions were of any benefit.

Multiple Samples

If more than two samples need to be compared, it would be quite possible to compare them in pairs using the methods described above. This, however, would be an unsatisfactory procedure for the following reason. If there were three samples, A, B, and C, there would be three pairs to compare: AB, AC, and BC. If we are testing at the 5% level, we have a 1 in 20 chance of being wrong in each of these comparisons. We have a chance of approximately 3 in 20 of at least one of the results being wrong. The situation gets worse rapidly as we increase the number of samples. Four samples produce six pairs, and five samples produce ten pairs, rendering the probability of being wrong unacceptably high.

A technique called *variance analysis* (ANOVA) is used in such situations, and it is here that the important role that variance plays in statistical routines becomes apparent. Variance, in spite of having often strange units, has the useful property of being additive. This we have encountered previously where, in order to calculate a mean standard deviation, we first obtained the variances from each standard deviation, then averaged the variances and obtained the mean standard deviation by taking the square root of the mean variance. You saw, similarly, in the "Difference between Means" section, that to get the variance of the difference between two values, we added the two individual variances.

If we have a number of samples, there will be variation of the data within each sample. In addition, the samples will differ from each other. In order to quantify the difference between the samples, it is necessary to separate the variation within the samples and the variation between the samples. The analysis of variance allows this to be done.

From the variances of all the samples, we can obtain a pooled variance. This gives a measure of the variation within the samples. In effect, we are supposing, temporarily, that the samples are in reality drawn from the same population, so each sample variance is an estimate of the population variance. The best estimate of the population variance is then obtained by pooling the several estimates. This is the measure of the within-sample variance.

We can then temporarily remove the variation within each sample by replacing each datum with its sample mean and calculating the variance of the total data. This gives a measure of the variation between the samples. In effect, we are asking what the best estimate of the population variance would be if each sample consisted of a set of identical values having the original mean but zero variance.

If all the samples could have been drawn from the same population, it would be expected that the variation within the samples would be similar to the variation between the samples. Thus the ratio of the within-sample variance to the between-sample variance indicates the extent to which the samples could have a common source. An example will make this clear.

Chapter 10 | Comparisons with Numerical Data

Five soccer players have scored goals, as follows, in a number of matches. The number of matches played is not necessarily the same for each player. The null hypothesis is that the five samples could have been drawn from the same population. In other words, there is no evidence that the performance of the five players differs significantly:

Player	A	B	C	D	E
Goals	3	3	0	1	4
	0	2	3	3	2
	3	3	0	1	2
		4	2	4	4
			0	1	3
Mean	2	3	1	2	3
Variance	3	0.67	2	2	1

Overall Mean = 2.18   Pooled Variance = 1.65

The pooled variance, following the pooling procedure explained in Chapter 7, is 1.65. This is the within-sample variance. The degrees of freedom associated with this variance are obtained by adding the degrees of freedom for each sample: that is, one less than the number of data. So, (2+3+4+4+4) = 17 is the number of degrees of freedom.

To get the between-sample variance, each datum is replaced by its sample mean:

Goals	2	3	1	2	3
	2	3	1	2	3
	2	3	1	2	3
		3	1	2	3
			1	2	3
Mean	2	3	1	2	3
Variance	0	0	0	0	0

Overall Mean = 2.18   Variance = 3.32

The variance of these values about the overall mean, 3.32, is the between-sample variance. The degrees of freedom associated with this variance are one less than the number of samples—viz., 4. Note that the sum of the degrees of freedom for the within-sample variance and the between-sample variance, 21—i.e., 17 + 4 —is equal to the total degrees of freedom for the total of 22 data values—i.e., 22 − 1 = 21.

The ratio of the two variances (3.32/1.65 = 2.01), together with their degrees of freedom, are referred to the table of F-values described in the section "Differences between Variances." An extract from the tables follows:

Significance Level	Degrees of Freedom of the Larger Variance		
5%	3	4	5
Degrees of Freedom of the Smaller Variance 15	3.29	3.06	2.9
16	3.24	3.01	2.85
17	3.2	2.96	2.81
18	3.16	2.93	2.77

In this example, the variance ratio, 2.01, is not sufficiently large to indicate a significant difference between the performances of the players. The null hypothesis is accepted.

The analysis of variance used in this way is referred to as a *one-way analysis* of variance, in that the variation between groups of samples is examined, each sample being of a similar type and possibly drawn from the same population. In Chapter 16, you will see that variance analysis can be applied to sets of samples that differ in some way.

MANAGING THE MANAGER

Premier Pressings is a company manufacturing steel pressings for engineering firms making automobiles, washing machines, gas boilers, and similar items. The company has units located in five different cities, each serving local needs.

The chief executive, George Robinson, was concerned that one of his units, Shempton, had been showing low profits over the past six months in comparison with the four other units. He had discussed his concerns with the manager of the Shempton unit, Tom Greeves, to establish what the problem was. The meeting was less than satisfactory: Tom was unable to offer any reasonable explanation for his poor results and claimed that it was a statistical quirk and that no doubt in subsequent months the effect would balance out.

Unconvinced, George decided on further investigation. He called on a senior draftsman from the Design Office who had some knowledge of statistics to have a look at the figures.

The draughtsman, Arnold Mason, could see immediately that the average profit over the six-month period was much lower that the profits for any of the other four units, although the variation, month to month, was quite large for all the units. He decided to first check on the consistency or otherwise of the results from the four other units. He listed the six profit values for the four units, 24 data in total, and carried out a one-way variance analysis. This gave him a value of the within-sample variance and a value of the between-sample variance. He calculated the variance ratio, F. Reference to tables of F-values showed that the result was not significant, so the four units could be considered to be producing results with similar amount of spread. He therefore calculated the mean and variance for the 24 values of profit.

The next step was to see if the Shempton results were significantly different from the combined 24 values. The mean and variance of the Shempton results were calculated. A comparison of the two variances gave an F-value that was not significant. However, the comparison of the two mean values showed a significant difference at the 5% level. This indicated that there would be a 1 in 20 chance of being wrong if it were maintained that the Shempton results were inferior to the others.

The CEO, armed with the results, summoned Tom to a further meeting and pointed out that there was good evidence that the Shempton results were not satisfactory. It was accepted that the evidence was not overwhelming; and, in view of a degree of uncertainty, Tom was told that he would be given a further six months to improve his profits. The exercise would be repeated in six months' time, and Tom's future would then be considered.

CHAPTER

11

Comparisons with Descriptive Data

Is Your Staff Female/Male Ratio OK?

Chapter 6 explained that descriptive data can be rendered numerical by expressing the numbers of items in various categories as proportions—thus enabling further analysis to be carried out on the data. In this chapter, a single proportion will be compared with a population, and two sample proportions will be compared. If the data is ordinal—that is to say, it can be listed in logical order—then ranking tests, which will be introduced, can be applied to achieve comparisons between pairs of ranks.

There is a particular advantage in having large samples of descriptive data, because several of the procedures used then allow the data to be dealt with as normally distributed data.

Single Proportion

A sample consisting of yes/no data will provide an example of dealing with a proportion. Suppose we know from previous investigations that the proportion of inhabitants of Newtown who were born in Newtown is 0.7. We can use this information to decide whether a sample of size 100, say, obtained in one area of the town is representative of the town or whether the sample shows a significant difference.

The null hypothesis is that the sample proportion, 0.8 say, is not significantly different from the overall proportion of 0.7 for the town. Our sample of 100 consists of 80 who were born in Newtown, whereas we would have expected 70 on the basis of the known results for the whole town. The procedure follows a pattern similar to that used in the first section of Chapter 10, where we asked whether a single value was likely to have been drawn from a population of known mean value. A Z-score was calculated by dividing the difference between the single observed value and the population mean by the square root of the variance. This gave us a measure of the difference in units of standard deviations.

Proportion is a binary measure: each person in our sample was either born in Newtown or not. So the proper distribution to use is the binomial, which we will look at in a moment. However, if the sample is large and the population proportion is not excessively large or small, the normal distribution can be assumed to be relevant. The variance of binomially distributed data is $np(1-p)$, where p is the population proportion and n is the number of data in the sample. The Z-score is therefore

$$Z = (\text{Single Value} - \text{Population Mean}) / (\text{Standard Deviation})$$
$$= (80 - 70) / \sqrt{(100 \times 0.7 \times 0.3)}$$
$$= 2.18.$$

This value shows that our sample differs significantly from the population at the 5% level. (See the selection of values for the normal distribution in the first section of Chapter 10.)

The binomial distribution differs from the normal distribution when the sample size is small, but unfortunately tables of the binomial distribution are not convenient to use. The values of probability vary with both the number of data in the sample and the population proportion, so there has to be a separate table for each size of sample and each value of population proportion. Furthermore, the values listed are cumulative probabilities. Figure 11-1 gives a more easily appreciated view of the binomial distribution by providing a selection of plotted values for a number of sample sizes and different proportions of the property of interest in the population. When the population proportion is small, the distribution is skewed, but it becomes symmetrical when the proportion is 0.5. As the sample size increases, the distribution approaches the normal distribution, as has already been stated.

Suppose we have a firm with just 10 employees, only two of which are female. Does this provide evidence that the firm is discriminating against female employees? The expected number of females assuming no discrimination is 5, so the null hypothesis is that a sample of 10 employees containing 2 or fewer females could have been drawn from a population having a proportion of females of 0.5.

Entering the values from our example in tables of the binomial distribution gives a probability of occurrence of 0.0547—i.e., just over 5%. We would have to conclude that there was no evidence at the 5% level of discrimination. Had there been just one female employee, the probability would be lower—0.0107, just over 1%— and we would consider that there was evidence of discrimination. With zero female employees, the probability would be even lower, but we would have to be careful. It would be quite likely that there was an underlying reason why the work was not suitable for or attractive to female employees.

In Figure 11-1(b), you can see these results diagrammatically. The bottom distribution is appropriate for a sample size of 10 and a population proportion of 0.5. The requirement for 1% significance is shown as zero occurrences and the requirement for 5% significance is shown as less than 2—i.e., 0 or 1.

Chapter 11 | Comparisons with Descriptive Data

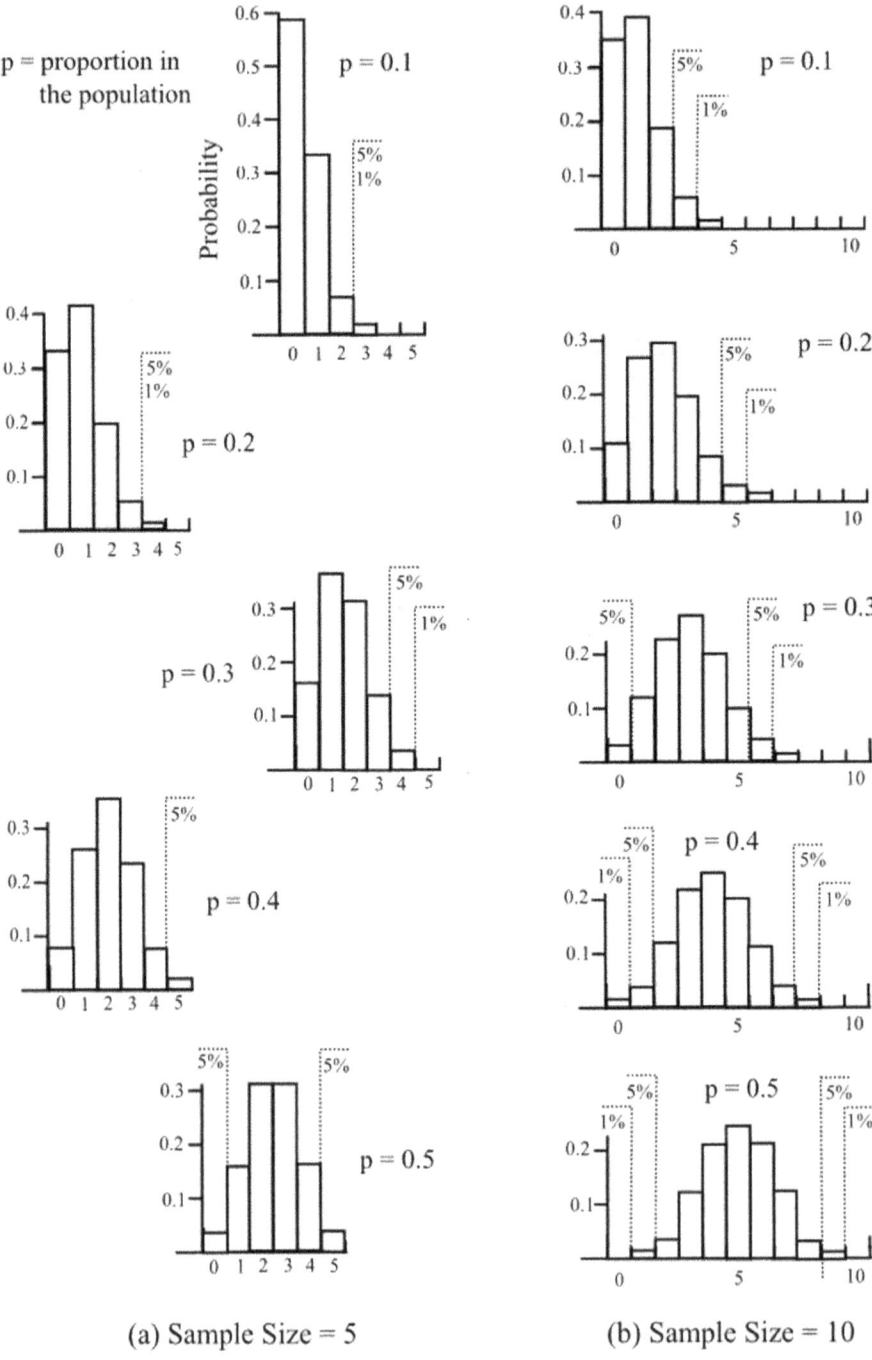

(a) Sample Size = 5

(b) Sample Size = 10

Figure 11-1. The binomial distribution showing the probability of a number of specified events in a sample when the proportion in the population is p, for a range of p values and for a sample size of (a) 5, (b) 10, (c) 20, and (d) 30

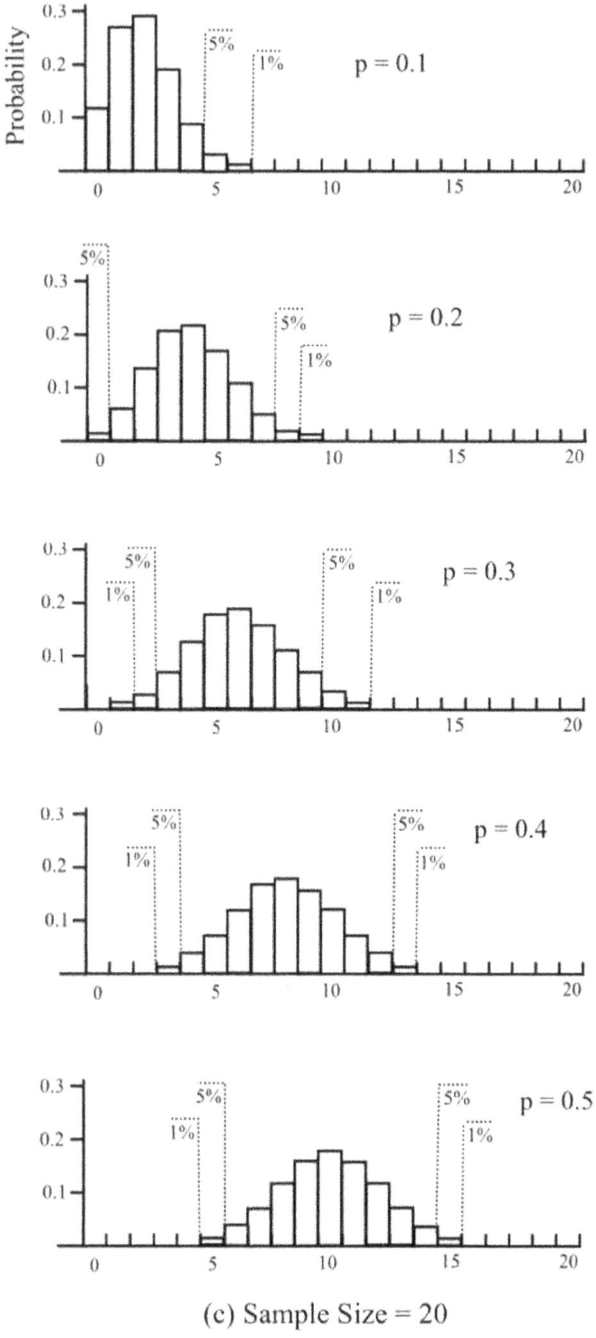

Better Business Decisions from Data

(c) Sample Size = 20

Figure 11-1. (continued)

Chapter 11 | Comparisons with Descriptive Data

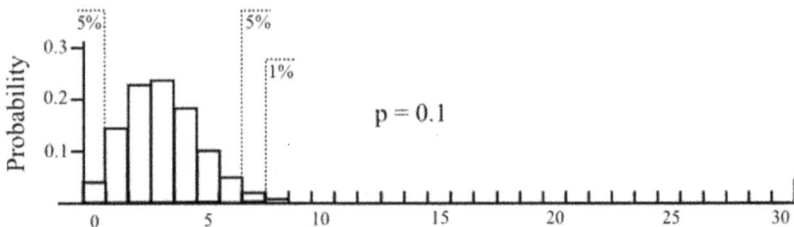

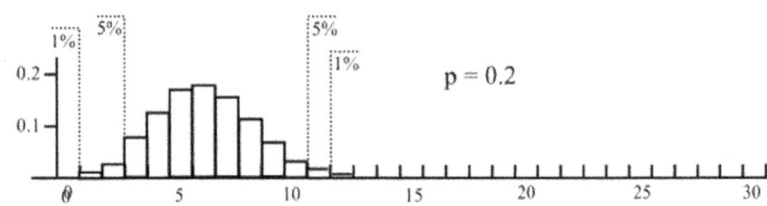

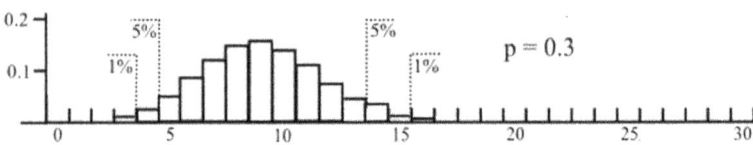

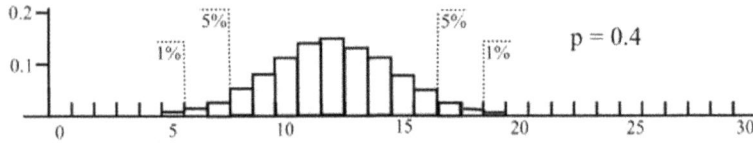

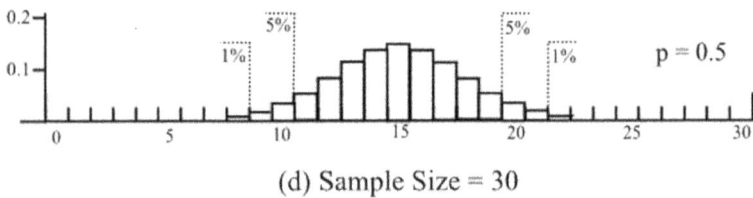

(d) Sample Size = 30

Figure 11-1. (continued)

Difference between Proportions

It may be that we have two samples and we wish to examine the difference between them. The null hypothesis is that the two samples could have been drawn from the same population. If the samples are large we can again use the normal distribution and deal with the data as for numerical data described in the "Difference between Means" section of Chapter 10. For samples of equal size, the variances of the two samples are added, and the Z-score is the difference between the numbers of occurrences in each sample divided by the square root of the combined variance. If the samples are of unequal size, the difference has to be the difference between the two proportions and there has to be an appropriate adjustment of the expression for the combined variance. Thus the Z-score takes a more complicated appearance,

$$Z = (p_1 - p_2) / \sqrt{(p(1-p)(1/n_1 + 1/n_2))},$$

where p_1 and p_2 are the two proportions in the samples, n_1 and n_2 are the two sample sizes, and p is the population proportion. If the population proportion is not known, a weighted mean of the two sample proportions is used.

Ranks

Ordinal data, which is descriptive data that can be placed in a logical order, can be compared by ranking tests. These are *nonparametric*—meaning that no particular distribution is assumed.

Suppose we have two categories that we wish to compare, and our sample data consists of an overall ranking of representatives of both categories. For example, we could have a list of singers ranked in order of preference by a panel of voters, and we wish to see if there is a significant preference for male or female singers. The list might look like this:

M F M M M F M F F F F M.

An appropriate test would be the *Mann-Whitney U-test*. An equivalent test, with a slight difference, is the *Wilcoxon rank-sum test*.

To take an example which we may follow through in greater detail, consider two teams of runners competing in a race: five runners from the A team and five runners from the B team. Our data consists of the order in which the runners finish, and our null hypothesis is that there is no significant difference between the two teams. The runners in order of finishing are

A A B B A B B A A B B B A.

Each data item is given its rank value and the values are totaled for each group, as follows"

A Team ranks   1, 2, 5, 8, 9, 13   Number, $n_A = 6$ Total, $R_A = 38$

B Team ranks   3, 4, 6, 7, 10, 11, 12   Number, $n_B = 7$ Total, $R_B = 53$

Two U values are calculated,

$$U_A = n_A n_B + n_A(n_A+1)/2 - R_A \text{ and}$$
$$U_B = n_A n_B + n_B(n_B+1)/2 - R_B$$

The statistic U is the smaller of U_A and U_B and is referred to the tables of critical values for the Mann-Whitney U-test. Use of the values above gives $U_A = 25$ and $U_B = 17$, so $U = 17$. The value needs to be equal to or less than the tabulated critical value to indicate a difference between the two sets, A and B, at the indicated significance level. Below is a selection of values from the tables:

		One Tail		Two Tail	
n_A	n_B	5%	1%	5%	1%
5	5	4	1	2	0
5	10	11	6	8	4
6	6	7	3	5	2
6	7	8	4	6	3
6	8	10	6	8	4
6	10	14	8	11	6
7	7	11	6	8	4
7	10	17	11	14	9

A two-tail test is appropriate because we are testing for no difference, rather than a difference in favor of A or B. It can be seen that our U value is too large to indicate any significant difference between the two sets of runners.

For large values of n, the normal distribution can be used. The appropriate mean value is $n_A n_B/2$, and the variance is $n_A n_B(n_A+n_B+1)/12$. Thus a Z-score can be calculated from the value of U and referred to tables of the normal distribution as shown in the first section of Chapter 10.

If the Wilcoxon rank-sum test is used, the rank sum from the smaller group, R_A, in this example 38, is the statistic to be referred to tables of critical values for the Wilcoxon rank-sum test to obtain the significance level. If the groups are equal in size, the smaller total is used. If the samples are large, the normal distribution can again be used. The appropriate mean is $n_A n_B/2 + n_B(n_B+1)/2$ and the variance is $n_A n_B(n_A+n_B+1)/12$.

The *Kruskal-Wallis test* is an extension of the Mann-Whitney test to cater to three or more samples. The test statistic has a complicated formula describing essentially the variance of the ranks. It is referred to tables of the chi-squared distribution, which was described in Chapter 7, to obtain the significance level. However, if the groups are too small (less than about 5), the statistic departs from the chi-squared distribution.

Ranks of Paired Data

If the two samples to be compared consist of paired values, the *Wilcoxon matched-pairs rank-sum test* can be used. Suppose we wish to compare a student's position in class in a range of subjects for two consecutive years. We are investigating whether there is an overall improvement in Year 2 compared with Year 1. The positions in class are as follows:

Subject	English	Math	French	German	Art	Physics	Biology	History
Year 1	3	4	6	1	1	8	6	2
Year 2	1	1	2	2	3	3	3	1
Improvement Year 1 − Year 2	2	3	4	−1	−2	5	3	1
Rank (disregarding + or −)	3.5	5.5	7	1.5	3.5	8	5.5	1.5
Sum of + ranks = 3.5+5.5+7+8+5.5+1.5 = 31								
Sum of − ranks = 1.5+3.5 = 5								
(Any zero differences are omitted.)								

The sum of the negative ranks, 5 in this example, is the statistic W, which must be equal to or less than the value in the tables of the Wilcoxon matched-pairs test. The number of pairs, n, is entered as 8. A small extract from the tables is shown below:

Number of Pairs n	One Tail		Two Tail	
	5%	1%	5%	1%
5	0	-	-	-
6	2	-	0	-
7	3	0	2	-
8	5	1	3	0
9	8	3	5	1
10	10	5	8	3

The one-tail test is relevant because we are testing for a significant improvement rather than a significant difference, and the value of 5 indicates a significant improvement at the 5% level.

Duplicate Ranks

If we have two separate rankings of the same items, there are a number of ranking methods that can be used. One of these employs the *Spearman rank correlation coefficient*, ρ (Greek letter rho) or r_s. I will illustrate the method by imagining seven different restaurants which are compared by two judges. We wish to know whether there is significant difference between the opinions of the two judges. The null hypothesis is that the two orderings are related and could have been drawn from the same population. The judges would therefore have similar opinions of the restaurants. The orderings might appear thus:

Restaurant	Judge 1	Judge 2	Difference	
	Rank	Rank	d	d^2
A	4	3	1	1
B	2	2	0	0
C	3	5	2	4
D	1	1	0	0
E	5	7	2	4
F	6	4	2	4
G	7	6	1	1
			Total	14

If two or more ranks were equal within a judge's ordering, the mean value, allowing fractions, would be substituted for each; but too many equal ranks render the analysis inappropriate.

The differences between the ranks from the two judges are squared and from the sum of the squares the correlation coefficient, ρ, is calculated. The value of ρ ranges between +1 and −1, with +1 indicating perfect agreement between the two rankings, and −1 indicating exactly opposite rankings.

The coefficient is calculated by

$$\rho = 1 - 6 \times (\text{sum of } d^2)/(n(n^2-1)),$$

where n is the number of items that are ranked. In our example,

$$\rho = 1 - 6 \times 14/(7(49-1)) = 0.75.$$

This value is referred to published tables of ρ to obtain the significance level. To give an idea of the required levels of ρ, the following table shows the values for a selection of n values and two significance levels:

Number of items n	One Tail		Two Tail	
	5%	1%	5%	1%
5	0.90	1.00	1.00	0.00
6	0.83	0.94	0.89	1.00
7	0.71	0.89	0.79	0.93
10	0.56	0.75	0.65	0.79
15	0.45	0.60	0.52	0.65
20	0.38	0.52	0.45	0.57
30	0.31	0.43	0.36	0.47
40	0.26	0.37	0.31	0.41

Our value of 0.75 can be seen to exceed the 5% significance level for a one-tail test but not for a two-tail test. In this example, a one-tail test is appropriate because we are investigating whether our two judges have ranked the restaurants in the same order. The second tail of the distribution is concerned with rankings that correlate but are in the reverse order to each other. We conclude, therefore, that there is evidence, at the 5% level, of agreement between the two rankings.

If n is greater than about 40, a Z-score can be calculated (as shown in Chapter 10) and tables of the normal distribution used to obtain the level of significance. The appropriate normal distribution has a mean of zero and a variance of $1/(n-1)$.

There are several other rank correlation coefficients, including the *Kendall rank correlation coefficient*, τ (Greek letter tau), which are calculated differently but which yield correlation coefficients that are interpreted the same as Spearman's and to which can be attributed levels of significance.

The word *correlation* in a strict sense means a linear relationship between two variables, and these ranking methods are also used to examine relationships. Here we have simply used the rank correlation coefficients to compare two samples that could be from the same population. In a sense, there could be considered to be a relationship between the two rankings: we could plot a graph of the rankings of Judge 1 against those of Judge 2. Perfect agreement between the two rankings would give a straight line with a rising slope of unity. If the two judges had given exactly opposite rankings, such a graph would give a straight line with a descending slope of unity. In Part V, we shall deal with relationships and meet ranking again.

CHAPTER 12

Types of Error
How Wrong Can You Be?

Whenever a significance level is quoted, there is a chance that the stated result is incorrect. If the null hypothesis is rejected when, in fact, it is correct, the error is referred to as a *Type I error*. So, if our null hypothesis is that there is no significant difference between the mean marks from the boys' results and the girls' results in the same examination, we may decide that there is a difference, at the 5% level, say. If in fact there is no difference, and our result is simply due to the random effect embodied in our 1-in-20 chance of being wrong, then a Type I error has occurred.

Alternatively, our result may show no significant difference, and we would accept the null hypothesis. If we are wrong and there is in reality a difference, a *Type II error* has occurred.

A Type I error is the easiest to recognize because its probability is defined when the significance level of the result is stated. In the above example, if we conclude, in agreement with the null hypothesis, that there is no significant difference (at the 5% level) between the boys and girls, we have a 5% chance of making a Type I error. The error would be a false alarm in indicating a difference when none existed. The probability of a Type I error occurring is denoted by α (Greek letter alpha). A Type II error arises when no significant difference is indicated, albeit incorrectly, and is accepted and is therefore a missed detection. A false alarm and a missed detection are useful ways of thinking of the two kinds of error: the designations I and II do little to suggest which is which (Figure 12-1).

Chapter 12 | Types of Error

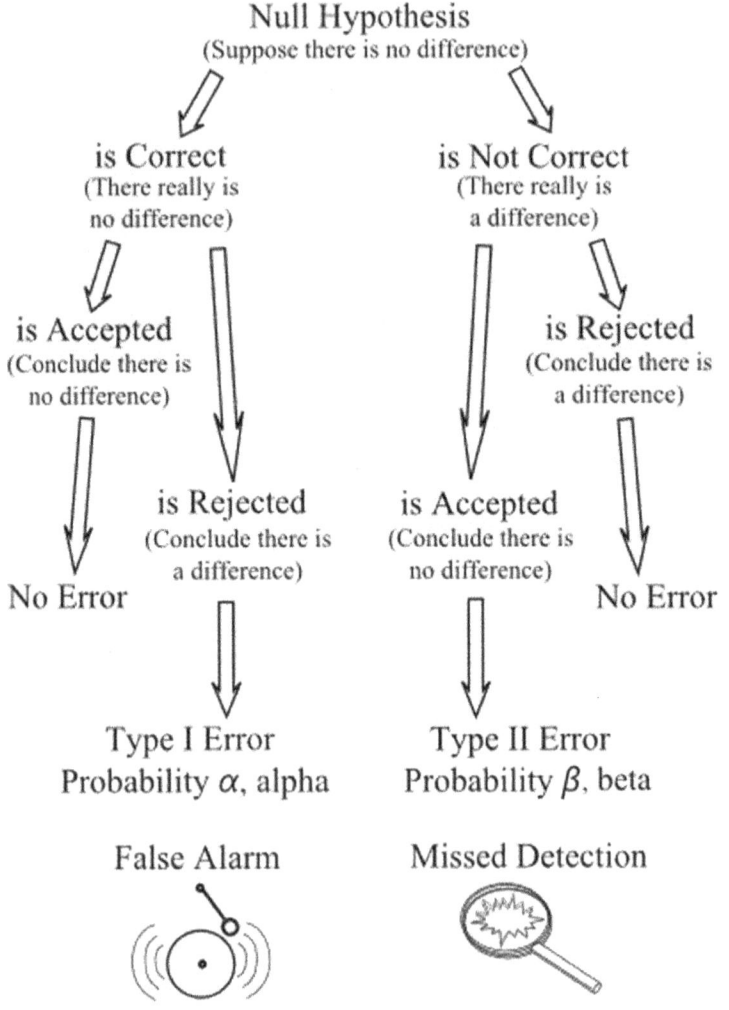

Figure 12-1. Type I and Type II errors, which arise when the null hypothesis is accepted though incorrect or when it is rejected though correct

An important purpose of hypothesis testing is to reject the null hypothesis when it is false. Thus the avoidance of a Type I error is important. A Type II error is generally less serious as it leaves the situation open for further investigation with improved resources. The *power* of a test is the probability of rejecting the null hypothesis when it is false—that is, it is equal to one minus the probability of a Type II error. The probability of a Type II error occurring is denoted by β (Greek letter beta), and the power of a test is therefore $1-\beta$. The power dictates the probability of being able to find a difference if one really exists.

Note that we cannot calculate the probability of making a Type II error without additional information, because we have no knowledge of how far the true situation is from the situation stated in the null hypothesis. We have to set up an alternative hypothesis in a quantitative way. For example, for our class of students we could propose that the girls are 3% better than the boys on average, and test this as the alternative hypothesis.

If we reduce the chance of making a Type I error by testing at a higher significance level, say 1%, then we increase the chance of making a Type II error. There is a trade-off between the two. In situations of acceptance sampling involving a supplier and a customer, there is a conflict of interest. Suppose apples are being supplied, and a sample is examined. The null hypothesis is that the sample is not significantly different from the population from which it was drawn. If a Type I error occurs, it is to the supplier's detriment, because the apples may be rejected when in fact they are satisfactory. If a Type II error occurs, the sample may indicate acceptance of the apples when in fact they are unsatisfactory. The customer is thereby disadvantaged. Reducing the probability of a Type I error increases the probability of a Type II error, and vice versa. However, by increasing the size of the sample, the probability of both types of error can be reduced. There is then a trade-off between the reduction of both errors and the cost of sampling.

A simple example will illustrate the two kinds of error. Suppose apples are obtained from a supplier whose apples are 10% bad. The customer accepts this level of quality in relation to the price paid. Keeping the numbers small to simplify the example, we assume that a batch of 10 apples is to be purchased. The customer decides to sample 3. If all 3 are satisfactory, the batch of 10 will be accepted. The null hypothesis is that the batch contains just one bad apple—i.e., 10%—in line with the expected proportion. The probability of all 3 in the sample being satisfactory is, by the multiplication rule, $9/10 \times 8/9 \times 7/8 = 0.7$. So there is a probability of 0.7 of accepting the null hypothesis and accepting the batch of 10. Thus the probability of a Type I error—i.e., the probability of rejecting the batch when there is only one unsatisfactory apple in it—is $1 - 0.7 = 0.3$.

We cannot calculate the probability of a Type II error without more information. We would need to know or suppose, for example, that the batch of ten apples might contain two bad apples. The null hypothesis that there is just one bad apple in the batch is now false. The probability of all three apples in the sample being satisfactory is $8/10 \times 7/9 \times 6/8 = 0.47$. Thus the probability of a Type II error—that is, the probability of the customer accepting the batch when the null hypothesis is false—is 0.47.

It is possible in practical situations to set up sampling arrangements to equalize the two types of error and thus equalize the supplier's risk and the customer's risk. In the above example, if the customer were to decide to sample 4 apples instead of 3, the probability of a Type I error would increase to $1-(9/10 \times 8/9 \times 7/8 \times 6/7) = 0.4$. The probability of a Type II error decreases to $8/10 \times 7/9 \times 6/8 \times 5/7 = 0.33$. Thus the risks are equalized somewhere between 3 and 4 apples being sampled with 4 apples being closer to the optimum.

REDUCING THE RISK

Hebdens was a large department store in the center of town, selling a wide selection of household goods. The store purchased a range of products from Plushcrocks, a manufacturer of ceramic goods such as plates, cups, saucers, and attractive, and very popular, ornaments. The goods were delivered to Hebdens in batches of 100. Five items from each batch were examined, and if all five items were free from damage or defects, the batch was accepted. This procedure was set up on an ad hoc basis at some time in the past.

In spite of this arrangement, Hebdens found themselves with a proportion of items that had to be scrapped or sold as seconds, and the number seemed to be rising, eating into the profits.

Roger Weyland, the quality control manager, decided to make a few calculations. It appeared to him that the percentage of unacceptable items had risen to over 5%, yet very few batches were ever rejected. At a defect rate of 5%, there would be, on average 5 defective items in every batch. The probability of the store accepting a batch when it contained as many as 6 defective items was 0.73 (73%, the customer's risk)—yet the probability of rejecting a batch when it contained just 5 defective items was 0.23 (23%, the supplier's risk). The arrangements were very much in favor of Plushcrocks, and Roger clearly needed to introduce a new procedure involving the examination of a larger sample of incoming goods.

Further calculations showed that if the number of items inspected was increased to 12, the risk of accepting the batch when it contained more than 5% defective items dropped to 48%, and the risk of rejecting the batch when it contained less than 5% defective items increased to 46%.

Roger took the matter up with Plushcrocks and, by demonstrating the equal risks for customer and supplier, he got agreement that 12 items would be inspected in the future and, unless all were defect-free, the batch would be rejected. The new procedure would not involve Hebdens in any appreciable increase in costs, but Plushcrocks would be faced with considerable additional work dealing with rejected batches. Roger realized that this was just the start. Armed with his calculations, he could continue to bring further pressure on Plushcrocks. Word went round that Plushcrocks had taken advice from a consultant statistician, with a view to improving their quality control arrangements!

PART V

Relationships

It is the function of creative men to perceive the relations between thoughts, or things, or forms of expression that may seem utterly different, and to be able to combine them into some new forms—the power to connect the seemingly unconnected.

—William Plomer

We now progress from considering a single variable to considering whether two quite different variables are related in some way. In the proper terminology, we are moving from univariate data to bivariate data and searching for relationships between two variables. We shall also consider relationships between more than two variables.

CHAPTER 13

Cause and Effect
Storks and Birth Rates

We human beings seem to have an inbuilt desire to seek out relationships between different observed effects, and deduce a cause-and-effect association. I suppose that survival depends to some extent on recognizing relationships and assuming that one effect causes another. As youngsters we learn of danger by relating climbing to the risk of falling. Crossing the road without looking is related to the possibility of being struck by a vehicle, and so on. However, we are inclined to imagine relationships where none exist, and, worse still, to imagine that these relationships imply cause and effect. The extreme situation is in the area of superstition: a remarkably high percentage of the population avoid the number thirteen or carry lucky charms. Astrology, which claims that events in our lives are affected by the positions of the planets, has a large following.

Of course, relationships can be a first step in indicating the presence of cause and effect. Science and technology have advanced, and still advance, by studying relationships. Meteorologists establish relationships between the features of air movements and the resulting weather. Chemists establish relationships between the constituents of substances and their properties.

In scientific investigations carried out under controlled conditions in a laboratory, a cause-and-effect link can be established beyond reasonable doubt. The same experiment can be repeated many times. Our chemist can assure us that he can predict a specific reaction if he knows the conditions that are being maintained. The meteorologist is on less certain ground, having to observe the effects without the ability to control any one of them or to remove unwanted effects that may play a part. Nevertheless, repeated observations can build up confidence that relationships are causally related, particularly if theories are available to explain the relationships. Indeed, theories, starting from hypotheses, develop from the confirmation of cause and effect and may progress to the status of laws.

The use of control groups is a common way of establishing a causal relationship, typically in trials of new drugs. The drug is administered to one group of patients while patients in a second group, the control group, are given placebos. The patients are not made aware of which group they are in. The validity of the results, of course, depends on the overall similarity of the two groups, which therefore need to be constituted by a randomizing procedure.

In general, unless we have evidence that changing one factor brings about a consistent change in another, we cannot assume a cause-and-effect connection. It is not sufficient to establish that the two factors are related. An example of correlation without a causal relationship is that the number of births in Copenhagen in the post-WWII period correlated with the number of storks nesting on the roofs of buildings. The correlation is consistent with the theory that storks deliver human babies but does not prove it. A more plausible reason for the correlation, however, is that increase in the city's human population was causally correlated with an increase in building which provided more nesting opportunities for storks. Similar correlations between storks and births have been reported from Germany and the Netherlands. Some correlations may be due not simply to a third common cause, as in these examples, but to a series of interconnected factors.

Sometimes a correlation may arise in a more subtle way. Suppose we suspect that a particular medical treatment is triggering an unpleasant side effect in patients. This could be based on an observed correlation between the use of the treatment and occurrence of the side effect. However, it may be that the side effect is not really a side effect but rather is a result of the ailment that the treatment is being used to relieve.

Blastland and Dilnot (2007: 163-174) provide a thought-provoking chapter describing situations in which correlation has been taken to imply causation. An example involves longevity and being overweight. Data from America showed overweight people living slightly longer than thin people. However, a factor not taken into account was that very ill people tend to be very thin. The inclusion of data from this category influences the overall picture, suggesting that being overweight leads to a longer life. The authors also point out that, because of the many false claims of causality, there arises among some of us an unfortunate condemnation of all claims, regardless of their validity.

Some proposed causal relationships are not easy to prove because we have no direct control over the effects involved. What do you make of the following, for example? Richard Wiseman (2007: 27-31) describes an experiment involving 40,000 people. Each was asked to rate himself or herself as lucky or unlucky. The results were found to correlate with the month of birth.

The self-described lucky ones were born in summer months, and the unlucky ones in winter months.

The experiment was repeated in the southern hemisphere (New Zealand), though with only 2000 subjects, and it was found that the birth rate for lucky people peaked in December—summer in the southern hemisphere. It was suggested that the temperature at the time of birth might influence the way the baby is looked after in its early months, or perhaps the mother's diet varies at different times of the year according to the climate. On the other hand, I suspect that many statisticians would like to see the results in greater detail before expressing an opinion. They might also want to know if the subjects in New Zealand knew of the UK finding before they took part.

Amazing coincidences occur regularly. We read of them in the newspapers every week. It is not too surprising, when we consider the enormous number of events that take place in the world and the large number of people there are to experience them. We must always remember that a relationship between events is not sufficient to demonstrate cause and effect. Correlation is a necessary condition for cause and effect, but it is not a sufficient condition. Statistics can demonstrate relationships within a specified level of reliability. But that is as far as it can go. Statistics alone can never prove a causal relationship.

CHAPTER 14

Relationships with Numerical Data

Straight Lines, Curved Lines, and Wiggly Lines

It is frequently required to compare two or more sets of data to decide whether they are related in some way. Some quantities are related because we have defined them to be so. Kilometers are related to miles in a precise way and the relationship can be expressed as a formula:

$$\text{kilometers} = \text{miles} \times 1.609.$$

Dollars are related to pounds sterling by a precise rate of exchange, which may vary from day to day and place to place, but which is nevertheless precise for a particular transaction. Generally, however, we are dealing with quantities which may show some relationship but rarely a precise relationship.

Scientific investigations under closely controlled laboratory conditions probably come closest to precise relationships, but even here there are small errors involved in making measurements which give uncertainties in the established relationships. At the other end of the scale we may be looking, for example, for a relationship between the way people vote in an election and how their parents vote. Here, it is likely that any relationship is uncertain, and the role of statistical analysis is to quantify the uncertainties.

Chapter 14 | Relationships with Numerical Data

When a relationship between two variables is sought, a distinction is made between the *independent variable* and the *dependent variable*. In Figure 14-1, the relationship between sales of ice cream and daily noon temperature is shown as a line graph. The temperature is the independent variable and sales is the dependent variable, sales depending on the temperature and not the other way round. Line graphs are commonly used, as here, to show relationships, and there is a convention in plotting them with regard to the choice of the quantities to be located on the two axes. The horizontal axis is used for the independent variable and the vertical axis for the dependent variable. Sometimes it is not clear which is which, both variables being dependent on other factors. We may have a choice as to which we treat as the dependent variable and which we treat as the independent variable. If we measure the temperature and humidity at a location at noon each day and plot temperature against humidity, the choice of axes for the two variables will be arbitrary.

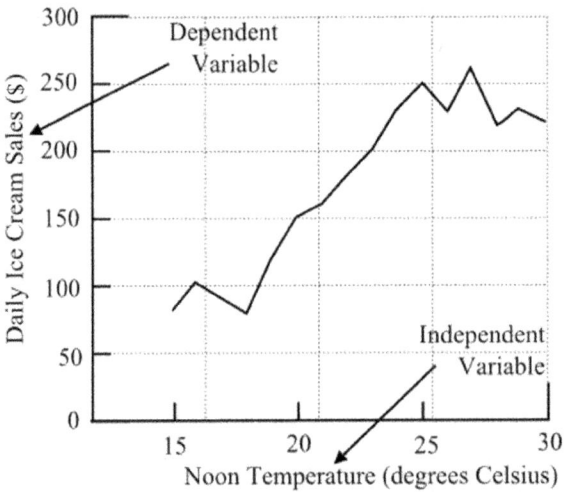

Figure 14-1. Graph of ice cream sales at various daily temperatures, illustrating the difference between the dependent and independent variables

The relation between two variables is the easiest situation to deal with; the difficulties increase rapidly as further variables are introduced. These difficulties are not only in the analysis but also in the decreasing reliability of the conclusions that can be derived.

The raw data that have been collected may allow many different explorations of relationship. If people of different ages are sampled, or if products of different categories are involved, the number of possible pairs of variables can be many. There is a danger that the investigators, rather than deciding at the outset what comparisons are to be examined, will compare everything possible with everything else. The result can be completely unreliable. If, for example, a statistical level of 5% is intended to be accepted, it is likely that 1 in 20 comparisons will spuriously exhibit this level of significance. Since the statistical tests to be described can now be rapidly carried out by computer programs, the temptation to search for any possible relationship is very great. When the tests had previously to be carried out by hand, time simply did not permit a far-reaching search for any evidence of relationship, however unlikely.

It does seem that we are being overwhelmed by claimed associations at the present time. The media are full of statistical correlations relating to what we think, what we do, what we eat and drink, what we should eat and drink, and so on. I wonder—cynically, I suppose—whether some manufacturers sponsor investigations to seek relationships between their product's characteristics and just about anything else that might boost the desirability of their product.

In viewing results obtained by others, it is not possible to know how many different pairings of variables were or were not examined. If the raw data are available, or if details of the sampling are known, suspicions may be raised if it appears that the results reported are particularly selective. If the reported results refer to cabbages only, yet a range of vegetables was included in the sampling, some explanation would be called for.

I need to point out that what I have said above applies strictly to relations between pairs of variables. It does not apply to investigations in which the aim is to study simultaneously the effect of several different variables. Such investigations are perfectly proper and will be considered in Chapter 16.

Linear Relationships

If two quantities are related precisely, the relationship can be represented by a line graph; and if the line is straight, the relationship is said to be *linear*. The line may pass through the origin of the graph, indicating that the two quantities are proportional to each other. Thus a graph of dollars plotted against pounds sterling, illustrating a rate of exchange, is a straight line graph passing through the origin (Figure 14-2). The formula describing the graph is

$$\text{pounds sterling} = R \times \text{US dollars},$$

R being the rate of exchange.

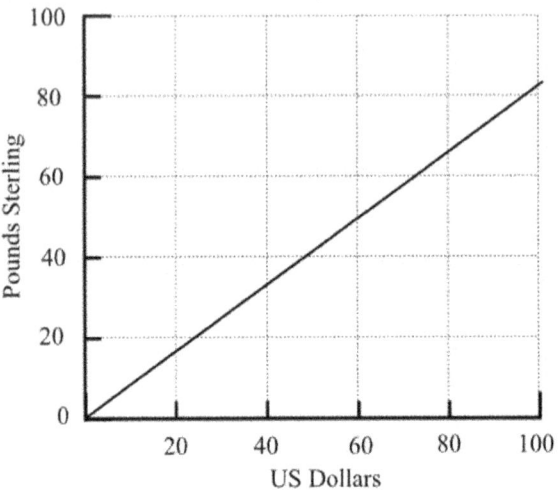

Figure 14-2. A straight-line conversion graph

Some linear relationships have straight lines that do not pass through the origin. For example, the cost of shipping goods to a particular destination might be $2 per kilogram plus $60. The formula has the form,

Cost ($) = 2 × weight (kg) + 60.

The graphs in Figure 14-3 show that as one of the quantities increases, so does the other. This is called *positive correlation*. *Negative correlation* describes relationships in which one quantity decreases as the other increases.

Better Business Decisions from Data

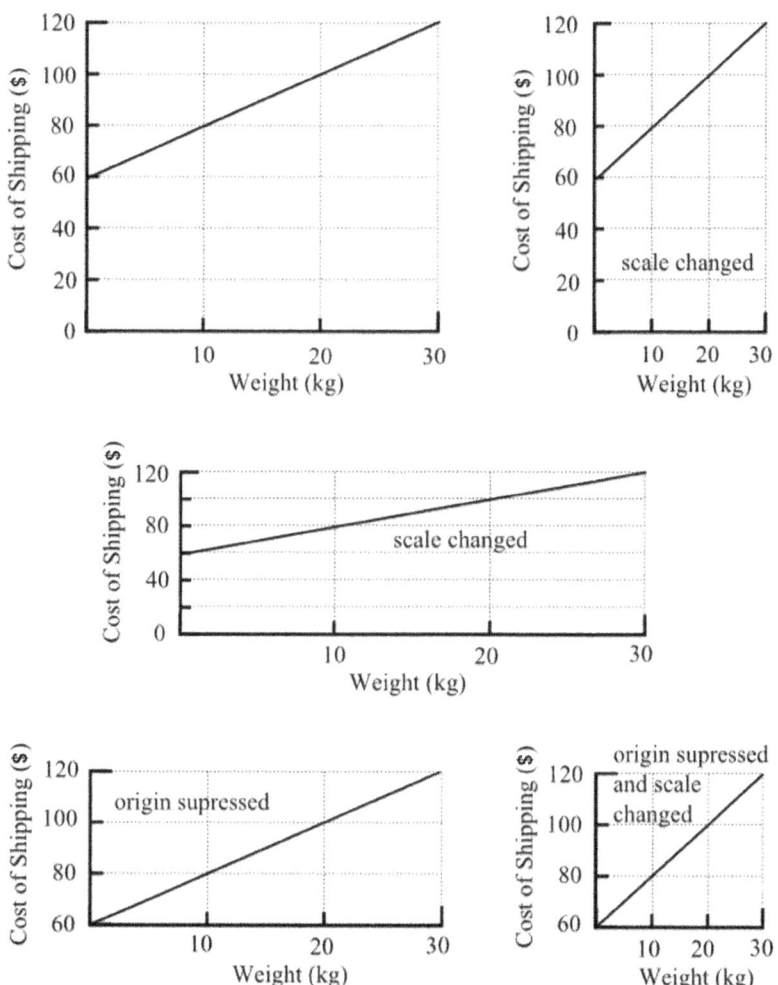

Figure 14-3. A graph of the cost of shipping goods of different weights, presented in several ways to illustrate the visual effects of changing the scale and suppressing the origin

Figure 14-3 illustrates also how the relationship between the variables can be made to appear different by changes of the scale used for plotting the graphs and by suppression of the origin.

When we are dealing with variables that are not precisely related, an initial examination of the data involves plotting a scatter graph. The individual data points are plotted on a graph whose axes represent the two variables involved. By eye, it may be possible to see a rising or falling trend indicating positive or negative correlation. A useful technique, illustrated in Figure 14-4, is to draw a horizontal line positioned so that half the data points are above the line and half are below. A vertical line is then drawn so that half the points are to the

Chapter 14 | Relationships with Numerical Data

left and half are to the right. A count of the points in each quadrant suggests correlation by any appreciable excess in either of the diagonally linked pairs of quadrants.

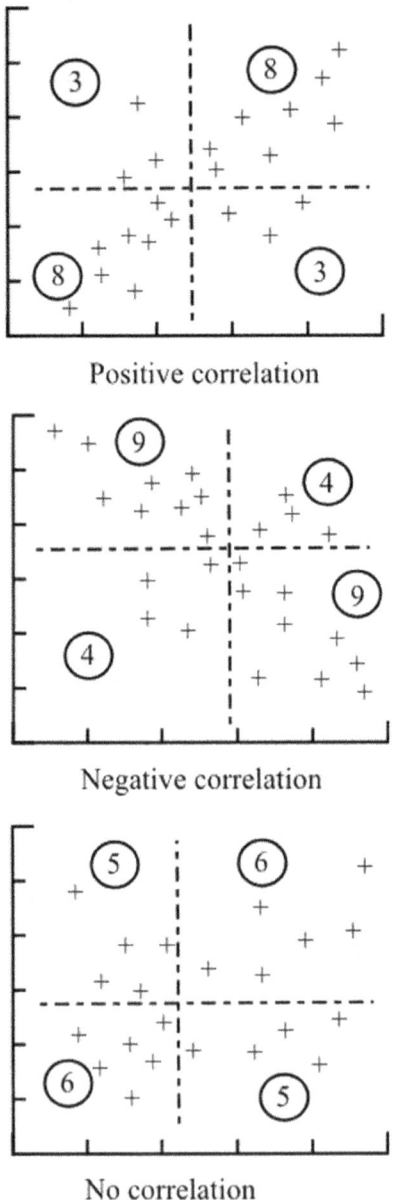

Figure 14-4. Examples of scatter graphs used to explore the existence of correlation between two variables

If there is evidence of correlation, a best-fit straight line can be located by eye. A transparent ruler allows the line to be located so that an equal or nearly equal number of points lie each side of the line and so that the distances of the points from the line are minimized. An improvement to the procedure involves calculating the mean value of each of the two quantities, plotting the values as a point on the graph, and ensuring that the line passes through it.

The gradient of the best-fit line—the steepness or *slope*, in other words—is the extent the line goes upward divided by the extent it moves to the right. Note that the gradient can mistakenly be taken as a measure of the correlation between the two variables, a steep line appearing to suggest strong correlation. The numerical value of the gradient is, in fact, arbitrary in depending on the units used in measuring the variables. For example, a formula for the time to cook a chicken might be

$$\text{Time (minutes)} = 45 \times \text{Weight (kg)} + 30,$$

and the gradient of the graph is 45. If hours are used, the equation is

$$\text{Time (hours)} = 0.75 \times \text{Weight (kg)} + 0.5,$$

and the gradient is 0.75. The extent of correlation between the two variables depends on the closeness of the points to the line, regardless of the line's gradient—provided that there is a gradient. Clearly, if there is no gradient, one of the variables cannot influence the other and there is zero correlation. A glance back at Figure 14-3 confirms that the gradient can be made to look large or small by changes of scale and can therefore misrepresent the extent of correlation between the two variables.

The position of the best-fit line can be determined by a statistical procedure called *linear regression*, which we now need to look at. The word *regression* is used here with the meaning of estimation, in that the line will be used to estimate the value of one variable from the value of the other.

Suppose we wish to know how fast a particular type of tree grows. We obtain data showing the height of a representative tree as measured each year up to five years old. The points are plotted in Figure 14-5 and the values are as follow:

Chapter 14 | Relationships with Numerical Data

	Year	Height (m)					
	x	y	$(x-x_m)$	$(y-y_m)$	$(x-x_m)(y-y_m)$	$(x-x_m)^2$	$(y-y_m)^2$
	1	0.1	−2	−0.6	1.2	4	0.36
	2	0.6	−1	−0.1	0.1	1	0.01
	3	0.9	0	0.2	0	0	0.04
	4	0.9	1	0.2	0.2	1	0.04
	5	1.0	2	0.3	0.6	4	0.09
Total	15	3.5			$2.1 = S_{xy}$	$10 = S_{xx}$	$0.54 = S_{yy}$
Mean	$3 = x_m$	$0.7 = y_m$					

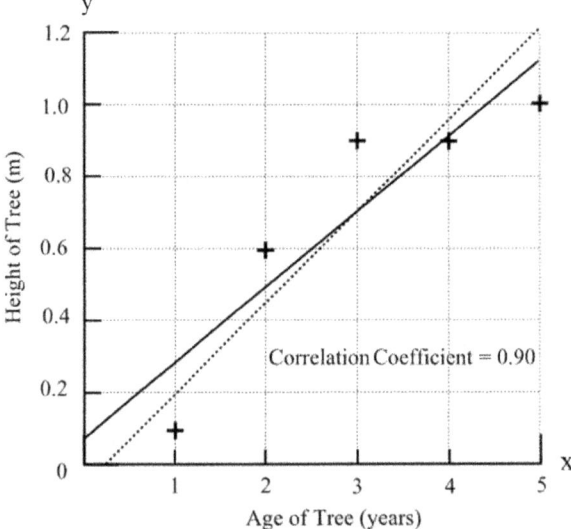

——— Regression line of y on x for estimating the height of a tree from its age
········ Regression line of x on y for estimating the age of a tree from its height

Figure 14-5. A graph of the height of a tree at different ages with its calculated simple linear regression lines

The difference between each value of x and the mean value of x is shown, together with the square of each difference. The y values are treated similarly. The product of each x difference and the corresponding y difference is included.

The equation of the best-fit line is given by the formula,

$$y - y_m = (x - x_m) S_{xy} / S_{xx},$$

which, inserting the values from above and rearranging, gives

$$y = 0.21x + 0.07.$$

The line, which is included in Figure 14-5, passes through the point located at the mean value of x and the mean value of y, and this will always be found to be so. The line is *best-fit* in that the squares of the deviations of the measured y values from the values predicted by the graph are minimized.

The observant reader will have noticed that although the value of S_{xx} appears in the equation, S_{yy} does not. This is because there are in reality two best-fit lines, the second one having a similar equation except for the replacement of S_{xx} by S_{yy} and the transposing of x and y. How could there be two best-fit lines? The reason is that it depends on how the graph is to be used. The line we have just calculated is called the regression of y on x and it is designed to give the best estimate of the y value when the x value is given. Thus, if we know the age of our tree, we can use the graph to estimate its height.

But we may want to use the graph to be able to estimate the age of a tree when we measure its height, which is a different process.

The requirement then is for the line representing the regression of x on y. The equation is

$$x - x_m = (y - y_m) S_{xy} / S_{yy}$$

which, when rearranged, gives

$$y = 0.26x - 0.07.$$

This second regression line is included in Figure 14-5. The line again passes through the point representing the mean values of x and y, but it has a somewhat different gradient compared to the previous line. The two lines are similar in this example; and, generally speaking, the greater the correlation between the two variables, the closer the two lines will be. Indeed, if there is perfect correlation, a conversion graph for example, there can be only a single line.

The above example was chosen to illustrate the usefulness of and the difference between the two regression lines. Often, however, it is sensible to use the graph in one direction only: this gives rise to the distinction between the independent variable and the dependent variable, which has been previously described. If we are free to fix the values of one of the variables, then this variable is the independent variable. The other is the dependent variable because its values depend on the fixing of the values of the independent variable. Relationships are commonly used to estimate the value of the dependent variable, and only one regression line is then required.

Sometimes it is known at the outset that the regression line must pass through the origin because, when one of the variables is zero, the other must be zero. The equation is now somewhat simpler, but we need a few additional calculations, as follow.

Year	Height (m)			
x	y	xy	x^2	y^2
1	0.1	0.1	1	0.01
2	0.6	1.2	4	0.36
3	0.9	2.7	9	0.81
4	0.9	3.6	16	0.81
5	1.0	5.0	25	1.00
Total		12.6 = S(xy)	55 = S(x^2)	2.99 = S(y^2)

The equation is

$$y = (S(xy)/S(x^2))x,$$

which gives

$$y = 0.23x$$

if we take x as the independent variable. In other words, we are estimating the height of the tree, y, from its age, x. If y is considered to be the independent variable, to allow estimates of age from a known height, then the equation is

$$x = (S(xy)/S(y^2))y,$$

which gives

$$y = 0.24x.$$

We might argue that the height of our tree is zero, or very nearly so, when its age is zero and that, therefore, these would be the preferred equations. However, taking a more practical view, we would say that our graphs are for use on trees that have achieved sufficient height to be considered trees; and, furthermore, the rate of growth might be very different when the tree is little more than a seedling and should not be allowed to influence the correlation within the range of practical use. In this case we would use the graphs of Figure 14-5.

Appropriate analysis yields regression lines, but the question remains as to how meaningful the correlation is. A *correlation coefficient, r*, can be readily calculated at the same time as the regression lines are being determined. The full name of the coefficient is the *product-moment correlation coefficient*, but it is often referred to as *Pearson's coefficient*. The coefficient has the property of always having a value between +1 and −1. A value of +1 indicates perfect positive correlation: all the plotted points lie exactly on the straight line and the line has a rising slope. A value of −1 indicates perfect negative correlation: the points again lie exactly on the line but the slope is descending. A value of 0 indicates no correlation, the plotted points being randomly scattered. A degree of judgment is generally necessary in interpreting the value obtained. A value of around 0.5 indicates some correlation but anything below about 0.4 would raise serious doubts. The equation for r is

$$r = S_{xy} / \sqrt{(S_{xx} S_{yy})}.$$

In the tree example above, the data gives $r = 0.90$.

The value of r^2 can be used to indicate the usefulness of the correlation. With r equal to 0.9, r^2 is 0.81 and shows that 81% of the variation in the dependent variable is due to the variation in the independent variable. Thus 19% of the variation is due to other factors.

The correlation that has been established relates strictly to the data in this particular sample, whereas we would want to use the correlation in studying other samples of similar trees. In order to justify the use of the correlation to represent the population from which the sample was obtained, it is necessary to determine the significance of the result. This can be done by using tables of critical values for the product-moment correlation coefficient. A selection of values is shown below.

	One Tail		Two Tail	
Size of Sample	5%	1%	5%	1%
3	0.988	1.000	0.997	1.000
4	0.900	0.980	0.950	0.990
5	0.805	0.934	0.878	0.959
10	0.549	0.715	0.632	0.765
15	0.441	0.592	0.514	0.641
20	0.378	0.516	0.444	0.561
30	0.306	0.423	0.361	0.463
40	0.264	0.367	0.312	0.403

Our value of 0.9 can be seen to be significant at the 5% level for both a one-tail and a two-tail test. If at the outset we were investigating whether there was a significant correlation between tree height and age—in other words, whether the true gradient of the graph was not zero—then we would apply the two-tail test. If we were investigating whether there was a positive correlation between tree height and age—in other words, whether the gradient was greater than zero—we would apply the one-tail test: the second tail corresponding to a negative correlation which would clearly be impossible in our tree example. The point was made previously that statistical tests are designed to establish the significance of hypotheses which are clearly defined at the outset.

It may seem odd that the testing for significance relies on comparing the gradient of the graph with the value of zero. We might have a gradient of 28, say, on one occasion and a gradient of only 0.28 on another. The first value is much further from zero than the second. However, as mentioned previously, the numerical value of the gradient is arbitrary because it depends on the units being used. The criterion for significant correlation is the likelihood of there *being* a gradient—that is to say, we are looking at the probability of the gradient having any nonzero value.

Confidence intervals can be obtained and represented by bands either side of the regression line. These indicate the reliability, on average, of predictions made from the line. Somewhat similar are *prediction intervals* with wider bands, showing the reliability of individual predictions at different position along the graph.

In some investigations, it may be known that individual points on the graph have different degrees of reliability. Some may be the mean values from large samples and others from small samples. Some may be from more accurate measurements than others. In such instances, each point may be shown with an *error bar* indicating the individual reliability. A vertical error bar is centered on the plotted point, the length of the bar indicating the confidence limits of the dependant variable. If the independent variable is subject to some uncertainty, there may be a similar horizontal bar centered on the point.

Note that predictions from regression lines are valid only within the range of the values represented. It is not possible to extrapolate a regression line to obtain values outside this range. Effort put into obtaining regression lines in order to extrapolate the data can give dangerously misleading results.

Numerical data can be treated in a ranking procedure as an alternative to obtaining regression lines. I described the method in Chapter 11. Each set of data is arranged in order and given rank numbers of 1 upward. The method is rapid compared with treating the numerical data as we did in the example of linear regression, but the main advantage arises when the data contains extreme values, usually a result of the data not being normally distributed.

Samples of salaries, for example, generally contain some very high values that will influence greatly a numerical correlation based on fitting a straight line. When the data are ranked in order of size, there are no extreme values. Note, however, that ranking tests are *non-parametric*: they do not assume any particular distribution of the data and are not as powerful as parametric tests. Also, although the ranking provides a measure of the extent of correlation, it does not give information regarding the way the two variables are related, other than showing whether the correlation is positive or negative.

Nonlinear Relationships

When the data are plotted, there may be evidence of a curved rather than a linear relationship. One way of dealing with the situation is to transform the data in order to achieve linearity. The following values show the growth in population of a town over a number of years:

Year	1700	1750	1800	1850	1900	1950	2000
Population (10,000's)	1.0	4.0	6.3	17.6	26.0	33.6	51.0

The graph, shown in Figure 14-6(a), is curved and the ever-steepening shape as time increases suggests that taking the square root of each value of population would produce a straighter line.

Square Root	1.0	2.0	2.5	4.2	5.1	5.8	7.1

Figure 14-6(b) shows the re-plotted data and it can be seen that the graph is approximately linear. Examination of significant correlation could be carried out as in the previous section.

Chapter 14 | Relationships with Numerical Data

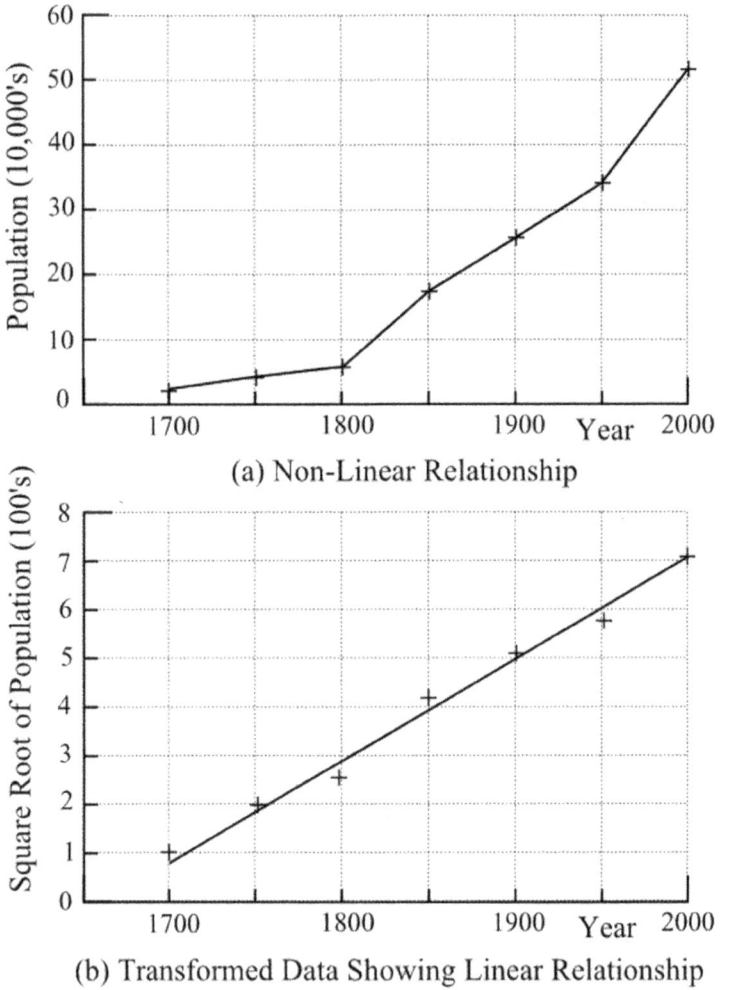

Figure 14-6. Graphs of the population growth of a town showing (a) the raw data and (b) the data transformed by plotting the square root of the population

Data can be transformed by applying any mathematical procedure. Commonly used transformations employ squaring, square rooting, cubing, cube rooting, taking the logarithm of one of the variables, and taking the logarithm of both variables.

In scientific work when a law relating the two variables is sought, transformations that are successful can suggest the physical processes underlying the law. To illustrate this, we can consider a well-known law relating the distance, R, of a planet from the Sun and the time, T, it takes to go once round the Sun. If we plot the two variables as shown in Figure 14-7(a), we get a curve. If we transform the variables by plotting the cube root of T against the square root of R, we get a straight line passing through the origin, Figure 14-7(b). (This is equivalent to showing that T^2 is proportional to R^3, which is the way the law is usually expressed. However, a plot of T^2 against R^3 has to be unacceptably large to accommodate the very wide range of the data.) We can then apply linear regression to locate the best line and use it to predict the path of any new minor planet that might be discovered. In reality, of course, the law relating T and R is well known (though not quite as simple as suggested here, because the orbits are elliptical and not perfectly circular) and the features of the orbit of any planet can be accurately calculated.

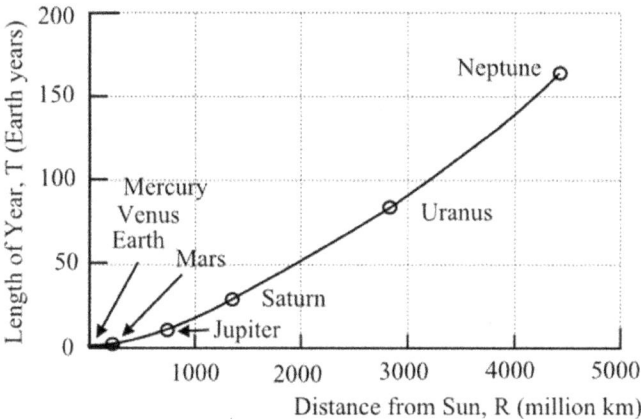

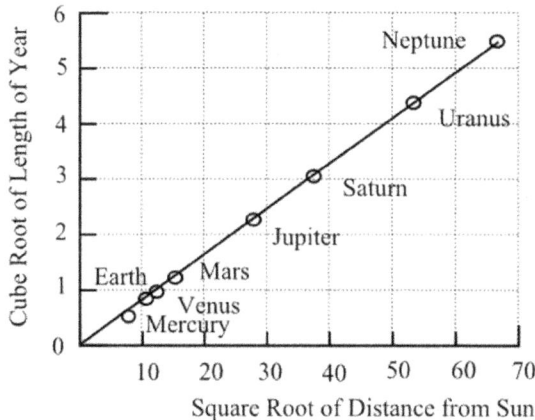

Figure 14-7. Graphs of a planet's length of year in relation to its distance from the Sun, showing (a) the raw data and (b) the transformed data

Sometimes, however, red herrings crop up. The Titus–Bode law was based on an apparent relationship between the sequence of the planets from the Sun and their distances from the Sun. Figure 14-8(a) shows a plot with the numerical sequence on the x-axis and the distances from the Sun on the y-axis. Note that Neptune had not been discovered when the law was proposed and that Ceres (a prominent asteroid) was considered to be a planet. The graph is curved, and a transformation looks useful. If we transform by taking the logarithm of the distance and re-plotting, we get, with the exclusion of Neptune, a linear relationship, as shown in Figure 14-8(b). The correlation is good: the correlation coefficient, r, has a value of 0.995. When Neptune was discovered, it was found to depart drastically from the supposed relationship. Nowadays, the Titus–Bode law is considered to be no more than a curious coincidence or, at best, a combination of several factors that combine to give an apparent simple connection.

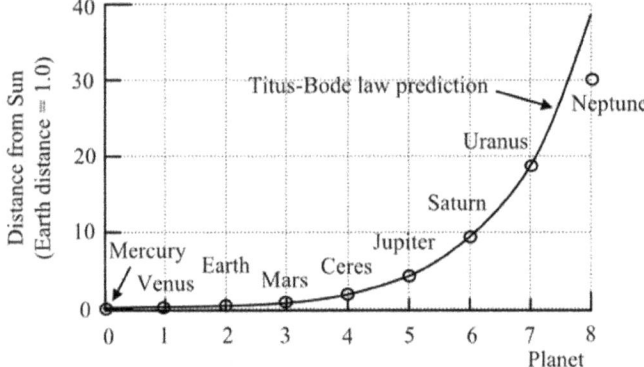

(a) Smooth curve fitting the data (except Neptune)

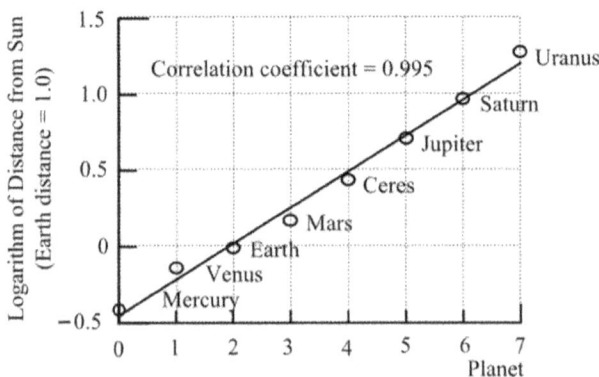

(b) Straight line fitting the transformed data (except Neptune)

Figure 14-8. Graphs of a planet's distance from the Sun in relation to its numerical sequence from the Sun (Titus-Bode law), showing (a) the raw data and (b) the transformed data

Achieving a linear relationship by use of a transformation is thus a useful and straightforward technique. It does suffer from the problem that minimizing errors in order to get the best fit is itself affected by the transformation. In other words, the best-fit line represents the best fit for the transformed variables but not necessarily the best fit for the variables themselves.

It should be noted that it is always possible to find the equation of a line that will pass through any distribution of points. An equation of the form

$$y = a + bx,$$

where a and b are constants, is always a straight line. An equation of the form

$$y = a + bx + cx^2$$

gives a curve which turns once. An equation of the form

$$y = a + bx + cx^2 + dx^3$$

gives a curve which turns twice, and so on. Such equations are called *polynomials*, and the fitting of such equations is referred to as *polynomial regression*. If we search for a polynomial equation with no restriction on length, we will always be able to obtain a curve that passes through all our experimental points. Clearly, this becomes a useless exercise: the final equation will have no meaning. We might just as well have drawn by hand a wiggly curve passing through all our points. Common sense dictates the extent to which it is reasonable to proceed down this path.

It is evident that there is not a unique best-fit line if we are to allow unrestricted curving of the line: it is always necessary to decide what is to be accepted in terms of the shape of the line or the form of the equation describing the line. Numerous computer packages are available for nonlinear regression. They are essentially trial-and-error procedures, and hence computer-intensive, progressing by iteration to a fit that meets the acceptable criteria and minimizes the errors of the experimental points in comparison with predictions from the line. This is, of course, what we saw with regard to linear correlation, where a straight line was the acceptable criterion and the mathematics minimized the errors of the individual points, though without the need for lengthy iterations.

Irregular Relationships

Two variables may not be related in any apparent, or even predictable, way but may nevertheless be related. Commonly, one of the variables is time. Many things vary with time: indeed, most things do. In the world of business and commerce, a great deal of attention is paid to how various quantities are changing. We wish to see how our profits are rising month by month or year by year. Or we look at the change in the stock market figures each morning in the newspaper. Such data are characterized by their to-and-fro variability, and because of this it is possible to draw numerous conclusions, some of which will be favorable from the point of view of the presenter and others of which will be unfavorable. Figure 14-9(a) shows the variation of the FTSE 100 financial index of shares from its inception in 1984. There is clearly a marked degree of positive correlation, but a search for a quantifiable correlation would be rather pointless.

In Chapter 6, I warned about suppressing the origin when presenting bar charts. The same warning applies to line graphs: the result can be extremely misleading, particularly when the origin is suppressed on the vertical axis—i.e., the dependent variable. We must bear in mind, however, that sometimes, particularly with regard to graphs showing changes with time, we must suppress the origin. Indeed, when did time start? The time axis clearly can start at any convenient point, and the vertical axis may have to start distant from zero. The graph in Figure 14-9(a) has a true origin, since the FTSE index started in 1984 with a value of 1000, and the graph is useful in showing the historical changes. But if you purchased shares within the past few weeks, you would be more interested in a graph such as Figure 14-9(b), which necessarily has its origin suppressed. The vertical axis is broken. A break is shown in the vertical axis, the index value; but to break the time axis would be pedantic in view of what has been said.

Better Business Decisions from Data

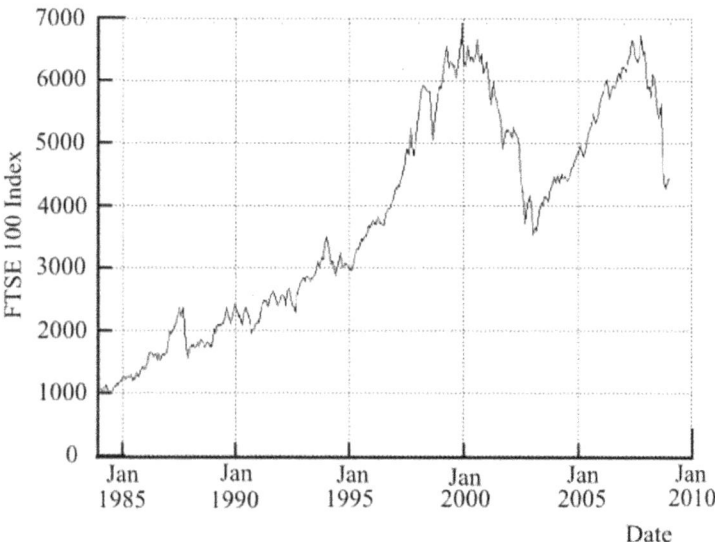

(a) The UK FTSE 100 index since its start in 1984 at a value of 1000

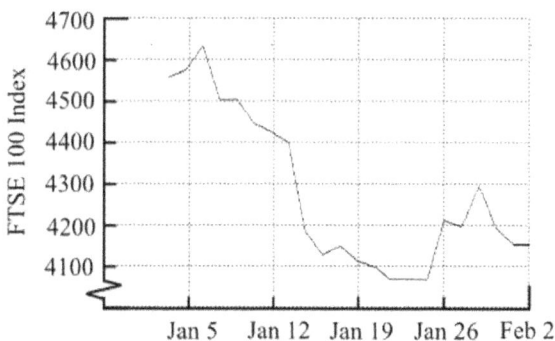

(b) The UK FTSE 100 index during January 2009

Figure 14-9. Graphs of the movements of the UK FTSE 100 index showing (a) the inclusion of the origin on the vertical axis and (b) an acceptable presentation of the suppression of the origin

Similarly, financial data relating to companies may be of interest only over the recent past and suppressing of the origin of graphs may be justified. The justification, however, can provide latitude within which misleading impressions may be given.

The table of figures below shows the monthly profits over a two year period for a small company. For simplicity, the figures are shown as small numbers in units of $1000.

Chapter 14 | Relationships with Numerical Data

	Jan	Feb	Mar	Apr	May	Jun	Jul	Aug	Sep	Oct	Nov	Dec
2008	1.3	1.1	1.1	1.4	1	1.2	1.3	1.6	1.2	1.3	1.1	1.4
2009	1.4	1.6	1.4	1.6	1.2	1.5	1.7	1.9	1.6	1.5	1.6	1.6

The data is shown as a line graph in Figure 14-10(a). The ups and downs provide opportunities for the company to present optimistic views from time to time and also for critics to present less favorable commentaries.

To present the data in a way that smooths out the fluctuations, a moving average can be used. This is particularly useful when it is recognized that there could be cyclic variations in the data—seasonal variations, for example.

The average employed can be the mean or the median. We will use a three-month moving average based on mean values. That is to say, we will average the values for the first three months, Jan to Mar, 2008; and then, moving along by one month we will average the values for Feb to Apr, 2008. The next average is for Mar to May, 2008, and so on. The results are shown plotted in Figure 14-10(b). The graph is now smoother, showing a gentle rise with time. The product-moment correlation coefficient is 0.88, compared to 0.70 for the original graph. A graph of the six-month moving average, shown in Figure 14-10(c), fluctuates even less, and the correlation coefficient has increased to 0.99.

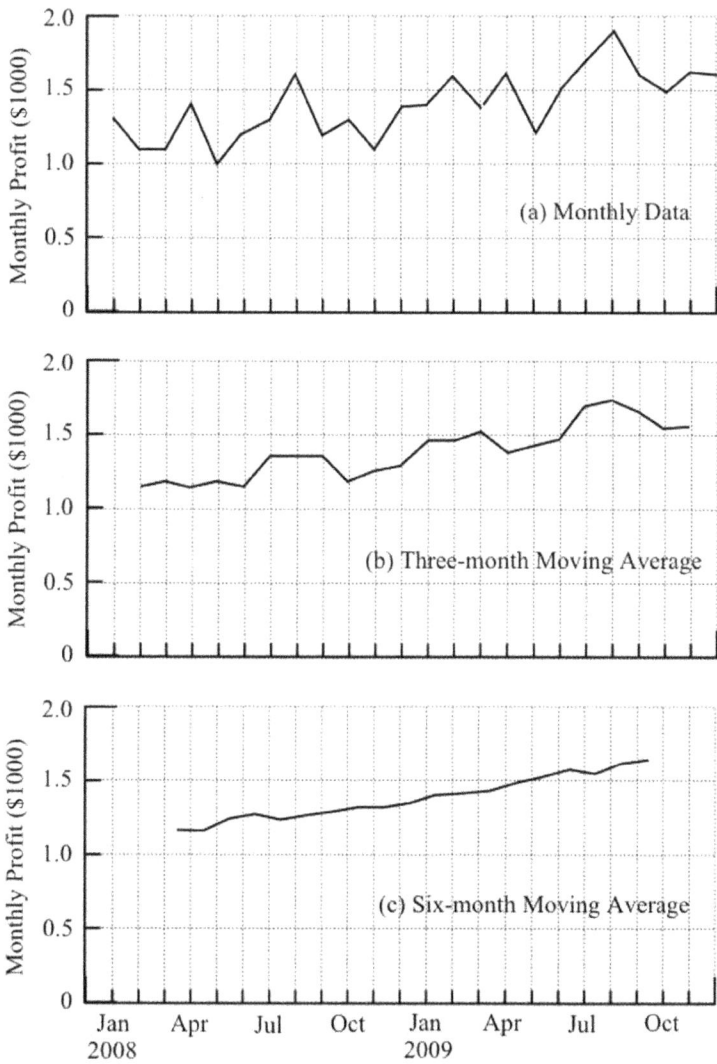

Figure 14-10. Graphs of the growth of profits of a small company showing (a) the raw data, (b) the three-month moving average, and (c) the six-month moving average

Figure 14-11 shows the data of Figure 14-10(c) with the origin suppressed, the vertical scale extended, and no break in the vertical axis. It can be seen that the effect is to suggest that there has been an improved growth in profits. Also, it becomes apparent that the omission of the origin on the vertical axis (the dependent variable) is more misleading than omission on the horizontal axis (the independent variable).

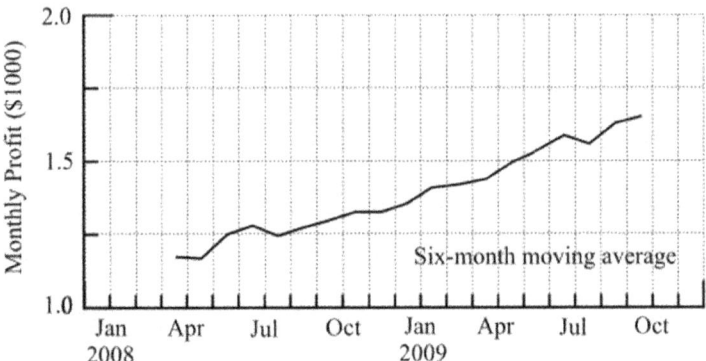

Figure 14-11. Data from Figure 14-10 (c) with the origin suppressed and the scale changed

Time is always plotted as the independent variable, and, as I previously pointed out, it is not feasible to show a true origin. Some other variables present the same kind of problem. Temperature is often the independent variable; the true zero, which is −273° Celsius, is never shown except in scientific publications relating to extremely low temperatures. In Figure 14-1, the temperature axis was shown with the origin suppressed and without a break in the axis. Note that 0°C and 0°F are not true zeroes: 20°C is not twice as hot as 10°C. Converting the two temperatures to Fahrenheit—50°F and 68°F, respectively—shows that the apparent doubling is not meaningful.

MARKET MARKETING

John and his wife Kate had a small business operating from market stalls in nearby towns. They visited each town once a week on the same day of the week. They sold a range of household essentials, such as kitchen and bathroom cleaning products, soaps, polishes, dusters, and brushes.

Although their overhead was low, they still had difficulty competing on price with the large supermarkets. They considered offering reduced prices for multiple purchases, as the supermarkets did, but were unsure whether this would lead to an increase in profit.

Kate asked her brother, Ted, for advice. He had some business experience and also had some knowledge of statistics.

Ted suggested an experiment. The goods would be sold on the basis of a percentage reduction when two of the same items were purchased. The purpose of the experiment was to find the optimum percentage reduction to apply. If the reduction was too low, say 10%, it would make little difference to sales or profit. If it was too high, 80% say, it would eat into the existing profit margin so much that increased sales would not compensate. Somewhere in between would be an optimum.

Ted suggested that John and Kate should start with a 10% reduction for two weeks and increase the reduction in 5% steps every two weeks up to a maximum reduction of 75%. The profit each day for each two-week period would be recorded.

The experiment was undertaken and the results passed to Ted for analysis. He first plotted a scatter graph of profit against percentage price reduction. He was not surprised to see that a best straight line would not be of any use: it would be approximately horizontal. However, he was pleased to see that there was indication of a profit increase in the central region of the graph. The task was to identify where the peak occurred. He made use of a statistical package to fit a low-order polynomial to the data and found that the peak value of profit was located at about 35% price reduction. John and Kate adopted a "one third off for a purchase of two of the same" practice and were pleased to enjoy a 3% increase in profits.

Ted pointed out that more could be done. In the original experiment, other variables had not been separated out. It would be possible to experiment further with a range of price reductions applied to different products and to the different towns that the couple traded in. This was just the beginning of a new marketing strategy.

CHAPTER 15

Relationships with Descriptive Data
Any Color as Long as It's Black

Much of the data involved in business operations is descriptive rather than numerical. In product development and marketing we have decisions to make regarding color, shape and packaging. Surveys will have resulted in yes/no answers to questions. Records will show whether a product is popular or unpopular, whether it sells or doesn't sell.

Nominal Data

If the data is nominal, we speak of *association* between the variables rather than *correlation*, and this can be examined by several means. Suppose we wish to know whether a particular medical treatment is effective in helping to cure a complaint. A sample of patients might give the following results:

	Treated	Not Treated	Total
Cured	100	30	130
Not Cured	40	30	70
Total	140	60	200

Chapter 15 | Relationships with Descriptive Data

Yule's coefficient of association, Q, can be calculated from the four values in the two-by-two table, making use of the products of the diagonals. With the above values,

$$Q = (100 \times 30 - 30 \times 40)/(100 \times 30 + 30 \times 40) = 0.43.$$

The value of Q is always between +1 and −1, the size of the value being related to the strength of the association. The sign, + or −, indicates the direction of the association: in our example, whether the treatment results in more or fewer cures. An improved version of Yule's coefficient, which involves a slightly more involved calculation, is the *tetrachoric correlation coefficient*. Yule's coefficient of association cannot be used when there are more than two rows or columns. Instead, the *polychoric correlation coefficient* is used.

The same data can be examined by a so-called *contingency test*. If the treatment had no effect, it would be expected that the proportion of cured to not cured would be the same for the treated and the not treated. The values, keeping the totals the same, would appear as follow:

	Expected Numbers		
	Treated	Not Treated	Total
Cured	91	39	130
Not Cured	49	21	70
Total	140	60	200

Thus 91/49 = 39/21 = 130/70. The issue then is whether the actual values depart significantly from these expected values. Our null hypothesis is that the two sets of values are not significantly different.

You saw in Chapter 7 how the chi-squared test can be used to compare two distributions. In effect, we have two distributions here: the distribution of sampled values and the distribution of expected values. Thus the chi-squared test can be used. The first step is to tabulate the differences between the actual and expected values. Each difference is squared and divided by the expected value. The sum of these values is the value of chi-squared.

	Difference d	Difference squared, d^2	d^2/expected value
Treated			
Cured	+9	81	81/91 = 0.89
Not Cured	−9	81	81/49 = 1.65
Not Treated			
Cured	−9	81	81/39 = 2.08
Not Cured	+9	81	81/21 = 3.86
		Total	8.48

There is only one degree of freedom, because the fixing of one of the four values in the table determines the other three. From the extract of the tables of the chi-squared distribution shown in Chapter 7, we see that the value of 8.48 is significant at the 1% level. Thus our null hypothesis is rejected, and we conclude that there is strong evidence for the effectiveness of the cure.

The example above uses a two-by-two table, having two rows and two columns. The procedure can accommodate a larger number of categories within the restriction of two variables. The variables could be, for example, color of hair and place of birth. The following table, a three-by-three, shows a possible set of data from a small sample:

	Hair Color			
Place of Birth	Brown	Black	Blonde	Total
England	11	2	4	17
Scotland	5	8	0	13
Wales	4	5	1	10
Total	20	15	5	40

If there was no relation between hair color and place of birth, we would expect the numbers to simply reflect the sizes of the various categories. Thus the table can be recast showing the expected number of individuals in each category. The expected number of brown-haired individuals born in Wales, for example, is shown as 5: a quarter of the total of 20 brown-haired individuals sampled, because a quarter of the total individuals, 10 out of 40, were born in Wales.

	Expected Numbers			
	Hair Color			
Place of Birth	Brown	Black	Blonde	Total
England	8.50	6.38	2.13	17
Scotland	6.50	4.88	1.63	13
Wales	5.00	3.75	1.25	10
Total	20	15	5	40

The decision to be made is whether the two tables are significantly different. If they are not significantly different, we can conclude that there is no evidence of hair color being related to place of birth. The differences between the two tables would be attributed to random errors in the sampling. If we find a significant difference, we would conclude that there is evidence of hair color being related to place of birth, and we would examine the data further to identify which combinations of hair color and place of birth were the source of the relationship.

To establish the level of significance, chi-squared is calculated as before. The difference between each sample value and its expected value is squared and divided by the expected value. These values, individual values of chi-squared, are added together to give an accumulated chi-squared for the whole data set. There are four degrees of freedom because fixing four of the nine values in the table determines the other five. In general, for contingency tables, the degrees of freedom are one less than the number of rows multiplied by one less than the number of columns. In this example, the value of chi-squared is 10.0, though the calculation is not shown; and from the tables of the distribution in Chapter 7, we find that the result is significant at the 5% level.

Ordinal Data

You saw in Chapter 11 how you can compare two sets of rankings to decide whether there is a significant difference between them. In the example that you looked at, two judges each put seven restaurants in order of preference. The identical technique, using Spearman's rank coefficient or a similar one, can be used to examine whether two rankings of different attributes are related. Indeed, we mentioned that these ranking techniques are in essence correlation techniques for examining possible relationships. Ranks can be allocated to data from different variables regardless of the nature of the variables, and it is this feature that makes ranking techniques so versatile.

Suppose, for example, that we suspected that our first judge in the previous example was influenced by the size of the restaurant rather than the quality of the food and the service. We could rank the restaurants in order of size and list them alongside the judge's ranking:

Restaurant	Judge 1 Rank	Size Rank	Difference, d	d²
A	4	4	0	0
B	2	2	0	0
C	3	6	3	9
D	1	1	0	0
E	5	3	2	4
F	6	7	1	1
G	7	5	2	4
			Total	18

Spearman's coefficient is calculated by

$$\rho = 1 - 6 \times (\text{sum of } d^2)/(n(n^2 - 1))$$

where n is the number of items that are ranked. In our example

$$\rho = 1 - 6 \times 18/(7(49-1)) = 0.68.$$

This value is referred to published tables of ρ to obtain the significance level. A selection of published values was included in Chapter 11. Our value of 0.68 with n equal to 7 does not reach the 5% significance level, so we conclude that there is no significant evidence that the judge was influenced by the size of the restaurant.

CHAPTER 16

Multivariate Data

Variety Is the Spice of Life

Practical problems often make it difficult to obtain homogeneous and similar samples. For example, samples may involve individuals of different ages and may have to be taken on different days of the week. Individuals differ in numerous ways, and real effects can arise on different days. It could be said, quite rightly, that samples differ because a variety of effects are always present, each creating a difference. In other words, no matter how we aim to obtain homogeneous samples, we will end up with multiple effects. In the past, when analysis involved lengthy procedures, this was a nuisance. Now, with the availability of computer packages that provide rapid and more versatile processing, multivariate data analysis is seen to be a great advantage and has in many areas taken over from the simplistic methods I have been describing.

The availability of rapid computer processing has brought with it other features. One is the increasing number of new methods that are appearing. New methods bring greater sophistication during processing but greater difficulty in understanding the detail involved, and controversy over their applicability to particular situations. An accompanying drawback to the ease of processing is that it becomes easy to search for any possible relationship that appears to be suggested by the data. As I have pointed out before, if enough correlations are sought, a number of spurious ones will be found, simply because of the probability governing the indication of significance. The relationships sought should be defined before the data is examined.

Chapter 16 | Multivariate Data

Chapter 4 mentioned the large databases that many organizations have. The data is potentially the source of unknown useful relationships; and sophisticated, computer-intensive procedures are used to extract those relationships. This process is referred to as *data mining*, and progress in developing and applying such methods has promoted data mining to an important subject in its own right. In a way, this compromises what I said above, that required possible relationships should be defined before the data is searched. The issue is discussed further in Part VII.

A drawback of computer processing is that the visibility of the processing is lost. The data is fed into the program, and the results are quickly displayed. In this chapter, it would be pointless to attempt to illustrate the processing of the data in detail. More useful to you will be a guide to the appropriateness of various methods, an outline of what each method does, and a guide to interpreting the results. Another drawback of computerized procedures is that anyone—even someone who lacks understanding of the methods, their restrictions, and their proper interpretation—can carry out analyses and produce conclusions.

The need for large samples has been mentioned a number of times. Here, because many different effects are involved, the samples need to be large in relation to each effect of interest. Note, though, that too large a sample may result in a large number of effects being found to be significant but with little practical use or meaning. In the sample, every feature is real. The larger the sample, the greater the number of variables that will be found to be significant. Ultimately, as the sample size approaches the total population, every feature of each datum becomes significant and reflects the fact that in the population, every feature is real.

You saw previously the difference between dependent and independent variables. A dependent variable is one that we observe rather than control, or the one we are attempting to predict. An independent variable is one that we fix or is fixed for us by circumstances. Thus, if we wish to see how illness varies with age, illness is the dependent variable and age is the independent variable. Clearly, illness depends on age, whereas age does not depend on illness. The distinction between the two kinds of variables is important in choosing the appropriate multivariate analysis method.

Previously we have separated numerical data from descriptive data in presenting the various techniques. The distinction becomes blurred when we are dealing with multivariate data. We may have both numerical and descriptive data involved in the same relationship. Also, we can in some methods render descriptive data numerical by the use of dummy variables. A *dummy variable* is a numerical code representing a descriptive variable. For example, if we have male or female as one of the variables, male could be coded as 0 and female as 1. With three levels of description, the coding could be 0, 1, and 2, and so on.

The various methods described in the following sections are ordered generally from numerical to descriptive; but as you will see, there is considerable overlap.

Multiple Regression

If there is one dependent numerical variable and several independent numerical variables, multiple regression may be used. We may, for example, wish to know how much a person generally pays when buying a car, in relation to the person's age, income, and savings. The principle is the same as in simple linear regression (Chapter 14). The squares of the differences between the observed values and the predicted values are minimized. In other words, the analysis is in terms of variance.

The form of the relationship used is

$$y = a + bx_1 + cx_2 + dx_3 + \ldots ,$$

where y is the dependent variable (i.e., the cost of the car in the example above), and x_1, x_2, x_3, ... are the independent variables (age, income and savings, etc.). The letters $a, b, c, d,$ .... represent constants, and the purpose of the analysis is to determine the best values for these constants. The form of the equation is linear—in other words, values of y plotted against one of the x values, the other x values being held constant, would yield a straight line.

However, this does not mean that curvature cannot be accommodated. If the data suggested that an increase in savings had an ever-increasing effect as the savings increased, we could add x_3^2, i.e. the square of savings, in the linear equation. The equation would then be

$$y = a + bx_1 + cx_2 + dx_3 + ex_3^2$$

The data may suggest other non-linear relationships, and transformation of the variables can be used to modify the equation appropriately. For example, $c(1/x_2)$ might take the place of cx_2 by transforming the x_2 data values to $1/x_2$. The dependent variable, y, may also be transformed if necessary. The equation can also incorporate possible interactions between the variables. For example, we might decide to include a term $f(x_1, x_3)$ to allow for interaction between age and savings. In other words, we would be allowing for the likelihood that the influence of savings would be different for different age groups. It must be remembered that the fit of the regression equation is based on minimizing the errors of the transformed variables and not the original variables.

When the constants $a, b, c, d, \ldots$ have been calculated and the regression equation has been obtained, we need a measure of the usefulness of the equation. The multiple coefficient of determination, R^2, is analogous to r^2 that we met in relation to simple linear regression with two variables. R^2 indicates, in a similar manner, the proportion of the variation in y that is accounted for by the equation. The closer the value of R^2 is to unity, the better the equation fits the data. Note, however, that although the equation may be useful, it may not be the best possible. It could be that a different selection of variables or a different transformation of variables would give a more useful equation.

Note also that as more variables are included the value of R^2 will approach unity. Indeed when the number of variables equals the number of data then $R^2 = 1$. There is also an increase in R^2 as the sample size increases. An adjusted value of R^2, the adjusted coefficient of determination, which compensates for the increase in sample size and number of variables, is usually quoted in the results provided by computer packages.

Unless the sample consists of the total population, it is necessary to establish the reliability of using the regression equation to represent the population. The variance ratio test, or F-test, described in Chapter 10, can be used to test at an appropriate significance level whether R^2 differs from zero, in other words whether there is a significant relationship. Additionally, each of the constants in the regression equation, $b, c, d, \ldots$, can be tested using Student's t-test to establish whether it differs significantly from zero and at what level of significance. A constant found not to differ significantly from zero indicates that the associated variable can be removed without affecting the usefulness of the correlation.

Descriptive variables can be included in multiple regression analysis by the use of dummy variables, though the dependent variable must be numerical. A technique known as *canonical correlation* extends the principle of multiple regression to dealing with several numerical dependent variables and several numerical independent variables. With the use of dummy variables, the technique can be extended to dealing with several descriptive dependent variables and several descriptive independent variables.

Analysis of Variance

You saw in Chapter 10 how analysis of variance (ANOVA) can be used to compare two or more samples in order to decide whether they could have been drawn from the same population. The method can be extended to analyze data that is influenced by more than one effect. For example, suppose we have test results for students in four subjects. We wish to investigate whether there is a difference between the results for boys and girls and whether ability in different subjects is related. Here we have two effects, or factors—subject and gender—and both of these are descriptive. These are the independent variables, while the dependent variable, which is numerical, is the mark obtained in the test.

Thus the data might be as follow:

	Marks Obtained in Test			
	English	Mathematics	History	Science
Boys	45, 52, 51,...	66, 58, 56, ...	59, 51, 46, ...	71, 67, 60, ...
Girls	70, 64, 55, ...	64, 61, 55, ...	62, 54, 43, ...	66, 62, 59, ...

For this type of analysis, it is necessary to have a numerical dependent variable and several descriptive independent variables. The analysis of variance will allow the total variance in the data to be partitioned between the various sources of variance. In this example, there is a variance attributed to the gender of the students and a variance attributed to the test subject. In addition, there is variance due to interaction between these two main effects. Interaction arises when the effect of gender is different in relation to different subjects: boys may be better than girls in science but poorer than girls in English. There is also a contribution to the total variance from effects that are not included in the analysis. This is the *residual variance*.

To illustrate the method we will outline the working through of an example with three effects and a replication of the data.

A company has three factories, and in each factory are three slightly different machines, versions 1, 2, and 3. On most days, the machines suffer from overheating of up to 3 degrees. The company wishes to see if the overheating is related to the version of the machines or to the circumstances of use in the three factories. The operating temperature of each machine is observed, and the excess temperature is recorded. In case the day of the week is relevant, records are taken on five days from Monday to Friday. The exercise is repeated the following week to give a measure of replication. The results are assembled as follows:

Chapter 16 | Multivariate Data

	Machine Overheating (degrees Celsius)								
Factory	F1			F2			F3		
Machine	M1	M2	M3	M1	M2	M3	M1	M2	M3
Day 1	0	1	2	0	1	1	2	2	3
Day 1	2	2	3	0	1	2	0	3	2
Day 2	1	2	3	2	1	3	1	1	2
Day 2	2	1	1	0	2	2	0	3	3
Day 3	1	1	0	1	2	1	1	1	1
Day 3	3	1	2	1	1	3	1	2	2
Day 4	2	0	2	2	2	3	0	1	3
Day 4	0	3	3	0	2	1	2	2	1
Day 5	2	3	2	2	0	2	2	0	0
Day 5	3	1	3	2	2	3	2	2	3

Note that the numbers here are all small integers. This is purely to keep the illustration simple. In a practical situation we would expect to have numbers consisting of several digits.

The ninety values listed have a variance which is due to a number of factors. The variability between factories, between machines, and between days of the week contributes to the overall variance. Interactions between each pair of variables and between all three variables may contribute. In addition, there are almost certainly other sources of variation that cannot be identified. The analysis of variance allows the total variance to be apportioned between the various factors. It is this additive property of variances that makes the analysis of variance such a powerful tool.

It would not be helpful to plow through the arithmetic in detail: computer packages are available to do the job. More useful is an explanation of what the calculation does.

The first three columns of the above table are the results from factory F1, thirty in total. If we were to temporarily replace each value with the mean value of the thirty, and do the same for F2 and F3, we would have a set of ninety values, the variance of which would reflect the variation due to any differences between the factories. Similarly, we can obtain three sets of adjusted values reflecting the variation due to machines and five sets of adjusted values reflecting the variation due to the different days of the week. Note that the degrees of freedom associated with the variances are reduced by this substitution of mean values. The variance of F has only two degrees of freedom because only three mean values are being used, despite the fact that there are ninety data.

The breakdown of the overall variance can be taken further. There are 9 sets of data which include the variation due to factories and machines. These are the 9 columns in the table. By again substituting the set mean value for each value in the set, a variance can be calculated. By removing the already obtained separate effects of factory and machine, we are left with a variance relating to interaction between factory and machine. That is to say, the behavior of the corresponding machine depends to some extent on which factory it is located in.

There are 15 sets of data that include the variation due to machines and days, and 15 sets of data that include the variation due to days and factories. There are 45 sets of data, albeit only 2 values in each set, that include the variation due to factories, machines, and days; and, finally, there is the complete set of 90 values that additionally includes variation due to other factors and random effects. Each set of values can in turn be temporarily modified by substituting the mean of the set for each member value, and the variance can be adjusted by removing the single factor effects, leaving the variance attributable to the interaction.

I must add that this is not the way one would actually carry out the calculations—as you would probably use a computer package—but it is a way of seeing what in effect is being done.

The results of all this can be laid out as follow:

Source of Variation	Variance	Degrees of Freedom
Factory, F	0.41	2
Machine, M	5.34	2
Day of Week, D	0.64	4
Interaction F-M	0.45	4 (2x2)
Interaction M-D	1.08	8 (2x4)
Interaction D-F	0.73	8 (4x2)
Interaction F-M-D	0.29	16 (2x2x4)
Residual	1.12	45 (89–16–8–8–4–4–2–2)
	Total 89	

The residual variance is a measure of the variation that would be observed in the absence of any effect arising from the particular factory, particular machine, or particular day of the week. In other words, random or unknown effects are producing a variance of this size. We can therefore test whether any of the other variances are significantly greater than the residual variance. The test to use is the variance ratio test, F-test. In the above example, only one variance is greater than the residual variance: the variance due to machine. So, this is the only one that needs testing. The variance ratio is 5.34/1.12 = 4.77, which is found to be significant at the 5% level. A relevant extract from the tables of the F-statistic is shown as follows:

Significance Level 5%	Degrees of freedom of the smaller variance	Degrees of freedom of the larger variance		
		1	2	3
	30	4.17	3.32	2.92
	40	4.08	3.23	2.84
	60	4.00	3.15	2.76

Thus we can conclude that the variation between machines is likely to be a real effect. We can also conclude that there is no significant evidence that overheating is more prone in one factory than another, nor that overheating is related to the day of the week.

Two additional points need to be mentioned regarding interactions. First, if an interaction is found to be significant, then the main factors in the interaction cannot be tested. The situation has to be investigated further. Second, if the interactions are not significant, then their variances are an additional measure of the residual variance. They can therefore be pooled with the residual variance.

By pooling some of the variances that are not significant, we can gain further appreciation of the versatile nature of the analysis of variance. Pooling the D, M-D, D-F, F-M-D, and residual variances gives a value of 0.89 for the revised residual variance. The results now appear as follow:

Source of Variation	Variance	Degrees of Freedom
Factory, F	0.41	2
Machine, M	5.34	2
Interaction F-M	0.45	4 (2x2)
Residual	0.89	81 (89–4–2–2)
	Total	89

The point of interest here is that if we had, at the outset, decided that the day of the week was unlikely to have any effect on the results, we could have treated the values obtained on different days as replicates. Thus we would have had 9 combinations of factory and machine and 10 data for each combination. The analysis would have been in terms of two main effects, F and M, and one interaction, F–M. The results would have come out exactly as shown above with a residual variance of 0.89.

It is useful to show the results of the machine overheating example by plotting a number of graphs. The significant effect of machine type can be seen in Figure 16-1, where the mean overheating temperature for each machine is plotted against the machine number. Similar graphs for the two non-significant main effects are also shown. There is no reason why these graphs should have a particular shape: any appreciable departure from a horizontal line might indicate a significant effect.

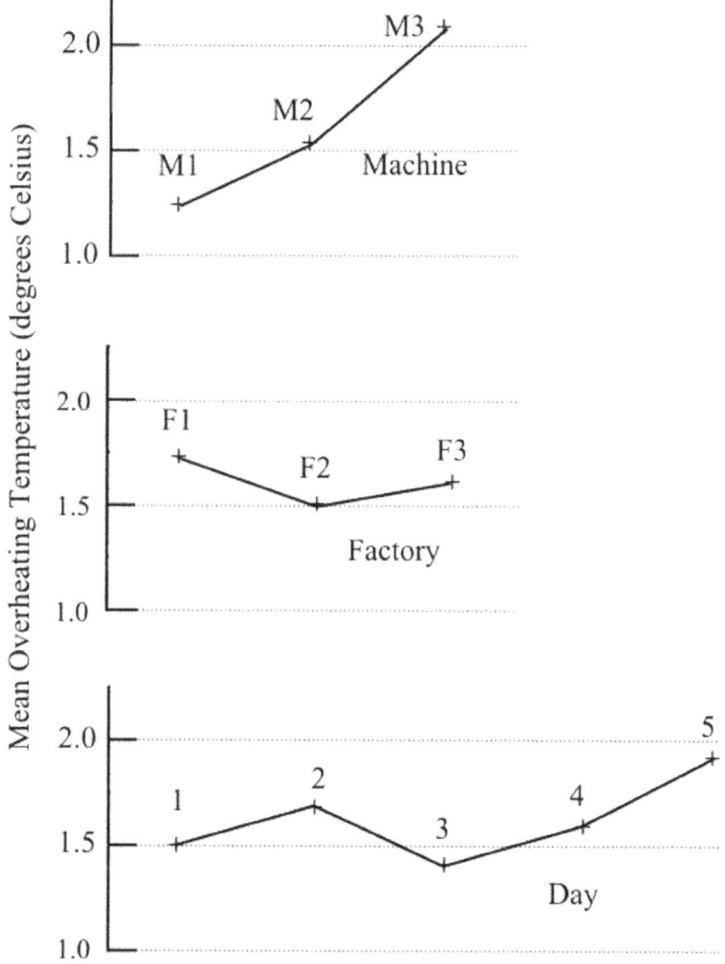

Figure 16-1. Comparison of overheating of different machines in different factories on different days

Latin and Graeco-Latin Squares

A version of analysis of variance uses Latin or Graeco-Latin squares, typically in agricultural experiments. If fertilizers are to be compared in terms of crop yield, for example, there is always the possibility that the fertility of the land used for the study may vary from place to place. Clearly, it is not possible to test all the fertilizers in the same place at the same time: each one is tested where the fertility may be different.

In the Latin square arrangement, the rectangular test area is divided into smaller plots, forming a grid of rows and columns. Each fertilizer is used once in each row and once in each column. Thus if we have four different fertilizers designated A, B, C, and D, the arrangement could be as follows:

	Columns			
Rows	A	B	C	D
	B	C	D	A
	C	D	A	B
	D	A	B	C

This corresponds to 16 data of the crop yield, 4 for each of the treatments A, B, C, and D. The crop yield is the dependent variable, and the fertilizer brand and soil fertility are the independent variables. The analysis of variance can be arranged as follows:

Source of Variation	Variance	Degrees of Freedom
Rows	XXX	3
Columns	XXX	3
Fertilizers	XXX	3
Residual	XXX	6
Total		15

The rows and columns variances reflect the variability in the soil characteristics across and down the experimental area. Note that there are no variances listed for interactions. This is a consequence of the Latin square design. Only one fertilizer is applied to a plot of a given fertility, giving a considerable saving in the number of plots required. The actual number of combinations of fertilizer and soil fertility is $4 \times 16 = 64$. The use of 64 plots would not be feasible: apart from the larger test area required and the extra cost, there would be additional variation in soil fertility because of the increased test area.

An additional effect can be included by the use of a Graeco-Latin square as shown below. The Latin letters A to D represent four treatments, as before, and the Greek letters α to δ represent a second treatment—pesticide, say:

Columns				
Rows	A δ	B γ	C β	D α
	B β	A α	D δ	C γ
	C α	D β	A γ	B δ
	D γ	C δ	B α	A β

As in the Latin square, each fertilizer is used only once in each row and column. Furthermore, each pesticide is used only once with each fertilizer. Squares of different sizes can be set up, but the arrangement is not possible for a square of side 6.

Although the description has been in terms of agricultural experiments, because that is where the practical applications have mainly been, the squares can be used elsewhere. They are particularly useful when it is essential, for reasons of cost, time, or accessibility, to keep the number of observations to a minimum.

Medical studies often fall into this category. If it were required to investigate four different treatments for an ailment, four suitable patients could be selected. Suppose it takes one month to assess the effects of each treatment. The columns in the Latin square shown above would be the four treatments, and the rows would be four consecutive months. The letters A, B, C, and D would represent the four patients. At the end of one month, all four treatments would have been tested; and after four months, there would be 16 sets of data representing the outcome of each treatment administered to each patient.

It can be seen from this medical example that the Latin square can be a very efficient means of investigation, particularly when interactions between the main effects are not considered likely. If there were to be appreciable interactions, the effect would be to increase the residual variance and make it more difficult to verify any significant difference between the treatments.

The Latin square can be modified by removing a row or a column. The resulting rectangular arrangement is known as a *Youden square*.

TIRE TRIALS

As chief accountant for ZIP Deliveries, Mark Groves was always looking for ways to cut back on expenditure. The company ran a parcel delivery service and had a fleet of about forty vans. The field was very competitive and costs were important.

Tires for the vehicles cost an appreciable amount, and that was what Mark was currently considering. At present the company was purchasing a cheap brand of tire, but perhaps it would pay to use a more expensive brand and achieve a longer life.

Three other brands were readily available, and Mark proposed an experiment to compare them with the brand currently being used. He had in mind a Latin square arrangement. Four vans would be fitted with new tires, each van with a different brand. The four vans, each with its regular driver, would constitute the columns of a 4×4 Latin square. Four daily routes, each of similar distance but, of course, different road conditions, would constitute the rows of the square.

For the experiment, each van would spend a month working each of the designated routes. The tire wear would be recorded by measurements of tread depth carried out by the garage maintenance team.

The Latin square arrangement ensured that the effect of the four different drivers and the effect of the four different routes would be separated from the effect of the different brands of tire.

Having got approval for the experiment, Mark took a standard 4×4 Latin square, put the columns in a random order, put the rows in a random order, and allocated the four brands to the lettered squares A, B, C, and D. This provided the schedule for the routes for the four vans, and the trial went ahead.

At the end of the trial period, Mark analyzed the results. He found that the variance due to the vans was not significant. The variance due to the routes was significant at the 5% level, which was perhaps not too surprising. Importantly, the variance due to the tire brands was significant, well inside the 5% level. Thus the difference between the different brands could be accepted as being real.

For each of the brands, Mark used the tire-wear values and the cost to calculate which brand would be most cost effective. It turned out to be one of the more expensive ones, so the exercise had not been a waste of time, much to Mark's relief. It was decided that the tire contract would be changed accordingly, and Mark had a smile on his face for the rest of the day.

Multidimensional Contingency Tables

You saw in Chapter 15 how the association between two descriptive variables can be compared by means of a contingency table. If we have more than two variables, we have in effect a table with three or more dimensions. Such tables can, of course, be laid out as several two-dimensional tables; but in order to explain how to proceed, it is useful to emphasize the multidimensional nature of the situation by attempting to give a perspective view of a three-dimensional one. This has been done in Figure 16-2.

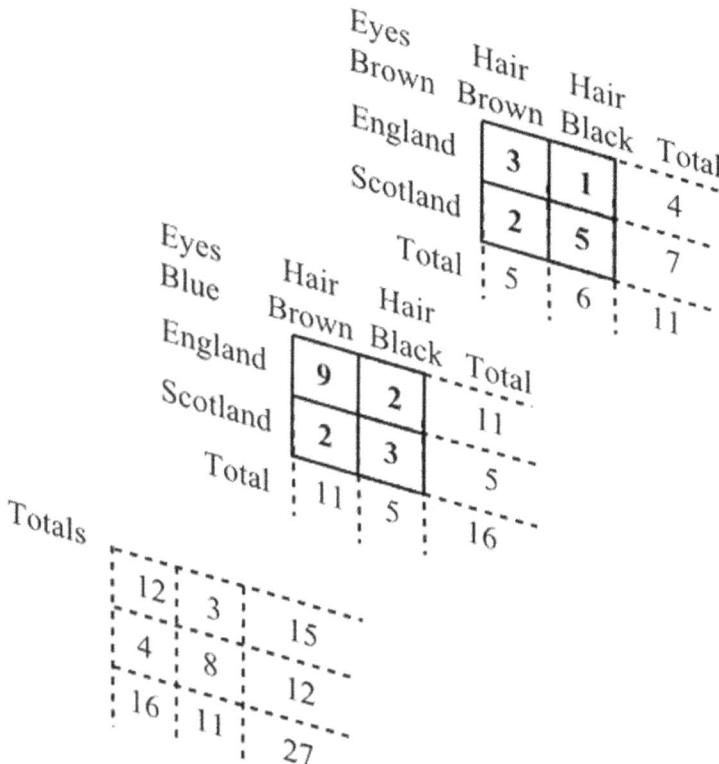

Figure 16-2. A three-way contingency table

The three independent variables are place of birth, color of hair, and color of eyes, and the dependent variable is the number of cases. The task is again to replace the actual sampled values temporarily with expected values based on the assumption that there is no significant effect from the variables. The values, in other words, are not significantly different from values that would be obtained from the overall proportions of each category. However, unlike the situation where we had only two variables, there is not a unique expected value. Judgment is needed to fix the best expected value.

Chapter 16 | Multivariate Data

To see where the problem lies, consider the table for blue eyes extracted from Figure 16-2. The expected values are as follow:

Expected Values			
Eyes Blue	Hair Brown	Hair Black	Total
England	7.6	3.4	11
Scotland	3.4	1.6	5
Total	11	5	16

For example, 7.6/11 = 3.4/5 = 11/16.

If we now look down from above on our three-dimensional table, the top layer appears as follows:

England	Hair Brown	Hair Black	Total
Eyes Brown	3	1	4
Eyes Blue	9	2	11
Total	12	3	15

And if we calculate the expected values, we get the following:

Expected Values			
England	Hair Brown	Hair Black	Total
Eyes Brown	3.2	0.8	4
Eyes Blue	8.8	2.2	11
Total	12	3	15

For example, 3.2/12 = 0.8/3 = 4/15.

Our expected value for England – Hair Brown – Eyes Blue is now 8.8, whereas our first calculation of expected values gave 7.6. The reason, of course, is that the first value is expected if Brown Eyes are excluded, and the second value is expected if Scotland is excluded. The same problem arises for each of the eight combinations of place of birth, hair color, and eye color.

The analysis that is used in these situations to overcome the problem is called *log-linear*. It is a lengthy iterative procedure that makes repeated estimates of the expected values and is thus computer intensive. The "log" in the title refers to the fact that the logarithms of the values are used to give additive properties in the processing. The technique is analogous to the analysis of variance shown earlier for dealing with numerical data when several variables are involved. There you saw that not only was there a main effect from each variable but we had interactions from each pair of variables, each triplet of variables, and so on. You also saw that the use of variance allowed us to partition the variability between the main effects and the interactions.

We have a similar situation here with our multidimensional contingency tables. Interaction here means, for example, that the effect of place of birth and hair color on color of eyes, acting together, is not the same as the sum of the effects acting separately. The processing involves an element of judgment. An approach from the top down would estimate the optimum expected values on the basis of three main effects. If the residual variability were too great, as indicated by its level of significance, the second-order interactions would be included, and so on. In the example, the third-order interaction involving all three variables cannot be dealt with, because the values as they were sampled may be the expected values. If we had a duplicate sample, the third-order interaction could be isolated from the residual variation. The example given in the "Analysis of Variance" section involved a duplicate sample and allowed this separation.

An alternative direction of processing is from the bottom up. Starting with the inclusion of all main effects and interactions, the significance of the highest-order interactions is checked. If not significant these interactions are removed from the activity of estimating the expected values. This continues until the only effects remaining are those with an acceptable level of significance.

A variation of log-linear analysis is *logit analysis*. This allows the use of a dependent variable that is not numerical but can take one of two descriptive labels: male or female, for example. The proportion of males (or females) is restricted to values between 0 and 1. The *logit*, or *log odds*, function transforms the proportion to a value having an unlimited range from minus infinity to plus infinity.

Multivariate Analysis of Variance

An extension of the analysis of variance (ANOVA) is the *multivariate analysis of variance* (MANOVA). You saw that the analysis of variance was able to deal with multiple effects but only when we had a single dependent variable and several independent variables. In multivariate analysis of variance, we are able to deal with several dependent variables.

As an example, suppose the bakery departments of two supermarkets are to be compared. Three different products are involved: loaves, buns, and cakes. The two dependent numerical variables on which the comparison will be based are profit and customer satisfaction. The variables are thus as follow:

	Supermarket A			Supermarket B		
	Loaves	Buns	Cakes	Loaves	Buns	Cakes
Profit	xxx	xxx	xxx	xxx	xxx	xxx
Satisfaction	xxx	xxx	xxx	xxx	xxx	xxx

For each level of each variable there will be a data sample, represented by xxx above. As the number of data groups increases, the need for large sample sizes increases. Each group must have a size greater than the number of variables and should have not fewer than about 20 data.

In the analysis of variance, partitioning of the variance produces values of the variance ratio, F, which can be used to evaluate the effect of each independent variable on the dependent variable. In multivariate analysis, we use a corresponding statistic to evaluate each effect on each dependent variable. There are a number of possible statistics: *Wilks's lambda*, the *Hotelling-Lawley trace*, the *Pillai-Bartlett trace*, and *Roy's maximum root*. The effect of interactions is examined first, as in the analysis of variance. If an interaction is found to be not significant, the constituent variables can each be tested for significance.

The processing is complicated and may involve additional routines to ensure reliability of the results: hence the need for a suitable computer package. Underlying statistical assumptions regarding the data also may have to be examined. The interpretation of the results needs considerable care. Because there are potentially many effects to be identified, the power of the test—that is, the ability to detect a relationship when it exists—may be low. In order to ensure that the power is sufficiently large to identify small effects, the required sample size may be prohibitively large.

Conjoint Analysis

Conjoint analysis is used to investigate customer evaluations of products or services. It differs from other techniques in that the investigator sets up at the outset combinations of features representing real or hypothetical versions of the product. These are the independent variables. Thus the sampled consumers merely rank the combinations rather than create variables by the nature of their replies. For example, a deodorant could be produced in the form of a roll-on, a pump spray, or an aerosol, each in one of three colors of container, and each in one of two sizes. This would give a total of 18 possible combinations. The three independent variables—form, color, and size—are descriptive, and the dependent variable is the preference of each combination as recorded by its rank order.

From the rankings supplied by each sampled consumer, the part-worth of each factor can be evaluated, taking account of interaction effects. It is not necessary to present each respondent with all combinations: a selection can be used to provide data for evaluation. A feature not present in most other methods is that an evaluation can be obtained for a single respondent. Results from several respondents can be aggregated to provide an overall assessment of the separate attributes of the product or potential product.

Proximity Maps

Association between descriptive variables can be visually presented by means of a map on which the degree of association between two items is represented by the distance between them. Greater degrees of association are indicated by closer spacing. Two- or three-dimensional maps can be shown as diagrams, of course, but if more than three dimensions are involved, only "slices" of the map can be visually appreciated.

Correspondence analysis is one such method. The data is represented in a contingency table, as discussed in Chapter 15 and the "Multidimensional Contingency Tables" section of this chapter. The analysis follows the procedure we described for multiway contingency tables in obtaining an expected value for each cell on the basis of no association. The difference between each actual and expected value is expressed as a value of the chi-squared statistic, which provides a measure of association. Distances for mapping are then computed in relation to the chi-squared values: the larger the value, the smaller the distance.

To illustrate the method in a simple manner, we can use the two-way contingency table from Chapter 15 that related color of hair to place of birth. The table is repeated here:

Observed Numbers				
	Hair Color			
Place of Birth	Brown	Black	Blonde	Total
England	11	2	4	17
Scotland	5	8	0	13
Wales	4	5	1	10
Total	20	15	5	40

Chapter 16 | Multivariate Data

The expected numbers, on the basis of there being no association, were calculated as follows:

Expected Numbers

Place of Birth	Hair Color			Total
	Brown	Black	Blonde	
England	8.50	6.38	2.13	17
Scotland	6.50	4.88	1.63	13
Wales	5.00	3.75	1.25	10
Total	20	15	5	40

The statistic chi-squared is equal to the square of the difference between the expected and observed values, divided by the expected value. It is calculated for each cell in the table as shown below. (Negative values, when the observed is less than the expected, are treated as positive in calculating the chi-squared totals.)

Place of Birth	Hair Color			Total
	Brown	Black	Blonde	
England	0.74	3.00 (neg)	1.65	5.39
Scotland	0.35 (neg)	2.00	1.63 (neg)	3.97
Wales	0.20 (neg)	0.42	0.05 (neg)	0.67
Total	1.28	5.42	3.33	10.03

These values provide a measure of similarity for each pair of variable levels, the largest values representing the largest positive association. Negative values represent negative association. (It may be noted that the sum of the above chi-squared values, 10.03, was used in Chapter 15 to show that there was a significant relationship between hair color and place of birth.)

Similarity

Place of Birth	Hair Color		
	Brown	Black	Blonde
England	+0.74	−3.00	+1.65
Scotland	−0.35	+2.00	−1.63
Wales	−0.20	+0.42	−0.05

We can use the similarity values to produce a map. Each of the nine values provides a distance that is used to separate the pair of variable levels: the larger the value, the smaller the distance. Figure 16-3 illustrates an approximate arrangement. Scotland-Black has the top position in ranking and the smallest separation, whereas England-Black has the bottom position and the largest separation. The map shows various degrees of association. Brown and blonde hair are closely associated with English individuals, whereas black hair is associated more so with Welsh and Scottish people. You will appreciate that the separations cannot be exactly as required: there has to be compromise to fit the variables together. In a practical application, a computer package would apply an iterative procedure to optimize the fit.

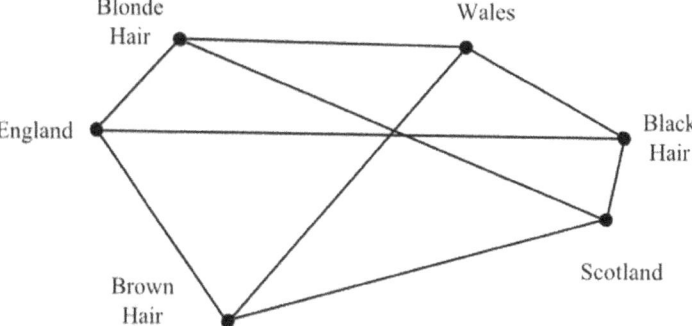

Figure 16-3. A map showing association between hair color and place of birth

The maximum number of dimensions that can be used is one less than the fewest number of levels for either variable: in this case, two. A realistic study might have more variables, each with more levels, and hence a map with a greater number of dimensions. To obtain the optimum set of distances that provides a consistent arrangement then requires a lengthy iterative procedure and is feasible only with the aid of a computer program.

Multidimensional scaling is similar to correspondence analysis in employing a multidimensional map to reveal association. It differs in that the variables are not defined at the outset; it is more a case of establishing the underlying variables from the analysis of the sample data. The technique represents perceived similarities or preferences between entities as the distances between them on a map. For example, six kinds of breakfast cereal could be compared two at a time by each volunteer in order to provide a sample. The comparison could be on a scale of 1 to 10, say. Six items produces 15 pairs for comparison; and to map the items in a consistent manner, with regard to correct relative separations, several dimensions are likely to be required for the map. Procedures for optimizing the mapping positions while minimizing the number of dimensions require judgment and repeated calculations.

The resulting map dimensions provide information as to the underlying features that prompt the recorded perceptions. It may be that degree of sweetness appears to lie along one dimension while "crunchiness" lies along another. It will be appreciated that considerable judgment is required in the interpretation. A feature of the method is that each respondent provides a sample which can be individually analyzed. Individual analyses can, of course, be aggregated.

Structural Equation Modeling

In the methods for dealing with multiple effects that have been discussed so far there has always been the limitation that there has been a single relationship between the dependent and the independent variables. It is sometimes the case that several interrelated relationships need to be established simultaneously. *Structural equation modeling* can be used when confirmation of a theory of such relationships is sought, but it is not useful at the exploratory stage.

A model based on theoretical judgments is set up, consisting of a number of variables linked by (assumed) causal relationships. Thus if we are concerned with the reputation of a school, for example, we may propose that success in examinations (a) depends on student ability (b) and teaching quality (c). Teaching quality depends on quality of teachers employed (d) and available resources (e). Quality of teachers employed depends on success in examinations and location (f). Student ability depends on available resources and location. In symbols, we have

$$a = w_1 b + w_2 c$$
$$c = w_3 d + w_4 e$$
$$d = w_5 a + w_6 f$$
$$b = w_7 e + w_8 f$$

where $w_1 \ldots w_8$ are weights to account for different degrees of influence. In effect, we have something similar to a set of multiple regression equations that are interrelated.

The processing is complex and not unique. It involves path analysis and is related to factor analysis and regression. The method has the ability to encompass latent variables that are not directly measured but that emerge from the measured variables. To achieve satisfactory results requires much care in setting up the initial model, establishing an acceptable goodness of fit, and interpreting and modifying the model.

Association: Some Further Methods

Some practical situations, like the example in the previous section concerning the reputation of a school, involve variables that are not only descriptive but subjective and difficult to define precisely. The levels adopted by the variables may also be subjective and difficult to define. Furthermore, there may be many such variables of interest. Such situations arise in marketing and product development. Hair brushes may vary in size, shape, color, shape of handle, feel of handle, and so on. Customer evaluation of the brushes may involve comfort in use, effectiveness in brushing, aesthetic appeal, and more. In sociology or psychology studies, attitudes and opinions can range between extremes with no clear means of scaling the in-between values. Degrees of friendliness, luck, ambition, pain, happiness, and so forth are difficult to scale.

Methods are available that can assist in reducing variables and their levels by identifying significant similarities. Many of these are interdependence methods in that there is no distinction between dependent and independent variables. The mathematics involved is usually complicated and requires considerable background knowledge. Furthermore, the planning of appropriate procedures and the interpretation of the results needs care.

Factor analysis is a method of analyzing relationships among a large number of variables in order to represent the data in terms of a smaller number of factors. All the variables are treated on an equal footing: there is no distinction between dependent and independent variables. As an example, we might consider customers' assessments of a dental practice under a variety of headings such as ease of booking an appointment (a), availability of suitable time slots (b), time spent in the waiting room (c), friendliness of staff (d), efficiency of staff (e), quality of treatment (f), and so on. Each assessment would be numerical, on a scale of 1 to 10, say. The correlation between each pair of variables would be determined, the six variables listed giving rise to 15 correlations. From these, an optimum grouping of the variables would be found, minimizing the variance within the groups and maximizing the variance between groups. It might be established, for example, that three groups—(a)-(b)-(c), (d)-(e) and (f) in the example above—adequately provide the required assessment. A similar method is *principal components analysis*.

Cluster analysis is similar to factor analysis but is used to group entities, rather than variables. The entities resemble each other in showing similar attributes. The characteristics of the clusters are not defined at the outset but arise in the process. People might be grouped according to their personal features or characteristics. The process is equally applicable to all kinds of things, such as cars, birds, or hats, for example.

In *multiple discriminant analysis*, groups are defined, and the process locates items in the appropriate group while maximizing the probability of correct location. The technique deals with a single descriptive dependent variable and several numerical independent variables. For example, the technique might be used to separate potential customers from unlikely customers based on several numerically designated characteristics.

This brief overview of methods for dealing with multivariate data is by no means exhaustive. The availability of computers that can perform iterative procedures at incredibly high speeds has given statisticians the means of employing and developing methods with greater and greater sophistication.

PART

Forecasts

Prediction is very difficult, especially about the future.

—Niels Bohr

So far we have been examining the use of statistics in describing present or past situations. Usually, of course, we gain such understanding in order to make decisions for the future—in other words, we are interested in forecasting. In this part, we shall see the ways in which statistics can help in forecasting.

CHAPTER 17

Extrapolation
Malthus Got It Wrong

Thomas Malthus, an English cleric, economist, and statistician, is known for his theories on population growth. He wrote in 1798 in his *Essay on the Principle of Population* that, because population increases geometrically (1, 2, 4, 8, ...) and food increases arithmetically (1, 2, 3, 4, ...), the population would eventually outstrip food supply. He warned of premature death visiting the human race. The onset of disaster would be prevented only by epidemics, pestilence, plague, famine, and preventive measures. His numerous writings on the subject gave rise to the *Malthusian doctrine*.

This doctrine is based on an extrapolation; and because it was proposed a long time ago, we can see that it was unjustified. It is relevant at the present time in providing us with a striking example of the dangers of extrapolation.

No one knows what tomorrow will bring. No one can predict the future with certainty. Of course, some events we can be fairly sure of: no one doubts that the Sun will rise tomorrow, but this is not the kind of event that statistics is asked to give a judgment on. Statistics is based on observations and measurements that relate to the past, but the purpose of statistics, apart from providing interesting historical facts, is to attempt to predict the future. Every shopkeeper who orders goods from his suppliers is indulging in forecasting. How can he be sure how many customers he will have tomorrow?

In the Mega Millions lottery, each number has an equal chance of being drawn. Although a few individuals may have doubts, most people would accept that this is true. In spite of this underlying knowledge, many people think a degree of forecasting is possible. They argue that each number will eventually appear the same number of times. In fact, the probability of each number being drawn exactly the same number of times is small, although the number of appearances of each number is likely to be approximately the same. If number 23, say, is lagging behind in number of appearances, some forecasters conclude that 23 now has a greater chance of being drawn. Others, perhaps, with a more cynical view, argue that there must be a reason why 23 is appearing less frequently and conclude that the trend is likely to continue. I happen to have a penny that I have tossed five times, and it has given five heads. Would anyone like to purchase it? It could win a fortune on its next toss! Our two groups of forecasters would, however, disagree about whether the next toss would result in a head or a tail.

Statistics alone cannot provide reliable forecasting. Common sense and judgment are needed, but both of these involve a degree of subjectivity. Objectivity is what is ideally required, and statistics can contribute in providing objective analyses. Forecasts based solely on subjective judgments can be useless or even disastrous. The gambling industry thrives on the fact that people are generally not very good at making forecasts. Suppose a successful jockey has not had a win in his last four races. Some would therefore be tempted to predict a win in his next race. Others would offer the alternative argument that his poor present performance is likely to continue. This situation has parallels in the business world. If the number of customers was unusually low today, does that allow us to say that tomorrow will bring extra customers to keep up the average, or does it allow us to argue that the trend will continue and produce fewer customers?

Forecasting is an essential activity, and in spite of the difficulties and pitfalls, we have to accept that it is always going to be with us. Forecasting the future can be based only on knowledge of the past and present. In order to use existing data to predict what the corresponding data will be in the future, we have to employ extrapolation to some degree. This creates a serious problem at the outset. We can never be certain that the same circumstances will exist in the future, and we can therefore never be certain that our forecasts will be reliable. From a strict mathematical view, we should never extrapolate data beyond the limits within which the data was obtained. Thus, if we observe that the population of our town has grown by an average of 1,000 per year over the past 10 years, we would be unjustified in deducing that the next ten years will bring a further increase of 10,000. We might, of course, consider it reasonable to bend the rule and assume that next year will bring an increase of about 1,000, the degree of extrapolation being relatively small.

We can distinguish different degrees of extrapolation to allow judgments as to the reasonableness of the extrapolations we encounter. Starting with a trivial situation, if there is perfect correlation between two variables, we expect no problems with extrapolation. If we know the volume occupied by a kilogram of sugar, we can reliably forecast the space required to store 1,000 kilograms of sugar. If we know that £1 can be exchanged for $2, we can predict with certainty how many dollars we will get for £100.

When a well-established scientific law relates a number of variables, it is possible to make reliable forecasts. The speed of a satellite circling the Earth is related to its height above the Earth, for example. If it were not for the ability to predict from such relationships, technology could not advance in the way it does. Of course, even well-used relationships have practical limitations. A spring extends in proportion to the weight applied to it, but if it is over-stretched the relationship changes.

Many laws, rather than being based on basic physical principles, are empirical and may have complex and changeable causes. The law of supply and demand, for example, can be justified experimentally and theoretically but may not always apply. Special circumstances can arise that upset expectations.

CHAPTER 18

Forecasting from Known Distributions
Why Does the Phone Never Stop Ringing?

The normal distribution has featured prominently in previous chapters because it is found to appropriately describe the data obtained in numerous situations. If there is good reason to believe in advance that the normal distribution will apply, then predictions can be made regarding future observations. Many other distributions are found to apply in certain circumstances, and, in a similar way, these can provide useful estimates of future outcomes. This chapter describes several of the commonly used distributions and gives examples of their use in forecasting.

Uniform Distribution

Forecasting from a uniform distribution is a trivial procedure, but it is worth considering it briefly to outline the steps involved. The score obtained from the throw of a fair die follows a uniform distribution. Each score from 1 to 6 has an equal probability of occurring. Figure 18-1 shows the distribution. The total area within the distribution is 1.0. If we wish to know what the probability is of obtaining a 1 or a 2, we add the areas within these two blocks. Thus the probability is 1/6 + 1/6 = 1/3.

Chapter 18 | Forecasting from Known Distributions

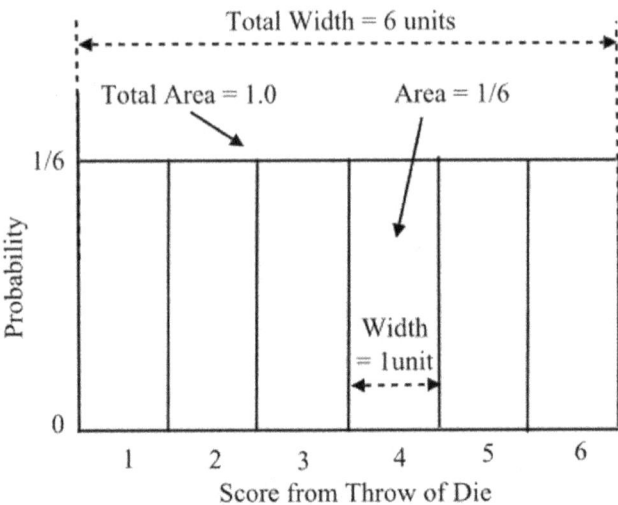

Figure 18-1. A uniform distribution

This is all very simple, but it does put us in a good position to see what happens when we consider non-uniform distributions.

Normal Distribution

You have seen that the normal distribution is a continuous symmetrical distribution with a central peak positioned at the mean value. The standard normal distribution has the central mean located at zero; the standard deviation, which controls the width of the distribution, has a value of unity. You also saw that the distribution describes the spread of data in many real situations, where there is a driving influence to render all the data the same but random errors from different and often unknown sources create a spread in the data.

Heights of people and their other physical dimensions—such as arm length, leg length, and so on—would be expected to be normally distributed. Manufacturers and retailers of clothing need information regarding future demand for clothes of different sizes. If the mean height and standard deviation of army recruits, for example, is known from past records, it is possible to forecast the likely future situation and ensure that uniforms are available in appropriate sizes.

Suppose the mean height of recruits is 174 cm and the standard deviation is 7 cm. We wish to know the proportion of recruits with heights between 180 cm and 184 cm. This represents a vertical strip on the normal distribution (Figure 18-2), the area of the strip indicating the probability of values between these limits being encountered. We have to convert our values to standard values so that we can use the published tables of the normal distribution, and we do this by calculating Z-scores, as we did in Chapter 10. For each of our limits, 180 cm and 184 cm, Z is equal to the difference between the limit and the mean value, divided by the standard deviation. For 180 cm, Z is 0.857; and for 184 cm, Z is 1.43. In effect, the Z-score expresses each limit in terms of the number of standard deviations it lies from the mean value.

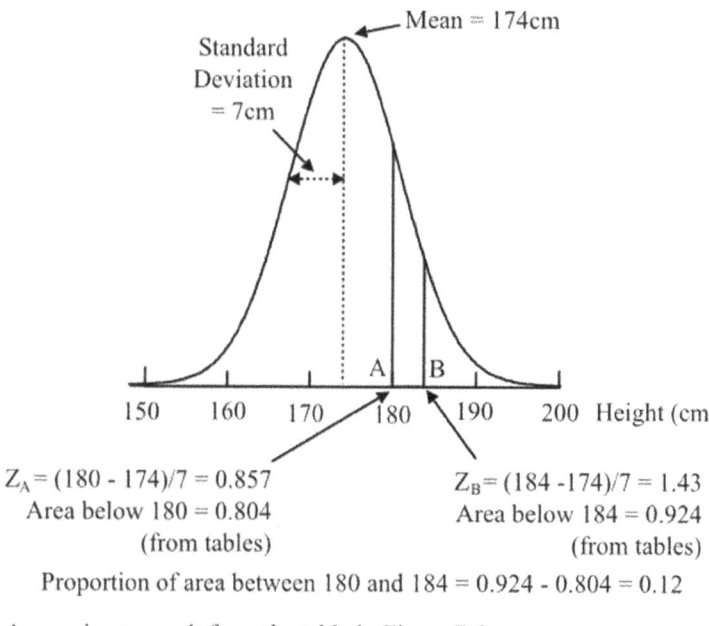

$Z_A = (180 - 174)/7 = 0.857$
Area below $180 = 0.804$
(from tables)

$Z_B = (184 - 174)/7 = 1.43$
Area below $184 = 0.924$
(from tables)

Proportion of area between 180 and 184 = 0.924 - 0.804 = 0.12

Approximate result from the table in Figure 7-9
$Z_A = 0.9$ and $Z_B = 1.4$ gives 10%

Figure 18-2. Use of the normal distribution to predict the proportion of army recruits within a height range

Referring Z to the tables gives the required area—i.e., the probability—and the difference between the two areas, derived from the two limits, gives the proportion of recruits. The calculation is shown in Figure 18-2 and gives the result that 12% of recruits are expected to be within our selected range. An approximate value can be obtained more easily by using Figure 7-9. Entering A = 0.9 (for a Z of 0.857) and B = 1.4 (for a Z of 1.43) gives a probability of 10%, which is approximately correct.

Binomial Distribution

The binomial distribution was described in Chapter 11. Here we will recall its features and show how it may be used in forecasting. The distribution describes the probability of observing a particular event when there are only two possible outcomes. Thus, if we have a series of yes or no answers to a question, the distribution describes the expected number of yes (or no) answers, given knowledge of the average number of yes (or no) answers in the population. If we toss a coin a number of times, the distribution shows the probability of obtaining a given number of heads or tails.

If the population proportion is known from theoretical considerations (as in our coin-tossing example) or has been estimated from a previously obtained large sample, we can use this to predict the characteristics of subsequent samples. If the samples are large, the binomial distribution can be approximated by the normal distribution, and we can proceed as in the previous section. For the Z-score, we take the difference between our sample proportion and the population proportion, and divide it by the standard deviation. The standard deviation of a binomial distribution is the square root of the variance, the variance being $np(1 - p)$, as you have seen previously, where n is the number of data in the sample and p is the population proportion.

If the sample is small, however, and the population proportion not approximately a half, the binomial distribution is skewed, as shown in Figure 11-1, and we have to proceed differently. To illustrate the procedure, consider the throwing of a die a small number of times. We will look at the probability of throwing a 3, so the two possible results are 3 or not 3. When we throw the die once, the probability of getting a 3 is 1/6 and the probability of not getting a 3 is 5/6. This is illustrated by the tree diagram in Figure 18-3, which will assist you in appreciating the results of further throws of the die. If we throw the die twice, the probability of two 3s is 1/36, the probability of one 3 is 10/36, and the probability of zero 3s is 25/36, making the total probability 36/36 (i.e., 1). Figure 18-3 includes the results of throwing the die three times and, additionally, shows the binomial distribution for each of the three stages. It is possible to calculate the results for any number of throws in this manner, but the calculations become tedious; it is customary to obtain the results by consulting published tables of the binomial distribution.

Better Business Decisions from Data

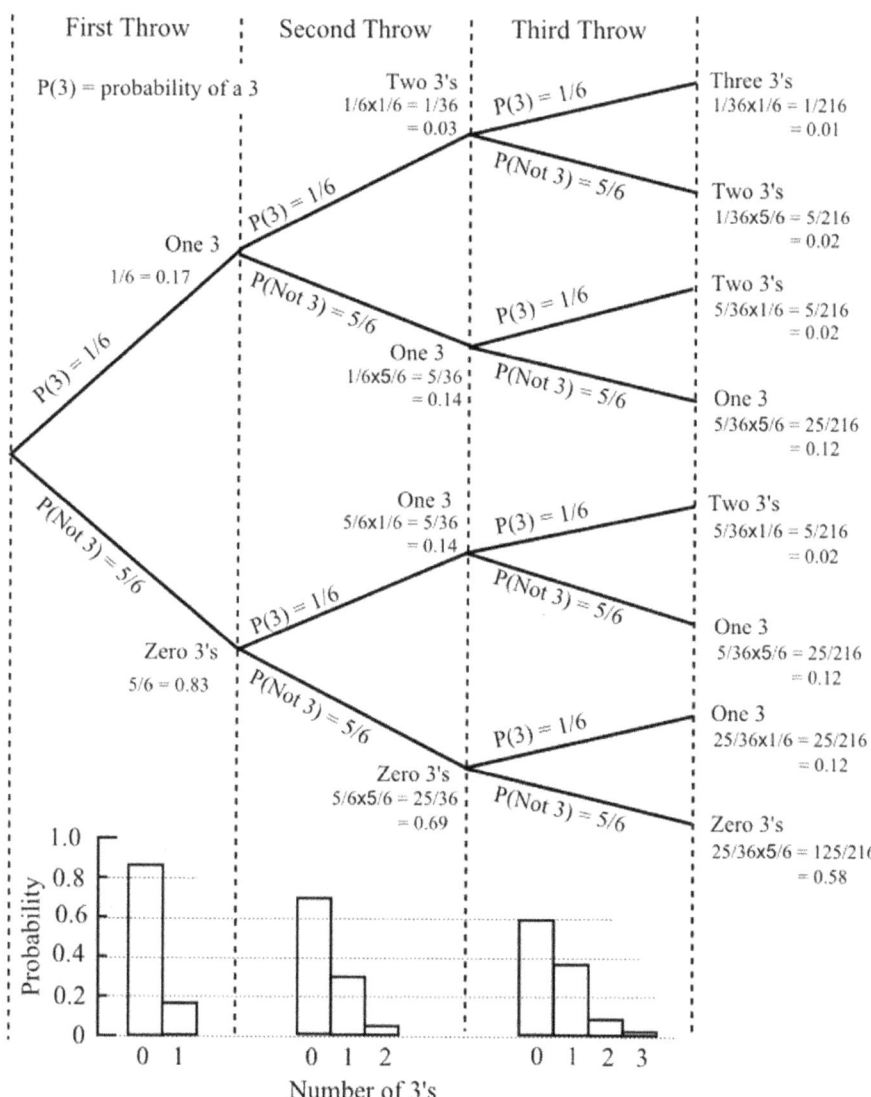

Figure 18-3. Tree diagram showing the probability of obtaining a number of 3s in several throws of a die

Chapter 18 | Forecasting from Known Distributions

A practical situation would be in applying the knowledge that 5% of cars on the road have no registration. This will have been obtained from records or from a large sample. The police may then wish to consider stopping a number of cars at random to check for any that are unregistered. The probability of, for example, 1, 2, or 3 cars having no registration, in a random sample of 20 cars, can be calculated using the same procedure that we used in the throwing of a die. For a sample size of 20 and a proportion of unregistered cars of 0.05, tables of the binomial distribution give the following probabilities.

Cumulative			
Probability of 0	= 0.3585	Probability of 0	= 0.3585
Probability of 1 or fewer	= 0.7385	Probability of 1	= 0.3773
Probability of 2 or fewer	= 0.9245	Probability of 2	= 0.1887
Probability of 3 or fewer	= 0.9841	Probability of 3	= 0.0596
Probability of 4 or fewer	= 0.9974	Probability of 4	= 0.0133
Probability of 5 or fewer	= 0.9997	Probability of 5	= 0.0023
Probability of 6 or fewer	= 1.0000	Probability of 6	= 0.0003
		Total	= 1.0000

The probability of there being no unregistered cars in the sample is 36%, and this provides a useful guide for the proposed sampling arrangement. It may be decided, for example, that a larger sample size should be adopted to increase the probability of detecting at least one unregistered car. The results are shown in Figure 18-4 as a probability distribution. Note that tables of the binomial distribution give cumulative probabilities. The probabilities for individual numbers, shown in the final column above, are obtained by subtracting adjacent cumulative values. Thus, the probability of 2 unregistered cars is the difference between the probability of 2 or fewer and the probability of 1 or fewer.

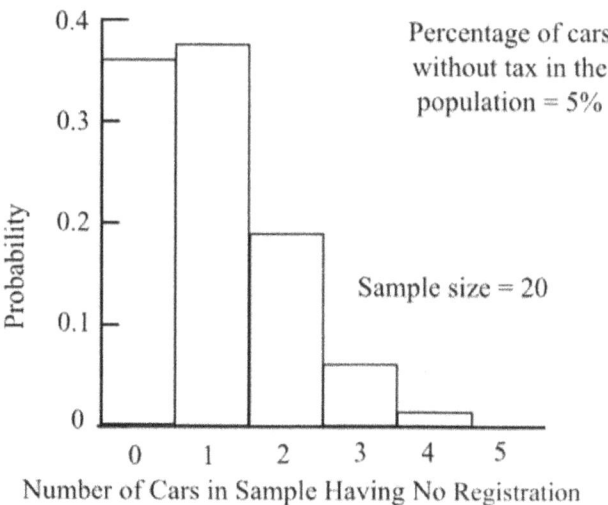

Figure 18-4. Binomial probability distribution of the number of unregistered cars in a sample of twenty

Instead of asking for the probability of a particular number of cars not having registration, we could ask how many unregistered cars, on average, we expect to find in a sample of 20. This is given by the expectation, which is equal to np, where n is the number in the sample (20) and p is the proportion (0.05). The expectation is therefore 1, a result that we might well have deduced at the outset.

Poisson Distribution

The *Poisson distribution* is relevant when we are dealing with events that are randomly scattered either in time or in space. The number of road accidents in a given period of time and the number of goals scored in a soccer match are examples of random events distributed in time. The number of defective links in a length of chain and the number of misprints on each page of a book are examples of random events distributed in space.

The best estimate of the population mean for a Poisson distribution is the sample mean, and the best estimate of the population variance is the sample variance. The variance of a Poisson distribution, surprisingly perhaps, is equal to the mean. When the mean value is large, the distribution approximates to the normal distribution, which can then be used for forecasting. If, for example, we knew that the mean number of telephone calls received by a switchboard per day is 200, we could proceed as in Chapter 10 by calculating Z-scores. Thus we could determine the probability of receiving as few as 100 calls in a day, say, or as many as 300.

Chapter 18 | Forecasting from Known Distributions

If, however, our concern was with the likely variation within shorter time periods, the mean number of calls would be small. The Poisson distribution departs seriously from the normal distribution when the mean is small, becoming extremely skewed. It is then necessary to consult tables to obtain the required probabilities. We might, for example, staying with our telephone calls, be interested in the number of calls received in each five-minute period, to reveal the extent to which callers might be kept waiting.

Suppose the mean number of calls in a five-minute period is 2.5. From tables of the Poisson distribution, we can read off the cumulative probabilities of various numbers of calls arriving in a five-minute period. Thus:

Cumulative			
Probability of 0	= 0.0821	Probability of 0	= 0.0821
Probability of 1 or fewer	= 0.2873	Probability of 1	= 0.2052
Probability of 2 or fewer	= 0.5438	Probability of 2	= 0.2565
Probability of 3 or fewer	= 0.7576	Probability of 3	= 0.2138
Probability of 4 or fewer	= 0.8912	Probability of 4	= 0.1336
Probability of 5 or fewer	= 0.9580	Probability of 5	= 0.0668
Probability of 6 or fewer	= 0.9848	Probability of 6	= 0.0268
Probability of 7 or fewer	= 0.9958	Probability of 7	= 0.0110
Probability of 8 or fewer	= 0.9989	Probability of 8	= 0.0031
Probability of 9 or fewer	= 0.9997	Probability of 9	= 0.0008
		Total	= 0.9997

The probability of a particular number of calls, shown in the final column, is obtained by subtracting adjacent cumulative values. Thus the probability of two calls is the difference between the probability of 2 or fewer and the probability of 1 or fewer. The probability distribution is shown in Figure 18-5.

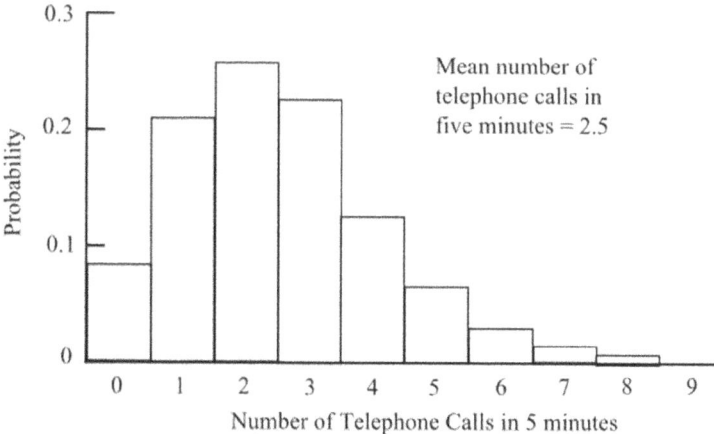

Figure 18-5. Poisson probability of the number of telephone calls in a five-minute period

Exponential Distribution

The *exponential* (negative exponential, to be precise) *distribution* is related to the Poisson distribution. Again, it concerns random events distributed in time or space, but the times or distances between successive events are recorded rather than the number of events in a given extent of time or space. If instead of recording the number of telephone calls arriving in each given time interval, as we did in the previous section, we recorded the time between each pair of successive telephone calls, then the data would consist of numerical values distributed according to the exponential distribution. The exponential distribution is continuous, whereas the Poisson distribution is discrete, and it is extremely skewed having a maximum probability at zero. As with the Poisson distribution, the variance is equal to the mean.

Figure 18-6(a) shows the exponential distribution of the time between successive telephone calls received, on the assumption of a mean time between calls of 2 minutes. This is equivalent to the rate of arrival of 2.5 calls in 5 minutes, which was used in the illustration of the Poisson distribution in the previous section. Because the time axis is continuous and not discrete, probabilities are obtained by evaluating areas under the curve. This was the procedure you saw to be necessary when using the normal distribution. Available tables, of course, remove the need for the rather complicated calculations.

In Figure 18-6(b), the cumulative probability is shown. You can see that shorter time intervals between calls are much more likely than longer time intervals. The probability of the interval being less than one minute is almost 40%. Nearly two thirds of calls are spaced at less than two minutes, though two minutes is the mean spacing.

Chapter 18 | Forecasting from Known Distributions

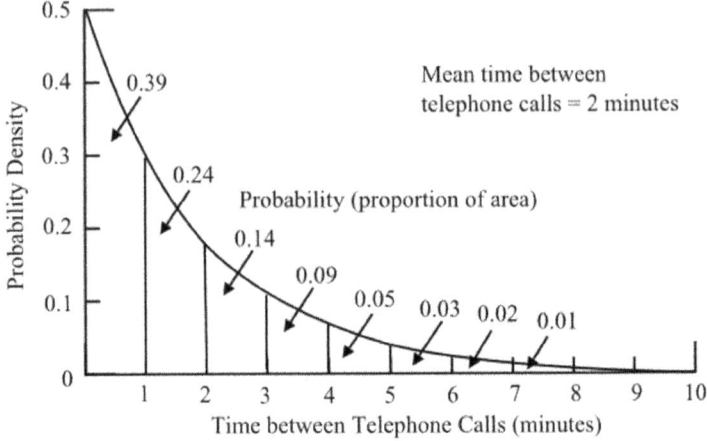

(a) Probability of Number of Minutes between Telephone Calls

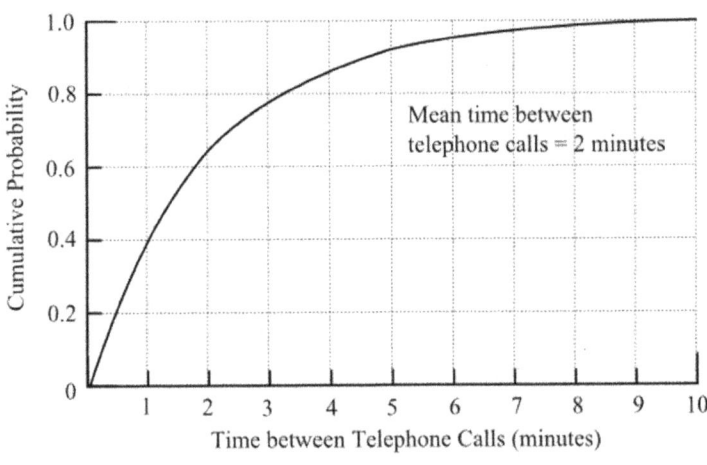

(b) Probability of Number of Minutes or Less between Telephone Calls

Figure 18-6. Negative exponential distribution showing the likely spacing of telephone calls

Geometric Distribution

The geometric distribution is relevant in situations where a number of attempts are made before success is achieved. Many games and sports, for example, are based on minimizing the number of attempts to hit a target or to throw a six. As with the binomial distribution, it is possible to construct the geometric distribution by combining probabilities. We can illustrate this by considering the achievement of a six when throwing a die.

Because the chance of throwing a six is 1/6, this is the chance of achieving success on the first throw. If success is not achieved until the second throw, the first throw must have been not a six, which has a probability of 5/6. The second throw yields a six with a probability of 1/6. The combined probability—that is, the probability of success at the second attempt—is 5/6 × 1/6 = 5/36. This is the application of the "and" rule: a not-6 and a 6. If success is not achieved until the third throw, we have to combine two not-6s with a final 6. Thus the probability is 5/6 × 5/6 × 1/6 = 25/216. These probabilities can be seen in the tree diagram of Figure 18-3, which we used in discussing the binomial distribution. Notice that the probability decreases as we consider each subsequent throw. The probability of success at each throw remains constant, of course, at the value of 1/6; but success at later throws requires failure at the preceding throws, and these failures involve a probability of occurrence.

As with the exponential distribution, to which it is related, the geometric distribution is extremely skewed, having a maximum probability at the first attempt. The geometric distribution is discrete, whereas the exponential distribution, as you saw, is continuous.

As a practical example, consider a door-to-door salesman. It is known from company records that the probability of making a sale at a house is 1/10. This is sufficient information for the following list to be constructed:

			Cumulative
Probability of sale at 1st call	= 1/10	= 0.1000	0.1000
Probability of sale at 2nd call, but not before	= (9/10) × 1/10	= 0.0900	0.1900
Probability of sale at 3rd call, but not before	= $(9/10)^2$ × 1/10	= 0.0810	0.2710
Probability of sale at 4th call, but not before	= $(9/10)^3$ × 1/10	= 0.0729	0.3439
Probability of sale at 5th call, but not before	= $(9/10)^4$ × 1/10	= 0.0656	0.4095
Probability of sale at 6th call, but not before	= $(9/10)^5$ × 1/10	= 0.0590	0.4685
Probability of sale at 7th call, but not before	= $(9/10)^6$ × 1/10	= 0.0531	0.5216
Probability of sale at 8th call, but not before	= $(9/10)^7$ × 1/10	= 0.0478	0.5694
Probability of sale at 9th call, but not before	= $(9/10)^8$ × 1/10	= 0.0430	0.6124
Probability of sale at 10th call, but not before	= $(9/10)^9$ × 1/10	= 0.0387	0.6511

The distribution is shown in Figure 18-7(a) as far as the tenth call. The distribution continues indefinitely: the salesman, poor fellow, may never get a sale, but the probability of not getting a sale after a large number of calls is very small.

Chapter 18 | Forecasting from Known Distributions

The cumulative values, which are shown in Figure 18-7(b), are probably of more interest to the salesman and to his company. These show the probability of a sale at the first call, or the second call, or the third call, and so on. The cumulative values approach the value of one as the number of calls increases, reflecting the fact that the probability of a sale increases with the number of calls and would become a certainty given an infinite number of calls.

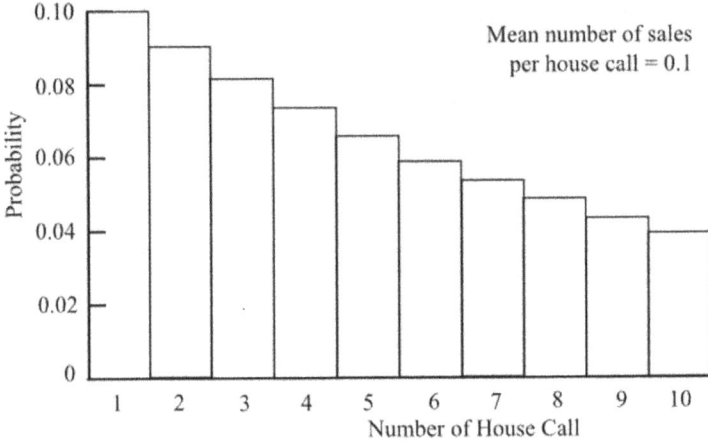

(a) Probability of making the first sale at a specified house call.

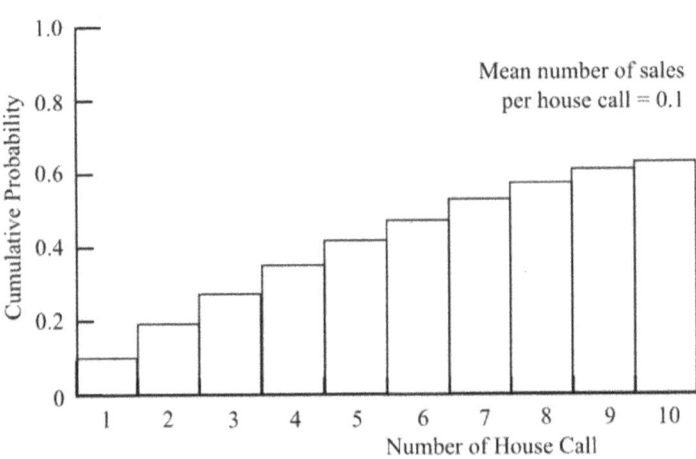

(b) Probability of making the first sale at or before a specified house call.

Figure 18-7. Geometric distribution of the first success in a sequence of house calls

Weibull Distribution

The *Weibull distribution* is a continuous distribution having a complex mathematical description. A shape parameter within the definition can take a range of values to give different forms of distribution. In one form the distribution is identical to the exponential distribution, while in another it approximates to the normal distribution.

The distribution is particularly useful in describing data that is positively skewed, having a peak at low values and tailing away to few but distant large values. Failure of components—for example, ball bearings—frequently follows this kind of distribution. Other applications include manufacturing and delivery times, and meteorological data such as wind-speed distributions. *Extreme value theory*, which deals with the low probabilities of unusual events—such as major floods, wildfires, freak waves, and large incomes—makes use of the Weibull distribution.

CHAPTER 19

Time Series
Yesterday Rain, Today Rain, Tomorrow...?

One of the most difficult areas of forecasting is in dealing with time series. Our profits have been x, y, and z over the past three years, so what will they be next year? Unfortunately, we might say, this is perhaps the area where forecasting is most necessary in the business and commercial world. In the United Kingdom, and probably elsewhere, documentation involving the sale of shares and other investment products has to carry the warning "past performance is no guide to future performance."

Regression

The problem is essentially to forecast data relating to the next time period from knowledge of the data from previous time periods. In Chapter 14, I explained the technique of regression analysis applied to relationships between two variables, and showed how a mathematical expression could be derived to describe the relationship. A time series can be treated as a relationship between two variables, and a mathematical relationship can be obtained using this technique. The relationship can then give predicted values for future times.

There are a number of problems associated with this approach. First, we will be extrapolating a correlation beyond the range of values within which it has been found to apply. Of course, as I have previously said, we have to extrapolate one way or another, and we are really looking for the least undesirable procedure. The second problem is that we are fitting the data to a straight line or a smooth curve with no justification. This is very different from the use of these correlation methods in establishing relationships between basic physical properties, which commonly vary smoothly with each other in line with well-defined laws. The third problem is that we have no way of knowing for certain how accurate our forecast will be.

With regard to the accuracy of our forecast, we can argue that provided our extension into the future is modest, in relation to the extent of our past data, the error is unlikely to be great. We can also put a value on the maximum possible precision of the forecast values. We will know the reliability of the correlation, and this is a measure of the precision of the correlation's estimate of the existing data points. The estimate of the future data points cannot be more precise than this, so we have a measure of the best level of precision to be expected. Put another way, the correlation cannot be better at forecasting future values than it is at predicting the known past values.

If you look back at the time series discussed in Chapter 14 and shown plotted in Figure 14-10, you will recall that a simple linear regression yielded a correlation coefficient of $r = 0.70$. By using moving averages, the correlation coefficient was increased to 0.99. This indicates strong evidence for the rising trend indicated by the data, but the rising trend alone is of little value in forecasting the monthly performance in the short term. In the long term, there is the problem of having to extrapolate well beyond the range of the existing data.

Autocorrelation

Autocorrelation provides a means of examining whether there are correlations between data from different times in the past. Pairs of data from different times are selected and compared. If the comparison shows a significant relationship, then there is evidence that the past values can be used to forecast future values.

We would expect the daily temperature to bear some relation to the temperature of the previous day. A correlation between the two over a number of days would provide us with a basis for forecasting the next day's temperature. It would not be perfect but, it would have a degree of success. If we considered the average monthly temperature and produced a correlation with the value for the corresponding month of the previous year, we would have better success. Indeed, this is the approach used in setting up projected monthly temperatures for various locations.

Of course, not everything that we have to deal with has the repeatability of weather and climate, but recognizable cyclic variations are not uncommon in data relating to business activities. We can use the following data showing the monthly profits of a company, in thousands of dollars, say, to illustrate a practical application. The data are plotted in Figure 19-1(a).

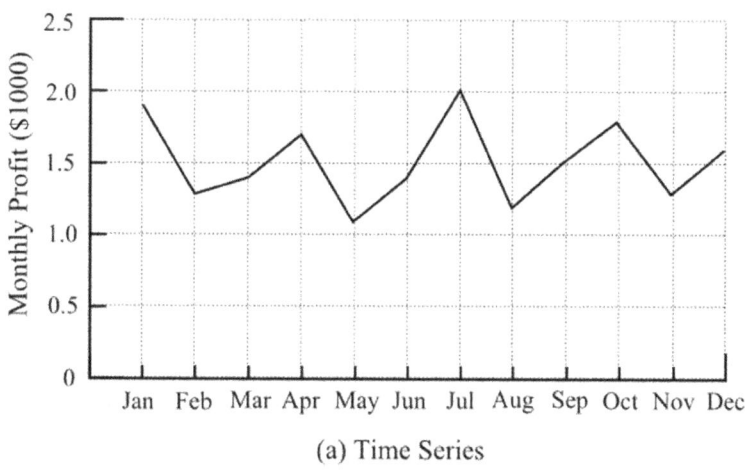
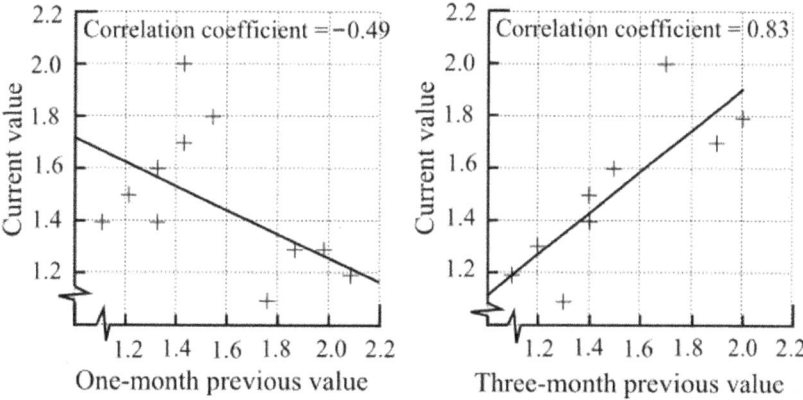

(b) Results of Autocorrelation

Figure 19-1. An example of autocorrelation

Jan	Feb	Mar	Apr	May	Jun	Jul	Aug	Sep	Oct	Nov	Dec
1.9	1.3	1.4	1.7	1.1	1.4	2.0	1.2	1.5	1.8	1.3	1.6

Chapter 19 | Time Series

A correlation between each value and the value for the previous month can be obtained by a simple linear regression analysis of the following two sets of data:

	Feb	Mar	Apr	May	Jun	Jul	Aug	Sep	Oct	Nov	Dec
Current	1.3	1.4	1.7	1.1	1.4	2.0	1.2	1.5	1.8	1.3	1.6
Previous	1.9	1.3	1.4	1.7	1.1	1.4	2.0	1.2	1.5	1.8	1.3

(one-month)

The equation of the regression line, following the procedure from Chapter 14, is calculated to be

$$\text{Current} = -0.45 \times \text{Previous} + 2.16$$

and is shown plotted in Figure 19-1(b). The predicted value for the next month—January of the following year—is obtained by inserting the value for December of 1.6 for the previous month. The prediction is 1.4. This would not be reliable, because the correlation coefficient for the data is −0.49, which is not significant at the 5% level. (See Chapter 14 for a selection of significance levels for the product moment correlation coefficient.) That is to say, the gradient of the regression line, −0.45, is not significantly different from zero.

The possibility of a seasonal effect can be examined by using the three-month previous values. The two sets of data are now as follows:

	Apr	May	Jun	Jul	Aug	Sep	Oct	Nov	Dec
Current	1.7	1.1	1.4	2.0	1.2	1.5	1.8	1.3	1.6
Previous	1.9	1.3	1.4	1.7	1.1	1.4	2.0	1.2	1.5

(three-month)

The equation of the regression line is calculated to be

$$\text{Current} = 0.79 \times \text{Previous} + 0.33$$

which, with the value of 1.6 for the previous month (December), gives a predicted value of 1.6 for the next month (January). The data is shown in Figure 19-1(b). The correlation coefficient is 0.83, which is significant at the 1% level. Clearly this is a better forecast than the previous one.

Exponential Smoothing

In Chapter 14, we showed an example of a time series and described how the use of a moving average has a smoothing effect on the shape of the graph. If we assume that the undulations in the graph are due to random effects, rather than meaningful effects, we could decide that the graph of moving averages would provide a means of forecasting future values. To achieve some improvement, we could then take the view that the more recent data points are more relevant in predicting the future than the older ones. We could therefore apply a weighting procedure in calculating the moving averages. This thinking leads us to the method of *exponential smoothing*.

In exponential smoothing, the forecast values for the time periods are calculated successively starting with the earliest. The value for each next period is obtained by adding a proportion, α (Greek letter alpha), of the current value to a proportion $(1 - \alpha)$ of the previous similarly produced forecast value. The proportion α lies between 0 and 1: a proportion of 1 leaves the current value unchanged, and a proportion of 0 replaces the whole of the value with the previous value. The formula is

$$F_{t+1} = \alpha D_t + (1-\alpha)F_t$$

where F_{t+1} = forecast for the next period

F_t = previous forecast applied to current period

D_t = current actual value

α = weighting factor

Because each forecast depends directly on the previous forecast, it consequently depends on all previous forecasts, though the dependency is greater the more recent the forecast.

The following is a small example, using a weighting factor of 0.2, to illustrate the procedure. Supposed sales figures are shown for six successive periods. Also shown is the forecast value for the seventh period.

Chapter 19 | Time Series

Period	Sales D_t	Forecast F_t	Forecast for next period F_{t+1}	Error $F_t - D_t$	Error squared
1	50				
2	46	50.0	49.2		
3	53	49.2	49.9	−3.8	14.4
4	52	49.9	50.4	−2.1	4.4
5	44	50.4	49.1	6.4	41.0
6	51	49.1	49.5	−1.9	3.6
7		49.5			
				Total	63.4
				Mean	15.9

The error in each period is the difference between the actual sales figure, D_t, and the forecast, F_t, which was calculated from the previous sales figure. The overall error is usually quantified by the mean squared error.

In carrying out this procedure, we had to make two choices. First, we had to decide on the weighting factor. A large value gives more weight to recent sales, whereas a small value gives more weight to earlier sales. Second, because we had no previous forecast value, we had to decide what to use as the first value for F_t. The example used the value 50, this being the actual sales figure in the previous period.

To achieve an acceptable forecast, the overall error needs to be minimized; but with two somewhat arbitrary choices to be made, it is not easy to achieve this manually. There are, of course, computer programs readily available that can rapidly run through a range of scenarios to work toward a minimum mean-squared error.

The method as described is referred to as *single exponential smoothing*, just one weighting factor being used. The method works well when the data are approximately constant as time progresses and the up and down variations are random. In many situations, however, the data points will show a trend, either increasing or decreasing with time. *Double exponential smoothing* is then required. A second constant, β (Greek letter beta), is introduced to adjust for the trend in each previous interval. The first smoothing constant is applied to the trend-adjusted values in a way similar to that of single exponential smoothing.

In addition to trend, time series often show periodic variation which could be daily, monthly, seasonal or annual. To include effects of periodic variation, a third smoothing constant, γ (Greek letter gamma), can be included to give *triple exponential smoothing*.

Exponential smoothing is essentially a trial-and-error procedure but is readily dealt with by the computer software that is available. It is worth pointing out, however, that there are a number of variants of the method, so not all computer programs produce the same results.

Notice that in exponential smoothing, unlike regression, no regard is taken of the expected shape of the fitted curve. The forecast is in essence based on the most recent value modified in accordance with how well each previous value would have forecast the next one in the series.

PLUMB WISE

Lawton Plumbing Supplies was located in an industrial park on the edge of the town. It was a small business run by the owner, Bill Lawton, supplying tools and plumbing consumables to local tradesmen and DIY enthusiasts. Kitchen and bathroom accessories were also stocked for sale to the general public.

Rising prices of copper and brass seriously affected the value of inventory, and much of it had become slow-moving because of the trend toward greater use of plastic pipework and fittings. Bill was nevertheless conscious of the need to retain his customers by always having what they needed in stock. He realized that his inventory control and forward-ordering practices were a mess and needed sorting out.

He talked to various colleagues about the matter, and it was suggested to him that he should spend some time examining his sales records and employ a rational routine guided perhaps by some form of time series analysis.

Armed with a book on statistics from the local library, Bill studied the possibilities. Because of the trend of decreasing copper and brass sales, and the increasing trend of plastic sales, he decided that exponential smoothing seemed to be useful. It promised the ability to deal with random fluctuations and an underlying trend. There might also be a benefit from the incorporation of a cyclic variation, because sales of pipework increased in the winter when many householders suffered from frozen pipes and central-heating faults.

At this stage, he needed help. Through his many contacts, he located a local IT expert who ran a computer repair business. For a modest fee, Bill had a suitable package installed on his computer and several short tutorial sessions.

Bill became quite fascinated by the process and used the technique to analyze sales records for much of his stock. He appreciated that the benefits would not be immediate but would improve with time, although it was quickly apparent that the system was recognizing the trends he was most concerned about. He was also shrewd enough to understand that no statistical analysis was going to give precise answers and that his practical experience in the business would still be required. Customer retention would always demand that safety margins be incorporated in his forward planning.

CHAPTER 20

Control Charts
Navigating around the Factory

Quality control procedures are used in production processes to ensure that the products continue to meet the appropriate specifications. Usually, periodic sampling of the products is employed; and control charts, sometimes referred to as *Shewhart charts*, are used to record the results in order to anticipate the onset of problems in the production processes.

Two types of chart are in use, the choice depending on how the product is checked. If it is checked by a numerical measurement, the process is referred to as *sampling by variable*. If it is checked by observation of satisfactory or unsatisfactory features, the process is referred to as *sampling by attribute*.

Sampling by Variable

Most products that are produced to a specification have requirements for specific dimensions. Suppose, for example, a factory producing steel tubes with an internal diameter of 50 mm has an acceptable tolerance of ±1.0 mm. So tubes that are smaller in diameter than 49 mm or larger than 51 mm are defective and unacceptable. At the outset, measurements on large samples of tubes will have determined that the manufacturing procedures are producing tubes with a mean diameter of 50.2 mm, say, which is well within the tolerance. The samples will also have provided measures of the standard deviation, 0.25 mm, say. The difference between the mean and the maximum permitted size is 0.8 mm, which is 3.2 standard deviations. From tables of the normal distribution, we find that 3.2 standard deviations either side of the mean will include all but 1 in 1000 observations. The company may accept that a rejection rate of about 1 in 1000 is acceptable. Reducing the rejection rate would involve increased costs in ensuring that the manufacturing processes gave more consistent output. Of course, depending on the type and cost of the product, other companies may settle for very different rejection rates.

Chapter 20 | Control Charts

During production, samples will be taken periodically and the results recorded on the control chart. The samples will necessarily be small, perhaps consisting of five items. Figure 20-1(a) shows a typical layout of a control chart. On the vertical axis is a scale in mm, and the established mean value of 50.2 mm is shown as a horizontal line. Along the horizontal axis is a scale indicating the time or date of sampling. The mean value from each sample is plotted, and its relation to the target value of 50.2 mm can be readily appreciated.

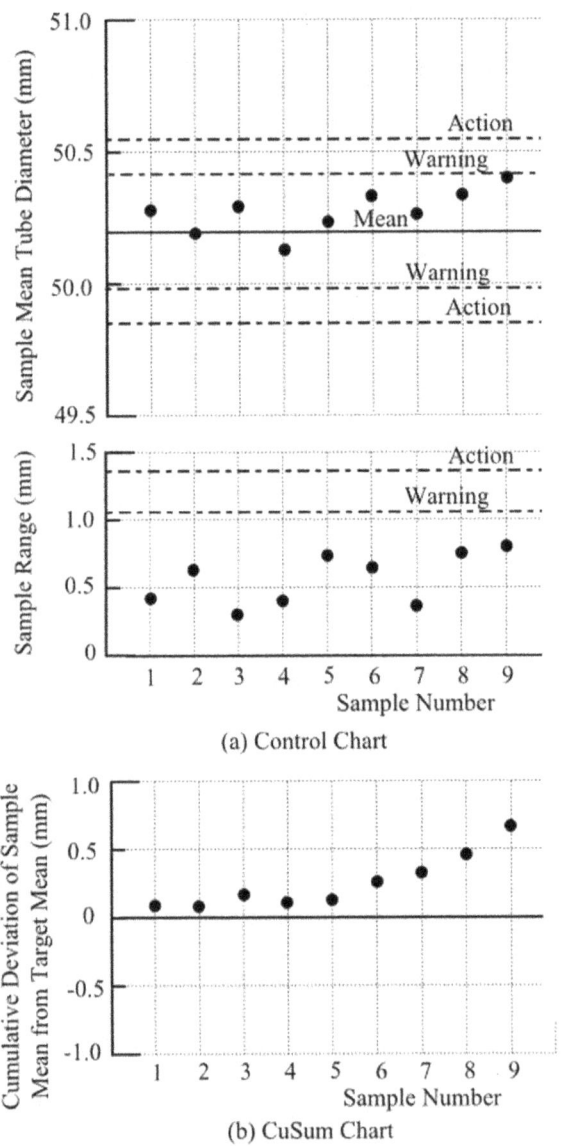

Figure 20-1. Control charts for sampling by variable

Either side of the 50.2 mm line are two more horizontal lines. The inner pair are the warning limits, and the outer pair are the action limits. If the sample means move toward one of the warning limits, the company will be forewarned of something amiss in the manufacturing processes and can instigate additional sampling or an investigation of the processes. Sample means reaching the action limits would indicate a serious problem. We shall shortly see how the warning and action limits are fixed.

Not only is it important to ensure that the mean value is being maintained, but it is also essential that the variability does not increase. In the lower part of the chart is a further set of horizontal lines to cope with variability. Again we have the target line, a warning line, and an action line. The target line could be set at the value of standard deviation, but because the calculation of standard deviation involves a degree of skill, it is common practice to use the range instead. The range from each sample can be easily recognized and plotted. The range of a series of values is related to the standard deviation, though it is a less precise measure of variability.

The warning limits are usually set so that there is about a 1 in 40 chance of the limit being reached on the assumption that the samples are still representative of the original products. The action limits are usually set so that the corresponding chance is about 1 in 1,000. The calculation of the limiting values is complicated by two factors. First, the samples are small, so the t-distribution is required rather than the normal distribution. Second, because the range is being used, a conversion has to be made from standard deviation to range, and the conversion factor varies with the number of items in the sample. To circumvent these difficulties, control-chart tables are published giving values of A and D for different sample sizes, which are used in the following expressions:

Mean: Upper Action Limit = mean + A_A × mean range
Mean: Lower Action Limit = mean − A_A × mean range
Mean: Upper Warning Limit = mean + A_W × mean range
Mean: Lower Warning Limit = mean − A_W × mean range
Range: Action Limit = D_A × mean range
Range: Warning Limit = D_W × mean range

The tabulated values of A fix the limits such that six standard deviations of the sample mean, three each side of the mean, lie between the action limits, and four standard deviations, two each side of the mean, lie between the warning limits. The D values correspond appropriately.

In the example above, the expressions yield the following values, which are included in Figure 20-1(a):

Mean: Upper Action Limit	= 50.2 + 0.594 × 2.326 × 0.25	= 50.55
Mean: Lower Action Limit	= 50.2 − 0.594 × 2.326 × 0.25	= 49.85
Mean: Upper Warning Limit	= 50.2 + 0.377 × 2.326 × 0.25	= 50.42
Mean: Lower Warning Limit	= 50.2 − 0.377 × 2.326 × 0.25	= 49.98
Range: Action Limit	= 2.34 × 2.326 × 0.25	= 1.36
Range: Warning Limit	= 1.81 × 2.326 × 0.25	= 1.05

The factor of 2.326 provides the conversion of the standard deviation of 0.25 to the value of the mean range, for a sample size of 5.

It is important to note that the tolerance plays no part in the setting up of the control chart. The tolerance, together with the mean and standard deviation from the initial large sample, determine the likely proportion of unacceptable items that will result, on the assumption that the production processes will not change in any way. The purpose of the control chart is to signal changes in the production processes that may, if not attended to, lead to an increase in unacceptable items. The control chart provides statistical control of the processes separately from decisions regarding the number of unacceptable items that can be tolerated.

An alternative form of chart, the *cumulative sum* or *CuSum chart*, is sometimes used. The difference between the sample mean and the target mean is accumulated, sample by sample, and plotted cumulatively, as shown in Figure 20-1(b). A change in gradient, either increasing or decreasing, indicates a departure from normal circumstances. An advantage of the chart is that small changes in mean show up more clearly than on a control chart.

Sampling by Attribute

Some products are either satisfactory or unsatisfactory and cannot be graded on a scale of defectiveness. Light bulbs, for example, either light up or refuse to. From what we have said previously, the situation will be recognized as a binomial one.

The periodic sampling must now involve larger samples than was the case with sampling by variable, discussed in the previous section. Clearly, a small sample would be likely to show no unacceptable items on a regular basis and would provide no useful information. Although the samples have to be larger, the checking of the items is likely to be much easier and quicker: checking a light bulb is more straightforward than measuring the diameter of a tube.

Suppose, staying with light bulbs, that the company accepts 1 defective light bulb in 100; and suppose that the periodic sampling involves 50 bulbs. The control chart, shown in Figure 20-2, records the number of defective bulbs in the sample.

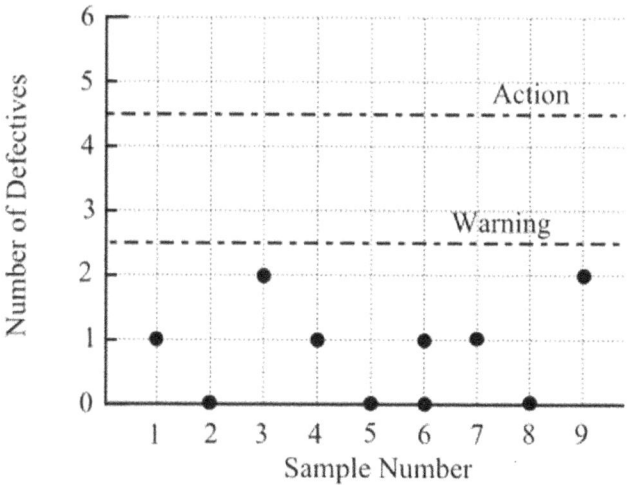

Figure 20-2. Control chart for sampling by attribute

On average, there will be 0.5 defective bulbs in each sample. We need to know the probability of there being 0, 1, 2, 3, ... defective bulbs in a sample in order to set up a warning limit and an action limit. From tables of the binomial distribution, we obtain the following values for a sample size of 50 and an average level of defects of 1%.

Probability of 0 defective	= 0.6050	=	60.50%
Probability of 1 defective	= 0.3056	=	30.56%
Probability of 2 defective	= 0.0756	=	7.56%
Probability of 3 defective	= 0.0122	=	1.22%
Probability of 4 defective	= 0.0015	=	0.15%
Probability of 5 or more defective	= 0.0001	=	0.01%
Total	= 1.000	=	100%

If the warning limit is set so that there is a 1 in 20 chance of the limit being reached, when there is in reality no change in the manufacturing processes, we require it to correspond to 5% probability. This arises between 2 and 3 defective bulbs, so the limit would be set between these values. Similarly, for the action limit, a chance of 1 in 1,000 corresponds to 0.1%, so the limit would be set between 4 and 5 defective bulbs. These limits are included in Figure 20-2.

CHAPTER 21

Reliability
Would You Trust That Bungee Cord?

Statistics plays an important part in reliability studies but represents only a part of the mathematical theory involved. *Reliability* of a component, machine, or system can be defined as the probability that it will perform its required function in the desired manner under the operating conditions when it is required to so perform. Reliability, R, is thus a probability with a value between 0 and 1, 0 representing immediate failure and 1 representing the (impossible) situation of never suffering failure. The probability of failure is $1 - R$.

Basic Principles

Machines and systems consist of many components. Components themselves consist of assemblies of parts. Failure of a single part may lead to failure of a complete system, or perhaps not. A broken chain link causes failure of the length of chain, but failure of a single strand of wire in a wire rope does not lead to failure of the rope. Analyses can thus be seen to be complex because of the number of items involved and because of the ways that the items interact in the functioning of the assembly. Simple systems can be analyzed using the rules of combining probabilities, and by looking at these we can appreciate what is involved.

In the case of the wire rope, suppose the probability of failure of one strand within the required operating period is 0.001. There are three strands in the rope, and the rope does not fail until all three strands fail. We have here a parallel situation: the three strands are physically parallel to each other and the failure mode is referred to as parallel. For failure of the rope, we require failure of the first, the second, and the third strands. This is an "and" situation; and as we saw in Chapter 3, the probabilities have to be multiplied together, assuming of course that the failure of a strand is independent of the failure of other strands. Thus 0.001 × 0.001 × 0.001 = 0.000000001 is the probability of failure of the rope. It should be noted that these values are not realistic.

The chain links referred to above are physically in series, and we can represent the failure probabilities as a series. If the probability of failure of a link within the required operating period is 0.001, then, with three links, the chain fails if the first or the second or the third link fails. This is an "or" situation; and, again as we saw in Chapter 3, we need to add the probabilities. Thus the probability of failure of the chain (albeit only three links) is 0.003. The observant reader may have spotted that there is an error here. The three events are not mutually exclusive. We have not taken proper account of all the possibilities: two or all three links may fail. Furthermore, if we consider just one link failing, we have to include, by the "and" rule, the survival of the other two. With 3 links, there is a total of 8 scenarios, which are listed here together with the probability of each:

	Link 1	Link 2	Link 3	Probability
1	Not fail	Not fail	Not fail	0.997,002,999
2	Not fail	Not fail	Fail	0.000,998,001
3	Not fail	Fail	Not fail	0.000,998,001
4	Fail	Not fail	Not fail	0.000,998,001
5	Not fail	Fail	Fail	0.000,000,999
6	Fail	Not fail	Fail	0.000,000,999
7	Fail	Fail	Not fail	0.000,000,999
8	Fail	Fail	Fail	0.000,000,001
Total 2 to 8 (at least one link fails)				0.002,997,001

Two things are apparent from the tabled values. First, the probability of at least one link failing, shown by the total probability for scenarios 2 to 8, is extremely close to our originally proposed value of 0.003. This reflects the fact that when the probability of failure of a component is very small, the probability of two or more components failing in the same time period is even smaller—i.e., insignificant compared to the precision attached to the single-failure probability. In real situations, the failure probabilities are much smaller than in our simple example: a chain of several hundred links, with each link having a failure probability within the operational period as large as 0.001, would be quite useless. Thus, when the "or" rule is encountered in reliability situations, the individual probabilities can usually be added without loss of precision.

The second point of interest from the above values is that the probability of at least one link failing can be more easily obtained by calculating the probability of all three links failing and subtracting this value from unity.

With assemblies of many components, there will be groups of series items and groups of parallel items, and these groups may be combined in series or parallel fashion with other groups. Figure 21-1(a) shows a hypothetical example of a sprinkler system consisting of power and water supply, sensors, relays, valves, and the sprinkler head. The analysis can be undertaken by means of a *fault tree*, shown in Figure 21-1(b). The various items are connected to show the reliance of each item on the functioning of others. The connections are labeled according to whether the reliance is series or parallel: in other words, whether the reliance is "and" or "or." Starting at the bottom of the tree, we would insert the individual failure probabilities for the components. We would work upward, multiplying at the AND gates and adding at the OR gates. The final failure probability would be subtracted from unity to give the reliability.

Chapter 21 | Reliability

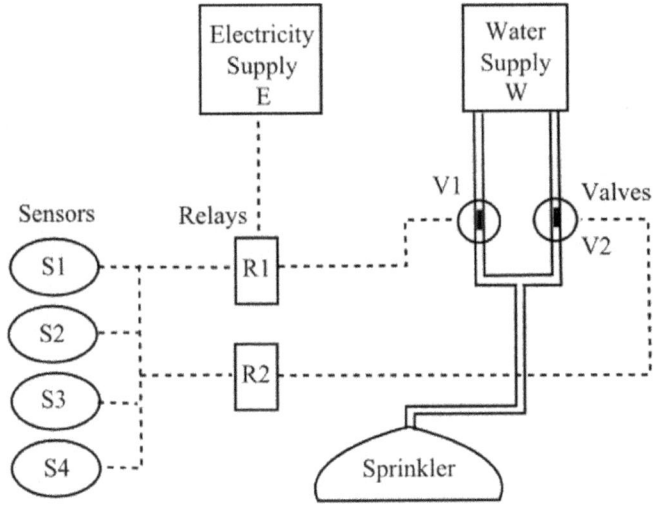

(a) The Sprinkler System

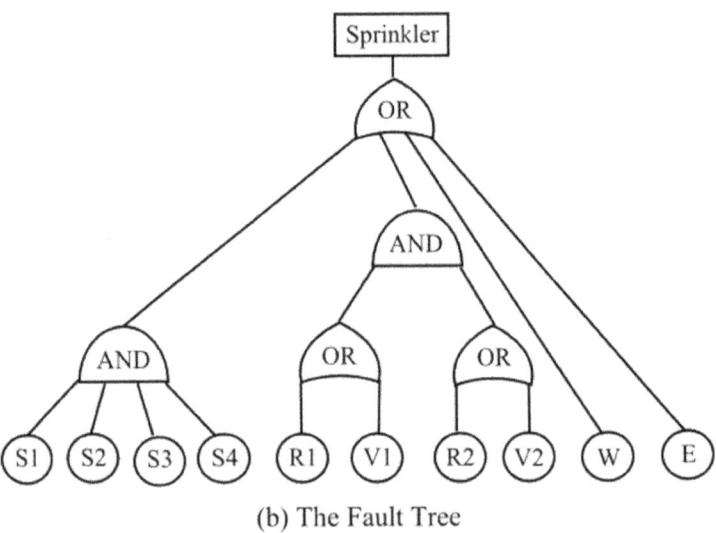

(b) The Fault Tree

Figure 21-1. A hypothetical sprinkler system and its fault tree

Items may be combined in ways that are neither series nor parallel. Figure 21-2(a) shows a bell that is activated by two parallel paths; but the addition of Z, as in Figure 21-2(b), renders the system neither series nor parallel (Smith, 1976: 66). X or Z ensures the activation of x, and Z or Y ensures the activation of y. X, Z, and Y are not in parallel since X does not activate y and Y does not activate x.

Compare the diagram with that in Figure 21-2(c), which shows X, Y, and Z in parallel and as a unit in series with the parallel arrangement of x and y.

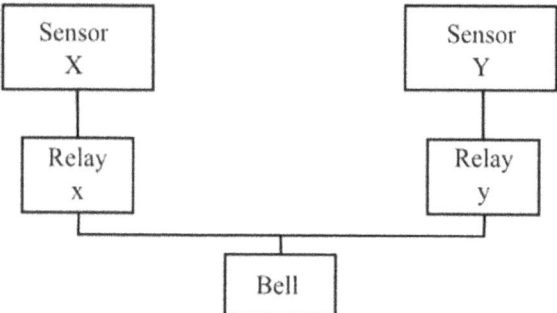

(a) Bell activated by two parallel paths.

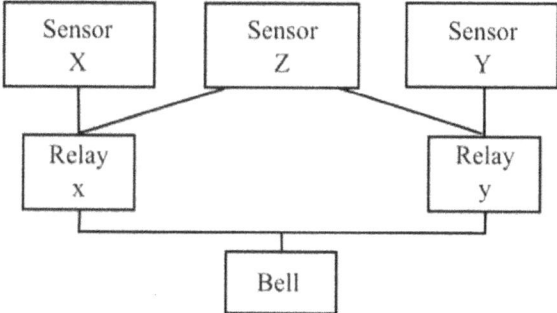

(b) Addition of Z renders system neither series nor parallel.

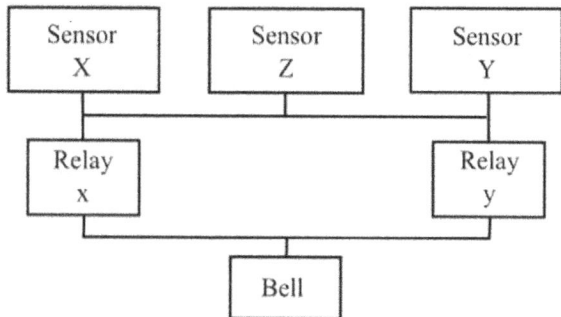

(c) Alternative wiring produces two parallel systems in series.

Figure 21-2. A diagram showing that some systems may be neither series nor parallel

Some such arrangements can be dealt with by conditional probabilities that you met in Chapter 3. In our example shown in Figure 21-2(b), consider first the condition that Z fails (probability P_z). Then we have in effect the arrangement shown in Figure 21-2(a), and we can calculate the failure probability (P_1) in the normal way. Next, consider the condition that Z does not fail (probability $1 - P_z$). X and Y are now irrelevant, and we need calculate only the failure probability (P_2) of x and y in parallel. Bringing the two situations together, there is now an "or" situation: Z fails, or Z does not fail. The failure probability of the system is therefore

$$P_z \times P_1 + (1-P_z) \times P_2$$

and the reliability is one minus this value.

Reliability Data

We discussed sampling at length in Chapter 4, and our main concern there was to ensure that the sample was representative of the population of interest. In reliability investigations this factor is still important, of course, but there is now an additional complication in that it is not easy to obtain the sample data. Some items, electronic components for example, are tested under service conditions for long periods until failure. A *mean time to failure* (MTTF) is obtained and can be used in predicting the reliability of assemblies. A general application of this approach has severe limitations. For many items, testing times would be long and expensive, and creating realistic service conditions would be difficult. When expected service lifetimes are very long, there simply is not the time available to test to failure. Accelerated testing, involving excessive forces, speeds, or environmental conditions, for example, must be used, though this means that the service conditions are not being reproduced exactly by the testing conditions. Testing times can be shortened by testing a number of items simultaneously and curtailing the tests when a percentage of the items has failed. Testing complete assemblies to failure is often a better option, but time and cost have to be considered.

When testing to failure is out of the question, historical evidence can be used. Items that have been employed for some time will generate data on time to failure. In novel, complex structures, it is likely that many of the components will have a history of usage in other applications that will give some guidance as to their expected reliability.

Distributions

Many different distributions are made use of in reliability analyses. The normal distribution may be appropriate for simple items failing in a well-defined manner; but as items and components become more complex, it is found more useful to assume that failure is a random event and that the probability of failure adopts a constant value. Thus the Poisson distribution, expressing the probability of a number of random events in a selected time period, and the associated exponential distribution, expressing the probability of specified time periods between random events, are used.

The Weibull distribution is often used. It was pointed out in Chapter 18 that this distribution has a deal of flexibility. It can describe a constant failure rate when failures are due to random events, and this is the likely situation during most of the lifetime of the assembly. There is generally a higher, but decreasing, failure rate when the assembly is new. This is the *burn-in* period, and the distribution can be used for this decreasing failure rate. Toward the end of the useful life (the *wear-out* period), the failure rate increases, and, again, the Weibull distribution can cope.

Practical Complications

In practice, most machines and equipment are not run until failure. Inspection and maintenance are carried out, and parts can be replaced or refurbished before failure occurs. Clearly this complicates calculations of reliability. The use of standby systems and the practice of derating equipment add to the complications.

It was mentioned above that failure is commonly assumed to be a random event except during the burn-in and wear-out periods. The burn-in period may be virtually eliminated by pre-service running and rectification, and the wear-out period may be virtually eliminated by maintenance.

ALARM BELLS

Luke Rogers was self-employed, running a small business in burglar alarms. He bought in components, designed systems for domestic and small business properties, and carried out the installation. He gave his customers a guarantee for two years, during which time he would respond rapidly to rectify faults and replace any required parts. To provide cover following this period, he sold maintenance contracts that were renewable each year.

He was having a problem with a large number of service calls to customers during the guarantee period. The fault was with a relay that was failing, often only a few months after installation. He had been somewhat foolish in purchasing a job lot of these relays very cheaply. The cost to him of a service call was considerable in terms of travel and time, whereas the cost of the replacement relay was, of course, negligible. A hidden but serious cost was the deterioration in his customer relations.

Chapter 21 | Reliability

The solution seemed to be to scrap the stock of relays and purchase a batch of more expensive ones; but Luke's daughter Louise, who was studying engineering at college, suggested that there might be a better option. She had some knowledge of statistics and knew about fault trees.

Using typical circuit diagrams of the installations and the data from the records of service calls, she produced an approximate fault tree. She could see that there were two relays in the circuit and they were effectively in series, so that if either failed, the system would shut down. The probability of either failing (an "or" situation) during the guarantee period, Louise calculated, was about 0.3. From this, she calculated that the probability of a single relay failing was 0.16.

Louise knew that components in parallel decreased the probability of failure (the "and" rule) and realized that if a pair of relays were wired together in parallel to replace the single relay, the probability of failure would decrease from 0.16 to 0.026 (i.e., 0.16 × 0.16). Replacing both single relays in the system in a similar way would give a probability of shutdown of the system of 0.052. The reduction of failure probability from 0.3 to 0.052, an 82% decrease, was impressive. Luke immediately introduced the doubling up of relays on all service calls, maintenance visits, and new installations until the poor-quality relays had all been disposed of.

It was noticed by her friends that Louise had a rather expensive new smart phone for Christmas that year!

PART VII

Big Data

I am one of the unpraised, unrewarded millions without whom Statistics would be a bankrupt science. It is we who are born, who marry, who die, in constant ratios.

—Logan Pearsall Smith

In the previous chapters, we have been concerned with small and large samples, the dividing line usually taken to be at about 30 data items. Now we need to discuss very large samples—not just somewhat larger, but enormously larger. The transition to what has become known as big data has not only introduced new methods and procedures but also created a new way of thinking about statistics. It has rapidly advanced from relying on limited sampling to a situation in which all of us, knowingly or unknowingly, are involved in providing vast amounts of data.

CHAPTER 22

Data Mining
Twenty-First-Century Gold Rush

Data mining is a means of producing predictive information from large amounts of data. It is one of the fastest growing methods of forecasting in the business world and is exciting in the prospects it offers for the future.

The Growth of Data

Storage of large amounts of data is not new: libraries have existed since ancient times. More recently, companies have kept details of suppliers, customers, and staff. Records of business transactions, of purchases and sales, of expenses and profits, and so on, were stored initially in books and files. Later, electronic storage on databases gave considerable savings in effort and space. Such data have traditionally been used to provide information regarding the past and present positions of the company, but not as a tool for forecasting. This situation has changed as databases have become much larger and computers have provided faster processing and greater storage capacity. The often-quoted *Moore's Law* says that computer capability doubles every two years or so. Without this phenomenal rate of growth, it would not have been possible to have the similar increases in the sizes of databases.

Databases have grown in two ways. If we visualize a database as essentially a two-dimensional table of data, the growth has been in the number of rows and the number of columns. Each row is an entry of new data, such as a new customer or a new sale or purchase. The numbers increase with time; and as storage becomes a decreasing problem, there is no pressure to eliminate older entries. The columns represent the variables: names, addresses, products, dates, etc. These have increased partly because, again, storage is no problem and partly because it has become easier to collect information. In retail activities, the scanning of barcodes on each item purchased allows the transaction to be recorded, along with other items in the same purchase, the time and date, and how the payment was made. If the purchase was paid for by the use of a store credit card, or if a loyalty card was presented, the customer's personal details can be recorded. The Internet has provided an enormous amount of data. Each click of a button or link adds to the store. Much of the information in databases has been accumulated simply because it became easy to collect and store it, not because it was seen to be needed.

Not only have databases grown, but the bringing together of many databases has produced data warehouses. A large company will typically have many databases. These might be at different company sites or used for different purposes at the same site. By linking the databases together, vast amounts of information are potentially available. In terms of computer storage, there are data warehouses as large as several petabytes. One byte is about the storage space of one character of text: a petabyte represents the information in all the books stacked along a bookshelf about 6,000 miles long.

The realization that not only could a great quantity of information be retrieved from data warehouses, but that it could reveal relationships between the different variables, gave rise to data mining. The revealed relationships could potentially provide a means of predicting future trends and opportunities.

The growth in available data accelerates each year. It is said that 90 percent of the data we had in 2013 did not exist three years previously. Onsite data warehouses became inadequate for the amount of data that large companies were accumulating. *Cloud computing*, in which the storage is undertaken by an external provider, came to the rescue. Organizations provided online storage and analysis of data for customers by using large networks of servers.

This was the start of what has become known as *big data*. There is no precise definition of big data: it means you have more data than you can handle yourself. For an organization such as Amazon or Facebook, that would be hundreds of petabytes, but it could be very much smaller for a small business. Big data could also be said to be data that cannot be handled by conventional database technology, either because there is too much of it or because it is unstructured.

Mayer-Schönberger and Cukier (2013) start their comprehensive account of big data with a useful indication of the amount of data involved. Google processes more than 24 petabytes of data per day. Facebook gets 10 million new photographs uploaded every hour, and users click a Like button or leave a comment nearly 3 billion times a day. Users of YouTube upload an hour of video every second. The number of messages on Twitter exceeds 400 million a day. Some estimates suggest that in 2013, about five exabytes of data were created in the world every few minutes (FT Reporters, 2013). This quantity is equivalent to the books on a bookshelf 30 million miles long.

Big data is often described in terms of three features: the three Vs. In addition to *volume*, there are considerations of *velocity* and *variability*. Velocity refers to the speed at which the data can be collected, stored, and analyzed and the findings applied. The data is from past transactions, and the conclusions need to be applied quickly if they are to be used to predict future events. The variability of the data is a characteristic that presents difficulties in the manner of storage and in the subsequent analysis. Numerical data is easily dealt with by traditional methods; but unstructured data involving text recognition, translation, voice recognition, video clips, and music is less easy to handle. A fourth V is sometimes included, referring to *veracity*. Clearly, truth and reliability are vital if results of analyses are to be utilized.

Because the amount of data is very large, testing the revealed relationships can be extremely reliable. The relationships can be tested using blocks of data that have played no part in their development. Of course, when the relationships are used to predict future events, there is still extrapolation. Anything may change in the future. It is important, therefore, to repeatedly revise the relationships and to apply the results without delay. For this reason, it is often better to make use of a readily obtained prediction rather than delay in searching for a more sophisticated one. Indeed, techniques have advanced from analyzing historical data to providing real-time results.

Data Warehouses

Data warehouses are produced by bringing together many databases of the traditional type, and we can look briefly at these to see how the assembled data warehouses differ. The traditional databases are transactional in that they allow operatives to input new data either automatically—from barcodes, for example—or manually. Operatives can also edit or delete data. Information from the databases is obtained by inputting appropriate queries.

The databases are *normalized*. This means the data are stored in many separate tables in order to ensure that any datum is stored only once. For example, the same supplier could be involved in many purchases, and it would be unwise to record the supplier's details repeatedly for each purchase. Errors could arise within the repeated entries, and a change of address would cause problems in updating. The result is that a separate table is used for supplier details. There are further stages involved in normalization to minimize anomalies and redundancies, and the final result is a multiplicity of tables linked in a fairly complicated network. The disadvantage of this kind of structure is that, when queries are required, the setting up and processing involved are relatively slow. The situation is acceptable when the database is not very large but becomes an increasing problem as the database grows.

Chapter 22 | Data Mining

The data from the databases are transferred to the data warehouse automatically and periodically. No data are added or altered piecemeal by operatives, so the normalized structure of the database can be largely abandoned. This allows a star structure of tables, as shown in Figure 22-1, which has fewer links between the tables. The central table, called the *fact table*, contains the numerical or descriptive data. The surrounding tables are allocated to the variables of interest, and each table links directly to the central fact table. The arrangement is designed to speed up the retrieval of information.

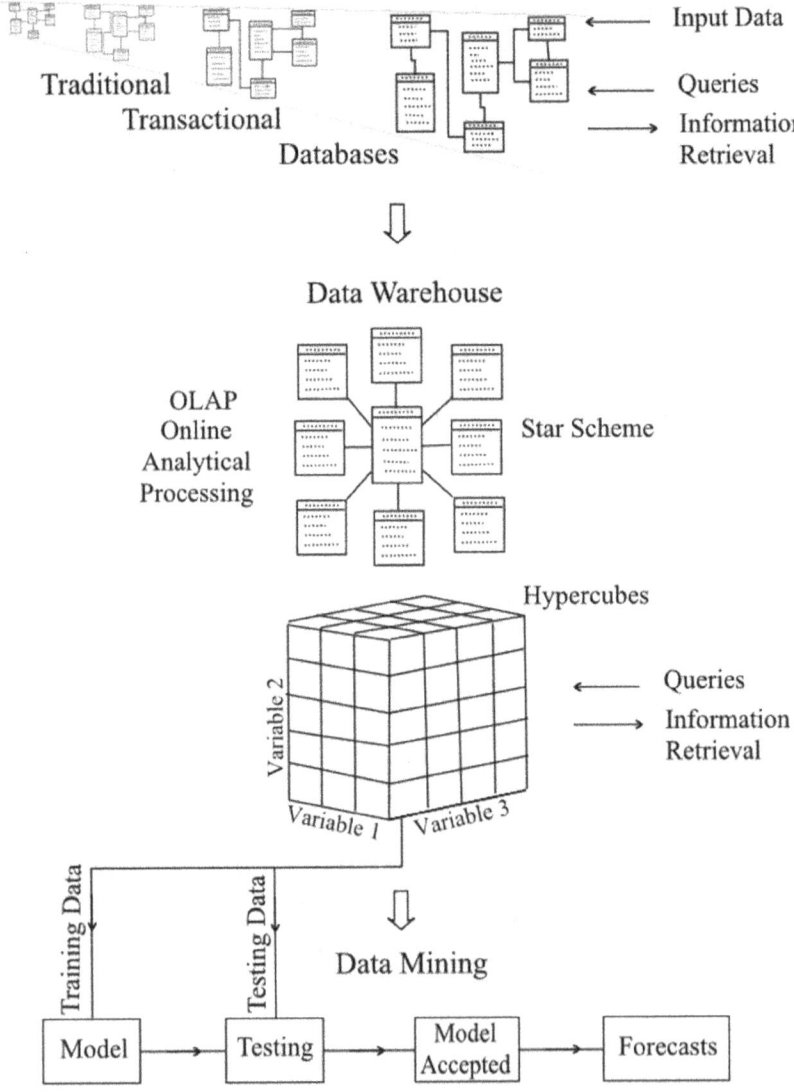

Figure 22-1. The development of data mining from traditional databases

In spite of these measures, the retrieval of information would not be acceptably fast without two further factors. One is the introduction of parallel processing of the data. A computer can do only one operation at once, though because it can do so very quickly, it may seem that it is multitasking. If the speed of processing is inadequate because of the vast number of steps to be performed, speed can be increased only by adding further computers or processors to work in parallel, simultaneously; and this is what has been done.

The second factor is the concept of *cubes* and *hypercubes* to allow automatic aggregation of data in readiness for retrieval. A diagram of a cube is included in Figure 22-1. Strictly speaking, it is a cuboid, as the sides are not of equal length; but the name *cube* has become the standard terminology. The three axes (sides) of the cube represent levels of three variables, and the cells of the cube contain the appropriate data. Summations can be carried out in the three directions at each level, and the aggregated values can be stored, ready for retrieval.

Thus, if we were interested in the sales of products in different outlets at different times, many of the totals we ask for would already be calculated and quickly obtained. We might want the number of an item sold in all outlets in 2011, say, and then request the total for a particular outlet in December 2011.

This example considers three variables only, but it is possible to set up hypercubes with many dimensions representing many variables. Unfortunately, it is not possible to draw them, even though it is no particular problem to define them mathematically as far as the computer is concerned.

In addition to aggregating totals, other readily calculated statistical indicators can be aggregated. Thus standard deviations and confidence limits can be made readily available, and also diagrammatic presentations of results, in the form of bar charts, for example.

Future Developments

The so-called *Internet of Things* is already with us to a limited degree, but its possible expansion is truly mind-boggling. Sensors can be attached to virtually anything to measure a range of properties and transmit data to a processing center. Details of any specified required action can then be transmitted to wherever the information is needed. Monitoring of engines and machinery in general has been around for some time, but current buzz is of domestic freezers that keep an inventory of their contents and signal when the stocks need replenishing. Flexible sensors fitted into clothing could detect when cleaning or replacement is required, or warn of a pickpocket or a lost bunch of keys. More important, and more feasible with present technology, is the proposal of benefits in health care by remotely monitoring patients in their own homes.

Two important advances that will eventually produce greater potential for big data are smaller devices for storage and processing, and faster processing.

The volume of space required to store or process a specified amount of data has decreased rapidly and currently halves every three years or so. Recent advances in nanotechnology are promoting research in manipulating units of storage at the atomic level. In 2012, IBM announced success in storing and retrieving 1 bit of data in the magnetic properties of just 12 atoms. Present technology requires about 1 million atoms per bit. In 2013, researchers from the University of Southampton, UK, demonstrated a laser method of achieving the storage of 360 terabytes of data on a small piece of fused quartz, a material that is exceptionally stable. Also in 2013, a team at Cambridge University stored 154 Shakespeare sonnets, a photograph, and a 26-second audio clip of Martin Luther King's "I have a dream" speech on a speck of synthetic DNA.

As size is reduced, the problem of electrical circuits overheating increases. This is because although the electrical currents are small, they are very close together, and local temperatures can be high. The use of optical fibers holds the promise of smaller devices, as the passage of light pulses along the fiber does not generate appreciable heat. However, the production of optical computers is still some way in the future.

With regard to the speed of processing, parallel arrangement of computers is the only way of increasing it at present. A major breakthrough is expected in the future, though how far away it is no one can say, when the first practical quantum computers appear. Because of the quantum behavior of elementary subatomic particles such as electrons and photons, it is possible for them to be in two states at the same time. This allows, in principle, a computer circuit to be free from the limitation that each unit must be on or off, registering one bit. Instead, the unit can remain in both states, referred to as a *qubit* ("quantum bit"). Parallel processing is potentially possible with such an arrangement, and much research is pursuing the possibility. We await the results with interest!

STOCKING UP FOR STORMS

Walmart had big data before anyone had heard of big data, and not only had it, but was using it to improve its business operations in ways that many companies would rush to follow in subsequent years.

Back in September 2004, Hurricane Frances was moving across the Caribbean and heading for Florida's east coast. Precautions were being taken. People moved to higher ground and prepared themselves as best they could.

Just three weeks earlier, Hurricane Charley had struck, and Walmart realized that in these difficult situations, shopping habits could be very different from usual. Executives could see that from the experience with Charley, it should be possible to predict demand and therefore supply goods in line with customers' requirements.

Even then, Walmart had some 460 terabytes of data stored on its computers. The data came from 3,600 stores in which about 100 million customers shopped each week. Checkout scanners recorded sales item by item.

The available data relating to Hurricane Charley was mined, and the results revealed the products that were required in quantities greater than normal. Electric flashlights, of course, were evident, as we would have expected. However, the top-selling item was beer. The product that no one would have expected to be on the list was strawberry Pop-Tarts. The increase in sales of these, prior to the hurricane, was not marginal but was in fact seven times the normal rate.

As a result of the analysis, deliveries of the predicted desirables were made to the Walmart stores in the path of Hurricane Frances, and it was reported subsequently that most of the goods stocked specially for the incident sold quickly.

CHAPTER 23

Predictive Analytics
It's Only Arithmetic!

The first step in interrogating the data for a possible relationship is the selection of a limited amount of data, called the *training data*, from which a model will be developed. The model is an idealized relationship, involving a number of variables, that is suggested by initial examination of the training data or by practical observations. Many different kinds of models are in use, having been drawn from different disciplines. *Predictive analytics* is essentially a statistical process in that the results obtained are not precise but are expressed in terms of probability. Thus, levels of reliability in terms of confidence limits are a feature. The various statistical methods that we have discussed in previous chapters have their use in setting up proposed models. In addition, techniques from studies of machine learning, artificial intelligence, and neural networks are in use. The development of new and improved models is an active area of research. The following sections are intended to give an indication of the kinds of models that are used and the way in which they work.

Simple Rules

A *rule* is an "if … then …" statement which may include few or many variables. We could have a rule, for example, that if an applicant for a mortgage is a self-employed plumber aged between 30 and 40 years, then it is 90% certain that he will not default on his payments. Rules are more appropriate when the variables are descriptive, although numerical variables can be dealt with by grouping values within defined limits as in the example quoted.

Chapter 23 | Predictive Analytics

The *1R* (One Rule) *rule* selects one variable from a number of possibilities on the basis of which variable gives the least number of errors. To illustrate the method, we will use the following data, which shows whether a particular item sells or not. We have data for 12 customers, male and female, on different days of the week at two different stores. This is an incredibly small sample but serves to illustrate the procedure:

Gender	Day	Store	Sells
Male	Saturday	A	Yes
Male	Sunday	A	Yes
Male	Saturday	B	Yes
Male	Weekday	B	No
Male	Sunday	A	Yes
Male	Saturday	B	Yes
Female	Weekday	A	Yes
Female	Saturday	A	No
Female	Sunday	B	Yes
Female	Saturday	A	No
Female	Sunday	A	No
Female	Weekday	B	No

For each variable, we note the majority result:

Gender	Male	5 out of 6	Yes
	Female	4 out of 6	No
	Total	9 out of 12	
Day	Weekday	2 out of 3	No
	Saturday	3 out of 5	Yes
	Sunday	3 out of 4	Yes
	Total	8 out of 12	
Store	A	4 out of 7	Yes
	B	3 out of 5	Yes
	Total	7 out of 12	

Gender is adopted as the variable for the rule because the number of total successes, 9 out of 12, is the highest of the three. So the rule is that the item sells if the customer is male but not if the customer is female.

With the use of simple statistics, the approach can be extended to produce several rules from the same data so that the effect of all the variables can be seen (Frank, 2009). The same data is set out differently here:

		Yes	No
Gender	Male	5	1
	Female	2	4
Day	Weekday	1	2
	Sat	3	2
	Sun	3	1
Store	A	4	3
	B	3	2
Total		7	5

We now express the Yes and No numbers as probabilities. Thus, 5/7, below, is the probability that when a sale takes place the customer is male. The fractions listed in the Total column are the probabilities of getting a sale or not in the whole of the data:

		Yes	No
Gender	Male	5/7	1/5
	Female	2/7	4/5
Day	Weekday	1/7	2/5
	Sat	3/7	2/5
	Sun	3/7	1/5
Store	A	4/7	3/5
	B	3/7	2/5
Total		7/12	5/12

These probabilities allow us to provide a rule for each of the various combinations of the variable levels by using the multiplication rule (the "and" rule) introduced in Chapter 3. For example, if we have a male on a weekday in store A, the relative probability of a sale is

$$5/7 \times 1/7 \times 4/7 \times 7/12 = 0.034$$

and the relative probability of no sale is

$$1/5 \times 2/5 \times 3/5 \times 5/12 = 0.020.$$

Note that these are not true probabilities in this form, as the two do not add to unity, but they are in the correct proportion so we can normalize the values to

Probability of a sale	= 0.034/(0.034+0.020) = 0.63
Probability of no sale	= 0.020/(0.034+0.020) = 0.37

The rule would therefore be that there would on balance be a sale, though the evidence is weak.

To take a further example, a female on a Saturday in store B leads to the following calculation:

Relative probability of a sale	= 2/7 × 3/7 × 3/7 × 7/12 = 0.031
Relative probability of no sale	= 4/5 × 2/5 × 2/5 × 5/12 = 0.545
Probability of a sale	= 0.031/(0.031+0.545) = 0.05
Probability of no sale	= 0.545/(0.031+0.545) = 0.95

There would be a greater degree of confidence in this rule than in the previous one.

The approach provides us with twelve rules, one for each of the twelve combinations of the levels of the three variables. Some rules will be more reliable than others. If it happens that the data contains contradictory entries, and this is likely in a reasonably large sample, the uncertainty in the derived rules will be greater.

There is a more serious problem with this simple technique. It will be recalled from Chapter 3 that for probabilities to be multiplied together in the "and" rule, the variables must be independent. It is likely that many of the variables in the database are not independent. In the above example it is likely that weekday shoppers are largely female. The effect of dependency between the variables is to bias the result. By multiplying the probability of the sale being to a female customer by the probability that the sale is on a weekday, we could be increasing the effect of the customer being female.

It is evident that a set of data can generate a large number of rules; and because of this, there is a danger of over-fitting. We previously discussed overfitting in relation to nonlinear regression, where we saw that it is always possible to obtain an equation that produces a curve passing through every point on a graph. Such an equation is of no practical use. Similarly here, we could end up with a set of rules that describes perfectly every situation represented in the training data. But the set of rules would then be merely an alternative representation of the training data and would have achieved nothing.

The usefulness of a rule depends on two characteristics: accuracy and coverage. As we saw above, *accuracy* can be expressed as the probability that the rule will give a correct result. *Coverage* indicates the relative occurrence of the rule in the database. In the data presented above, only one quarter of the data involves purchases during weekdays, so the coverage of rules involving such purchases is only 25%. Rules having high accuracy and high coverage are clearly desirable, but low-coverage rules can be extremely useful if each occurrence is very profitable.

More sophisticated methods are available for determining rules. A common feature is that they operate on a bottom-up procedure. The data is split on the basis of the levels of one variable giving two groups, say. A split on the basis of a second variable in a similar way gives four groups.

PRISM is a commercially available system that builds up rules by repeatedly testing and modifying the rule under construction.[1] It starts with a simple "if A then Z" rule, selecting A on the basis of the proportion of correct predictions. Improvement is obtained by selecting B in a similar way, giving "if A and B then Z." The procedure continues, bringing in C, D, E, etc. as required, until the rule is perfect. The resulting rules are numerous, and some will be contradictory. The ambiguities have to be dealt with, possibly by selecting on the basis of coverage.

Decision Trees

A decision tree is a well-known structure and is popular on account of it being very easy to follow. Figure 23-1 shows a tree built from the data we used in the previous section. At each stage in the tree, the data is separated according to a criterion—in other words, by answering a question. The aim is to ask the right question at each stage so that the data is separated appropriately in order to make useful predictions.

---

[1] PRISM is an acronym for "PRogramming In Statistical Modeling" (http://sato-www.cs.titech.ac.jp/prism/)—no relation to the United States National Security Agency's Internet server surveillance program.

Chapter 23 | Predictive Analytics

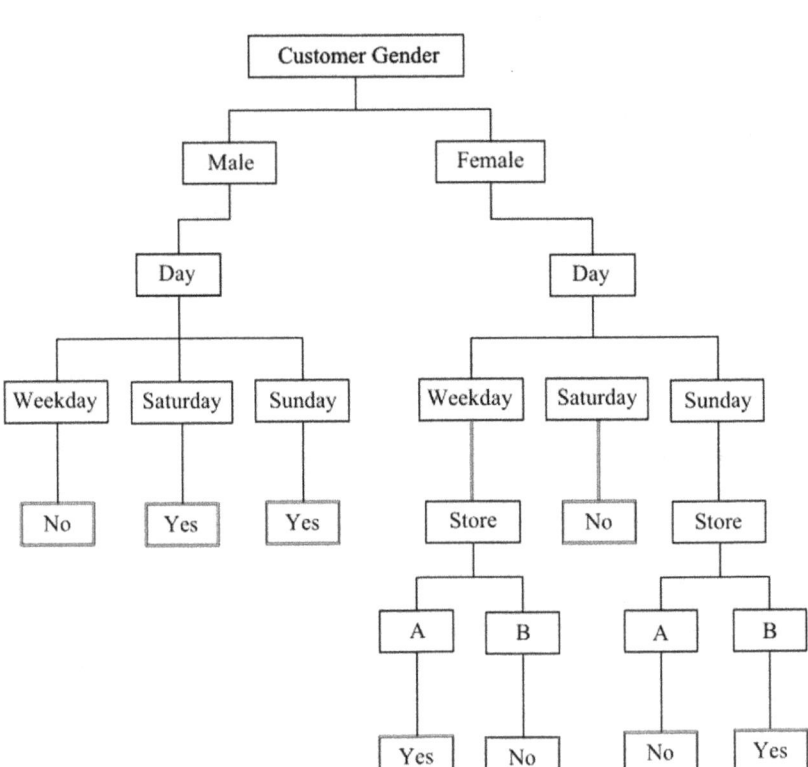

Figure 23-1. A simple decision tree

The key issue, therefore, is the choice of the best question to ask at each stage. *Classification and Regression Tree* (CART), which is a commonly used method, examines all possible questions and selects the best. The best is the one that decreases the disorder of the data; and for this reason the term *entropy*, which is a measure of disorder, is used. A complex tree is in effect constructed, but repeated validation at each stage and avoidance of over-fitting result in an efficient structure.

Another method is *Chi-squared Automatic Interaction Detector* (CHAID). As the name indicates, the Chi-squared test (Chapter 7) is used to decide which questions are to be asked to form the splits in the tree. Contingency tables are set up and, you will recall, the data has to be descriptive. Continuous numerical data can be grouped in categories in order to be dealt with. The trees, unlike the ones resulting from CART, can employ multiple splits, which leads to wider arrangements and eases interpretation.

Decision trees generate rules, but there is a difference between these and the rules obtained by the methods we looked at in the previous section. Decision trees work from the top down, searching for the best possible split at each level. For each record, there will be a rule to cover it and only one rule. In the example shown in Figure 23-1, taking each route from the top down will repeat the records that were used to build the tree. This is, of course, a case of overfitting, justified here in order to show the principle with a small amount of data.

Association

Each record in a database shows association between the variables at the specified values or levels. If we look back at the first record in the example data we used to illustrate the development of rules, we can see how this applies. We had "If male and Saturday and store A, then yes." Thus we have association between four variables in the record. In fact, we can break down the association to give many more associations in the form of rules:

> If male then Saturday
>
> If Saturday then male
>
> If male and Saturday then store A
>
> If male and Saturday then store A and yes
>
> and so on

A total of 50 rules could be stated on the basis of the associations revealed in this single record. This is a very large number; but, of course, it is unlikely that many of the rules would be of practical use. Because so many rules can be generated, it is necessary to have a rationale for weeding out the ones unlikely to be useful and for selecting productive ones.

The selecting is on the basis of accuracy and coverage. Accuracy will show the likelihood of the rule giving the correct answer, and coverage will indicate how often the rule is likely to apply.

We can use the full list of twelve records from the previous example to show how the procedure is applied. The number of levels included in the data is as follows:

Gender	Day	Store	Sells
2 levels	3 levels	2 levels	2 levels

The number of possible two-component groups—e.g., "Male, Saturday"—is 30.

The number of possible three-component groups—e.g., "Male, Saturday, A"—is 44.

The number of possible four-component groups—e.g., "Male, Saturday, A, Yes"—is 24.

Chapter 23 | Predictive Analytics

Note that these numbers are not readily apparent: They arise from summing the possible combinations of the levels of the variables.

We can reduce the number of groups of interest by considering coverage. Male and Saturday appear in three of the twelve records so coverage is 3/12, or 25%. Similarly, the following values are obtained by comparing the records with the complete set of combinations:

Coverage	2 components	3 components	4 components
0	0	12	15
1	6	19	6
2	12	10	3
3	9	3	0
4	2	0	0
5	1	0	0
Total	30	44	24

We might decide at this stage that it is worth considering only those groups with a coverage of 4 or 5, and make a further judgment on these on the basis of accuracy. The three selected groups are all two-component, so each group gives us two possible rules. These are as follows:

Coverage 5.	Male, Yes	
	Rule: "If Male then Yes"	Accuracy 5/6 = 83%
	Rule: "If Yes then Male"	Accuracy 5/7 = 71%
Coverage 4.	Female, Store A	
	Rule: "If Female then Store A"	Accuracy 4/6 = 67%
	Rule: "If Store A then Female"	Accuracy 4/7 = 57%
Coverage 4.	Store A, Yes	
	Rule: "If Store A then Yes"	Accuracy 4/7 = 57%
	Rule: "If Yes then Store A"	Accuracy 4/7 = 57%

Note that, if we had been considering groups with more components, there would have been many possible rules for each group because of the ways that the members of the group can combine on either side of the if-then statement. We mentioned that just one of the four-component groups gives rise to 50 possible rules.

It is worth pointing out that the rule having the highest accuracy with the maximum coverage—i.e., if the customer is male then the item sells—is the rule that we found using the 1R rule when we discussed simple rules.

It is very laborious working through the coverage of the groups and the accuracy of the rules by hand, even when there are few data—but it is, of course, a simple task for a computer program.

Clustering

Clustering is the grouping of data in such a way that the levels of the variables in each group are more similar than the levels of the corresponding variables in the other groups. Suppliers, for example, could be grouped according to the type of goods supplied, on their location, or on the value of goods supplied. Patients could be grouped according to their various symptoms. If any one of the variables was used for grouping, it is unlikely that the other variables would show an identical grouping. The aim is to establish which variable or combination of variables gives the optimum overall grouping.

Thus the manner of grouping is not decided at the outset. The grouping technique fixes the grouping, and the situation is referred to as *unsupervised learning*. There is no preconceived pattern to be imposed on the process, and it may not even be evident when the grouping is completed what the logic is that has fixed the optimum outcome. However, a decision has to be made as to how many groups would be desirable. Clearly, without some restriction on number, the optimum arrangement would be an enormous number of groups with one member in each. This would be a case of overfitting and would not serve any useful purpose.

The grouping progresses on the basis of the proximity of one record to another. The proximity is taken to be the distance separating the records. If we think initially of two variables, x and y, a two-dimensional graph would allow the plotting of each record, and the points might show clustering in some regions—small x and large y, say. The distance between each pair of points would be the length of the straight line joining the two points, and this would be a measure of the association. For three variables, we could draw a three-dimensional graph, and the required measures would again be the lengths of the lines joining the points. Although we cannot draw beyond three dimensions, there is no problem mathematically in having an unlimited number of dimensions, to cater for all the variables, and calculating the distances between the various points. The grouping is optimum when the distances within the groups are minimized and the distances between the groups are maximized. The variables, of course, have different units (dollars, weeks, meters, etc.), and an equivalence has to be defined to allow the distances to be calculated. The equivalence could be on the basis of the range of each variable.

Many variations in the iterative routine work toward the optimum grouping. The group centers, which may be initially chosen randomly, are modified according to the resultant calculated distances. Some systems work from an initially defined number of groups and allow subsequent changes to the number. Other systems produce a hierarchy of groups, either starting from a coarse grouping and breaking it down, or starting from the separate records and progressively reducing the number of groups. Although we have referred to an optimum grouping in the discussion, it should be noted that no system can guarantee a perfect unique solution.

Closely related to clustering is the *nearest neighbor technique*. The concept of proximity in multidimensional space is again used; but rather than attempting to rationalize the data by grouping, the aim is to establish similarities between records to provide predictions. It is thus a form of supervised learning, unlike clustering.

Neural Networks

A *neural network* is so named because of the similarity to the network of neurons in the brain. The analogy is extended to speaking of the neural network as being able to learn in the way the brain learns, although the analogy should not be taken too far. It is not correct to assume that the neural network is a black box that can simply be fed the data, which it will learn to process and then output the answers. Nonetheless, neural networks emerged from the discipline of artificial intelligence, whose aim there is to mimic the working of the brain.

The similarity is apparent in the schematic layout of the neural network. It consists of nodes connected by links so that data moves from input nodes to the output node. Figure 23-2 shows schematically a simple arrangement to illustrate the principle.

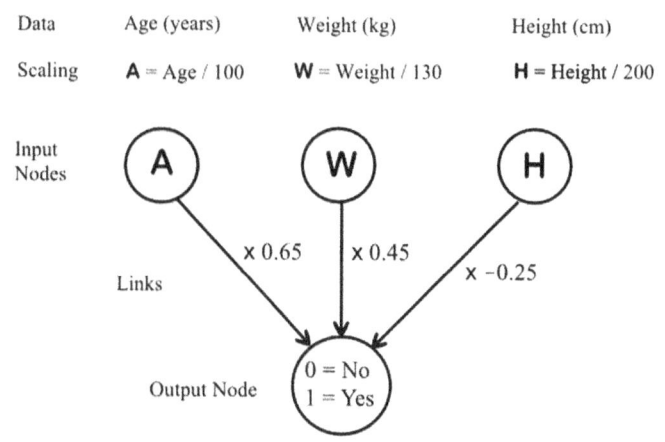

Figure 23-2. A simple neural network illustrating the principle

There may be a layer of nodes between the input nodes and the output node, and these are referred to as *hidden nodes*. There is an input node for each variable, and the input data is usually scaled to give a value between 0 and 1. The link to the next node will perform a multiplication on this value before passing it on. The multiplication is effectively a weighting factor. The next node will be accepting several values from other input nodes. The added values will then be passed to the output node. The number of nodes to be used has to be decided at the outset, and the number of links may number tens of thousands. The output data are numerical and must be converted back to the required variable values or levels.

The records from the training data are fed in one at a time, and the output is compared with the required value. The error leads to modifications in the link weights, large errors producing large changes and small errors producing small changes. As the process continues, the link weights are revised and the system approaches acceptable outputs short of overfitting. For overfitting can present problems, particularly as it is difficult to see how the processing has taken place. Indeed, there is no logical approach to the process that one could describe, other than that the arithmetic contrives to get the right answers. Because of the complexity in understanding the processing and the required conversion of the output, there have been moves to package neural network programs to suit specific applications.

The simple arrangement of Figure 23-2 has just three input nodes accepting the age, weight, and height of a subject we wish to assess for the possibility of hospital treatment being required in the following year. Each of the input variables (within reasonable limits) is scaled to give a value between 0 and 1. The output is 0 for no and 1 for yes. A set of possible link-weighting values is shown. The outputs for three example sets of input data can be seen to lie between 0 and 1 and may be interpreted as the probability of hospital treatment being required.

Ensembles

With a choice of many different methods and models to use, it is difficult to know at the outset which is likely to be the best for a given set of data. However, it has been found that combining two or more different models can give better predictions than any of the individual models. In effect, a voting procedure is taking place.

These combined models are referred to as *ensembles*. A remarkable finding with regard to ensembles is that that they do not appear to suffer from overlearning (Siegel, 2013: 148-149). *Overlearning*, or *overfitting* as I have described it previously, arises when the analysis has become sophisticated to the point where it is describing the data so fully that the results are sensitive to the detailed features of the data. Siegel likens this advantageous property of ensembles to the behavior of crowds. A group of people guessing, and averaging the result, will usually get closer to the right answer than most of the individuals. Watson, the IBM computer that beat two expert contestants on the US television quiz show *Jeopardy!* in 2011, was programmed with an ensemble of hundreds of models.

MANHOLE CONTROL

New York City has more than 94,000 miles of underground electrical cables. Manholes provide access to the cables, and periodic faults cause manhole fires, explosions, and smoking manholes. There is an enormous amount of data relating to past events and inspections dating back to the 1880s. The records have been collected and stored by Consolidated Edison, the power utility serving New York City.

In order to radically update the company's inspection and repair programs, it was decided that the past records could be used to identify the manholes most at risk of a serious incident and those least at risk. This would improve the reliability of the system and public safety.

A team consisting of scientists from Columbia University and engineers from Consolidated Edison took on the task of processing the available data. The raw data was very varied, in that it included records of past events, engineers' records of dealing with events, inspection records, manhole locations, and cable data. Because of the length of time over which information had been collected, there was no consistency in the manner of recording or even in the identification of locations and components.

The raw data was processed to provide an accurate event history over a ten year period for each manhole and a potential 120-year cable history. Combined with inspection results, the data was processed by machine learning algorithms to produce a predictive model aimed at predicting failures of individual manholes.

The model was tested using training data. Data from three boroughs were used: Manhattan, Brooklyn, and the Bronx. Predictions for 2009 were obtained from earlier data and compared with the actual manhole explosions and manhole fires. The top 10% of manholes predicted to have a serious event contained 44% of the ones that did have a serious event, and the top 20% contained 55% of the ones that had a serious event.

The exercise was seen to be of great value in providing a better procedure for electrical grid inspection and repair that could improve public safety and energy reliability. The project demonstrated the value of using all available data, no matter how mixed and confused—big data, not just a selection. The project also demonstrated the value of collecting data for future prediction and not simply as historical records.

CHAPTER 24

Getting Involved with Big Data
What Would You Like To Know?

In the previous chapter, we saw that the procedures for extracting information from big data can be quite simple. In contrast, the setting up of computer systems for applying the procedures to large amounts of data in a reliable and rapid manner requires considerable expertise. Following a summary of the potential applications of big data, we will discuss how businesses can become part of this new and exciting development.

Applications

There is hardly any area of human activity where big data is not having an impact, and the trend is likely to continue at an increasing rate. Any summary of the applications tends to end up as a very long list of examples.

Search engine providers such as Google and Yahoo were probably the first to use big data methods. Documents are located by text retrieval on the basis of keywords and similarities.

Retail sales provide appropriate applications. Large supermarkets, such as Walmart and Tesco, have incredible amounts of data, as each sale of each item is recorded via the barcode. It may be that certain items tend to be sold together in the same transaction, or certain items may sell better at certain times. Pricing and stocking can be altered to take advantage, and sales promotions can be timed appropriately. If purchases are made with the use of store cards or loyalty cards, the items sold can be linked to the customer and thus to the purchasing habits of customers in relation to gender, age, address, and so on. Tesco is installing face-scanning devices in its petrol stations to register the gender and likely ages of its customers.

If a retailer sends vouchers and details of products or special offers by post to potential customers, most of the approaches, of course, will produce no result. But there will be stored data available showing the features of those that have been successful in the past. It thus becomes possible to target customers of the type that are most likely to respond positively. Sales of financial products such as credit cards, insurance, or investment opportunities can be targeted in a similar way. The strategy can be applied by all kinds of businesses involved in sales. Amazon, for example, sells a large proportion of its books by sending recommended titles to customers on the basis of previous purchases. Retention of customers can be improved by identifying and targeting those most likely to depart.

The Internet can provide large amounts of data for the retailer. Every click on a website gives information not only about a sale but also about initial interest in a product, repeated interest, an immediate rejection, a rejection when the price is revealed or when the delivery charge appears, and so on.

Companies providing transport of mail, parcels, and goods generally make use of barcodes and thereby potentially accumulate much data. Information regarding the nature of the goods, their sources, and their destinations allows future resource needs to be anticipated and areas of growth to be identified. Scheduling of deliveries and route planning can be improved.

Financial institutions and banks can use historical data to identify the level of risk in offering loans to particular customers or even the possibility of fraud. The spending habits of credit card customers can reveal those most likely to be interested in other financial products. Fraud detection can also be employed by tax authorities and those responsible for government contracts. Possible fraudulent insurance and warranty claims can be detected.

In the fight against crime, areas more likely to be hit by specific kinds of criminal activity can be highlighted. Likelihood of terrorist attack can be determined, and the probability of repeat crimes from prisoners pending release can be quantified.

Product development is an expensive process, and if the product misses its target market, the result can be disastrous. Traditionally, sampling of prospective customers has been used to establish the desirable features of proposed products; but sampling is expensive, and its effectiveness is limited by the size of the sample. Predictive analytics offers the possibility of relating features of the new product to its desirability among specific types of customer as revealed by previous purchasing patterns.

Medical records show the characteristics and previous medical histories of patients who later develop specific conditions. Relationships can be identified that give warnings of possible future ailments. Similarly, the efficacy of different treatments may be compared. Successful predictions have included the spread of influenza, occurrence of premature births, and risk of death while undergoing surgery. Diagnosis of breast cancer has been improved.

The control of industrial processes reaps benefits such as reducing the number of defective items and avoiding operational problems. Faults in machinery and large industrial installations are often preceded by symptoms such as vibrations, temperature rises, or noises of various kinds. Information that distinguishes between serious and benign symptoms or that indicates a probable time to breakdown is of considerable value. Preventive maintenance scheduling can benefit from such information. In a similar way, the diagnosis of problems with cars and other vehicles from reported symptoms of malfunctioning is possible. The likelihood of failure of electric cables, washing machines, and office equipment has been predicted.

In the energy industries and utilities, monitoring of customer usage with regard to time and location can improve the efficiency of generation and supply.

Charities have benefited from increased donations and lower costs by targeting likely donors. People most in need of help have also been located.

Governments hold vast amounts of data. Some of it is centrally held—census and tax records, for example—and is usefully processed, but much of it is spread over numerous local sites. Combining data stores offers the potential of useful predictions in infrastructure planning, crime fighting, and health care, for example.

Mayer-Schönberger and Cukier (2013) and Siegel (2013) describe many applications in fascinating detail. The latter has a summary table of 147 specific cases of predictive analytics that have produced benefits, usually financial, for the organizations involved.

It should be noted that some of the applications mentioned above are not, strictly speaking, forecasting. Rather, they are searching for answers that are known, by someone somewhere, at the present time. Search engines, for example, locate information that already exists, though for the user the information is for future use. In the case mentioned in the preceding chapter of Watson's success in playing *Jeopardy!*, the answers to the factual questions were of course known in advance to the contest producers, and Watson's task was to determine those answers from the information contained in its few terabytes of disk storage.

AIRCRAFT CRAFT

Rolls Royce has risen from a position of financial difficulties in the 1970s to being a successful global company. It is the world's third largest maker of aircraft engines and the second largest maker of large jet engines. About half of wide-bodied passenger jets and a quarter of smaller aircraft under production are powered by Rolls Royce engines. Also important is its business in marine engines and in the energy industries.

A major factor in its success story has been the collection and application of data. Its jet engines are fitted with monitoring systems that collect temperatures, pressures, flows, rotational speeds, and vibration levels at various locations within the engine. The successful series of Trent engines can be fitted with about 25 sensors. Signals from the sensors are collected during takeoff, climb, and cruise and are transmitted to the company's headquarters in Derby, via radio or satellite link, during each flight of the aircraft. Any unusual engine conditions trigger additional transmissions.

At Derby, the collected data is analyzed automatically using algorithms based on neural networks. Unusual features are studied by skilled engineers to obtain a diagnosis on which decisions can then be made. It may be necessary to notify the maintenance team at the destination airport that there is a need to undertake checks or, alternatively, to give assurance that the engine performance is satisfactory. Either way, the procedure leads to fewer delays and improved passenger safety and satisfaction. Gradual deterioration of an engine can also be identified and inspection schedules agreed on after discussions with the operating company. Sudden changes in engine performance may require more immediate examinations which, again, can be programmed to suit the operator's options without compromising safety. The procedures have led to improved working lives for the engines.

Rolls Royce's utilization of data puts it in a commanding position when it comes to the servicing side of the business. When it sells an engine, it is effectively selling a service for the life of the engine. It would be difficult for another company to break into this corner of the market.

The Big Players

Chapter 1 started with matters that could be handled with pencil and paper. Subsequent chapters concerned calculations that require a pocket calculator, a spreadsheet, and eventually computer packages. This chapter reaches a stage when it is time to get assistance from experts. In spite of what you may have read or been told, handling big data is not easy. The subject is full of new terminology and much jargon, and the procedures require knowledge of programming and other specialized subjects.

The best-known technology for handling big data is probably *Apache Hadoop*, which was developed by Yahoo in the period 2006 to 2008. It is now an open source data-storage framework that can handle 10 to 100 gigabytes of data and above (Dumbill, 2012). It uses a file system—the *Hadoop Distributed File System* (HDFS)—which is distributed among numerous servers. In real time, it can capture, read, and update large amounts of unstructured data such as social media, clicks, event data, and sensor data. In fact, Hadoop can accept any kind of data, either for processing or long-term storage. There is much replication and redundancy in the system so that server failures do not cause problems.

Hadoop is not a single defined entity but rather an evolving ecosystem embracing numerous auxiliary modules and programs.

Moving data is expensive, so the data processing is carried out where the data resides, though the tasks are distributed to the numerous servers. The processing is by means of *MapReduce*, which was originally developed by Google. The "map" in *MapReduce* refers to the filtering and sorting of the data, and the "reduce" refers to a summarizing process. Results of processing are returned to HDFS. MapReduce is used in other databases apart from Hadoop.

Java programming for loading files in HDFS is tedious. The task is made easier by the use of Pig or Hive. *Pig*, from Yahoo, is a programming language that can deal with semi-structured data. *Hive*, from FaceBook, is a module that allows Hadoop to be used as a data warehouse, accepting queries in a form similar to SQL, a commonly used programming language for database management.

Improvements in data access are provided by HBase, Sqoop, and Flume. *HBase* is a database that runs on top of HDFS providing billions of rows of data for rapid access. HBase can also be used as a source and destination of data for MapReduce. *Sqoop* imports data from databases into Hadoop via HDFS or Hive. *Flume*, from Google, is used for streaming data into HDFS.

Zookeeper organizes the various components, while *Oozie* manages the work flow. *Mahout* is a machine learning component.

Other add-ons are used in Hadoop applications, some of which are part of Hadoop and some of which are not. It can be seen from this brief summary that the choice of components for particular circumstances is a job for experts.

The kinds of problems suitable for analysis are varied. Risk exposure can be modeled for the banking and insurance industries. Customer churning can be analyzed. Product preference for Internet sales, retailing generally, advertising, and manufacturing can be identified. Sensor data is used to predict failures for telecommunications operators and data centers. Search analysis for Internet commerce and websites is dealt with. Threats, fraud, and spam can be identified. There is a facility for data from any kind of business, on which various analyses can be tried in the search for patterns.

Apache Cassandra is another open source database management system. It was developed at Facebook, and its long list of important users, such as Twitter and Netflix, vouches for its versatility and reliability. It is a distributed system that automatically replicates to multiple centers. There are no single points of failure. In comparison with Hadoop, it scores in dealing with real-time data and less so in terms of analysis.

Large companies such as Google, IBM, Microsoft, HP, Amazon, SAP, and Oracle make use of open source facilities, together with their own components, to offer a commercial service to businesses. Cloudera, Teradata, 1010data, Fujitsu, Kognitio, Microstrategy, and NetApp are some of the other companies offering similar services.

CREDIT WHERE IT'S DUE

In 2009, United States legislation was introduced to protect subprime borrowers. It required lenders to provide fairer rates and fees for their borrowers. Traditionally, lenders in the subprime market depended on rates and fees for their profitability.

Premier Bankcard is an organization providing credit cards for individuals with damaged credit histories. The company is committed to helping individuals receive a second chance with regard to their finances. The new legislation created problems. On the one hand, if too many cards were issued to customers who had not reached a satisfactory level of creditworthiness, there would be losses and pressure from the regulators. On the other hand, too much emphasis on those well on their way to recovery would lead to loss of customers moving to prime card issuers.

Premier decided to employ SAS Business Analytics to identify its best customers: the ones who lie between the two extremes and are on their way to creditworthiness. Aspects also covered in the analyses were rapid response to customer and market data, by daily review and daily forecasting, and fee justification analyses to meet the regulations.

The approach had the beneficial feature of being based on Premier's own data, and not on imported data or performance models.

The characteristics of the ideal customer were identified. It was found, for example, that the best customers had been with Premier on average for five years. Knowing who the best customers are means they can be targeted effectively. Customer retention was seen to be important. Retaining one customer for an extra month makes for Premier nearly $12. An improvement of 10% in retention strategy produced $4.8 million.

The results achieved a revenue increase of $50 million, an additional $24 million from better customer retention and a decrease of $1 million is losses resulting from fraud.

The Smaller Options

With so much publicity being given to big data, many small and medium-sized businesses that are not involved are considering whether they should be, and perhaps wondering what they want from it. Most of these businesses will not have in-house expertise and will rely on commercial providers of big data analysis. Furthermore, some such businesses will avoid involvement with the big players described above and will prefer to start in a more modest way. There are dozens of consultants who can provide big data analysis. These are the smaller players, employing between a handful of staff up to several hundred. Often they will have developed modules to carry out fairly standard analyses of data that can be readily adapted to the needs of different businesses, and this clearly reduces the costs involved. The Internet, of course, provides details of these consulting firms, often with example case studies of their activities, and there are useful directories that include comparisons between the various firms. SourcingLine is a company that provides rankings and reviews of consulting companies in the field of big data analytics.

A business looking for assistance will have plenty of data in the form of past records of activities, and this would clearly be the starting point. Analysis of the existing data is likely to be straightforward, although it is important to be clear about what questions are being asked of the data. It will not be exciting, for example, to be told that more sandals are likely to be sold in the summer and more boots are likely to be sold in the winter.

The initial results will provide a useful introduction but will be of limited value unless new data is fed into the system as it becomes available. Streaming of real-time data is essential for rapid application of the results of analysis and effective control of business operations. If the company recognizes a particular problem for which a solution is required, the data analysis firm can develop a suitable model or use one that it may have available. The model can be supplied and staff trained to use it, applying it as necessary to different sets of data. Any additional problems will require further appropriate models.

So far, the business is probably not locked into an agreement with the solution provider and can shop around, but further analysis of a more advanced nature may require commitment to a more permanent arrangement. The business will supply full details of its activities and request a system that will produce modules capable of analyzing and dealing with predictions and problems. Included will be predictions of potential future problems and the ability to deal with them as they emerge.

With regard to the choice of data analysis company, the same criteria will apply as when engaging any other form of consultancy. Issues such as cost, extent of lock-in, time scale, and security of data will be considered. There may be advantage in commissioning a company that has assisted or specializes in similar businesses and may have appropriate expertise and software readily available.

TURNING CHURNING TO EARNINGS

2degrees is a New Zealand mobile telecommunications company. In four years it won one million customers in the face of long-installed competition.

With no in-house expertise but with a recognition of the value of big data analysis, the company decided to enlist the help of 11Ants Analytics. *Churning*—that is, customers leaving and moving to a competitor—was a specific problem. Indeed, it is a common problem in the mobile phone business. 2degrees chose to use a suite of modules consisting of a customer analyzer, a customer-churn analyzer, and a model builder. The use of these available modules from 11Ants Analytics meant the work could go ahead quickly.

The results were impressive. Customers most at risk of churning were identified by time on network, days since last top-up, whether the customer number was ported or not, customer plan, and calling behavior over the previous 90 days.

An experiment was run for three months. The customers were classified by their likelihood of churning. The 5% of customers chosen by the 11Ants Churn Analyzer as being most likely to churn were found to be 12.75 times more likely to churn than customers chosen at random. The 10% of customers chosen as most likely to churn were found to be 7.28 times more likely to churn than customers chosen at random.

2degrees could now focus on those most likely at risk and reduce its expenditure on retention marketing. The smaller number to be targeted meant that the retention offers could be more generous. The added benefit was that customers not likely to churn were not annoyed by messages asking them to stay. Also, offers could be aligned to the customers' usage—minutes for talkers, texts for texters.

CHAPTER 25

Concerns with Big Data
The Small Print

Beneficial innovations always have downsides. We accept large numbers of deaths from road accidents and occasional air disasters for the benefits of faster travel. We accept the risk of nuclear war for the benefits of nuclear energy. Big data is not unique in having problem areas—but we are not contemplating the end of civilization!

Security

Data is valuable. It is not just the conclusions from the processed data that have an economic value; the data itself has value because of its potential. OpusData, for example, is a company that sells access to data from The Numbers, a large database containing financial details on about 15,000 movies and 18,000 actors, directors, and technicians. Traditionally, of course, there have been small businesses that have collected data, fairly laboriously, to supply to industries and media organizations for a fee. As the stores of data get larger, the value increases exponentially. It has even been suggested that data stored by a company should be attributed monetary value, which should then be added to the company assets.

In the wrong hands, data can result in serious problems for companies, governments, and the general public. Security is therefore paramount, particularly when a business entrusts its data to cloud storage and processing by a different company. Although companies take extreme precautions, it is well-known that leaks of sensitive material have always occurred and still do occur. They can range from a laptop being left on a train to hackers accessing bank accounts. In February 2014, Barclays Bank reported that it was investigating the loss of several thousand files containing customers' details. It had been alleged that the files, which included the customers' attitudes to risk, had been sold to rogue City traders.

Some businesses, understandably, are put off from engaging with big data because of concerns about security.

Privacy

Each one of us is extensively documented by data stored by various organizations. Our details are hoovered up in the course of purchases, online searches, social website interactions, financial transactions, and so on. In addition, there are the more obvious traditional repositories of our data, such as electoral registers, employment and tax details, passports, and licenses of various kinds.

In the past, when the data lay dormant, it didn't really matter; but now, without consent, the data is being used for various purposes that the general public is only just beginning to realize. Sometimes the data are anonymized by the removal of names and addresses, but numerous studies have shown that it is often a trivial analytical task to identify individuals by combinations of particular characteristics in the records and links to other databases.

Amazon's privacy policy puts no restrictions on its collection of data from users of Kindle devices and reserves to Amazon the freedom to sell analytics of readers' reading profiles and habits with third parties, such as publishers. The potential for systematic and abusive privacy invasion is a mounting concern for many consumers as the use of big data increases. Information about what we are doing and what we are likely to do in the future is becoming widely known. A downside of this is that we risk being judged on the basis of probability rather than actuality. A thirty-year-old artist who listens to jazz and lives in a poor part of town may be unfairly denied a bank loan on the basis of a prediction of risk from the bank's big data analysis. An office worker who has no interest in sport and regularly eats fast food may be denied medical insurance. It was reported that American Express fixed credit card limits based on where a customer shopped, regardless of the individual's record (Croll, 2012).

Suggestions of what the future holds are reminiscent of George Orwell's *1984*. A married couple chatting at home discover a difference of opinion. The television is switched on and is listening to their conversation. The information is processed, and in the next commercial break an advertisement for marriage counseling appears (FT Reporters, 2013). More serious are issues of possible legal action against individuals on the basis of probability. Should a person be released from prison if there is an 85% chance of his committing a further murder? Should drivers of fast cars be fined for potential speeding? These kinds of questions may sound rather silly, but we can already be prosecuted for actions justified on the basis of probability. Not wearing a seat belt while driving and smoking in public buildings are examples of actions that are harmful—but only potentially harmful.

We are beginning to see reactions to the invasion of privacy by big data. Cornell University students are opposing New York State's cooperation with inBloom, an organization that seeks to assemble student details in a single database. Of the nine states that joined with inBloom, eight have already pulled out because of issues of privacy. The *Washington Post* reported that there is considerable concern regarding the activities of the Patient-Centered Outcomes Research Institute (PCORI), which is collecting detailed patient medical records. The aim is to assemble the data for analysis to improve diagnosis and treatment.

There has been similar opposition in the UK. The introduction of identity cards has been strongly objected to. CCTV cameras have had to be removed in a suburb having a high population of ethnic minorities, after public protests. In 2012, the government introduced legislation for the compulsory destruction of samples and profiles of DNA, and fingerprint records, of anyone arrested but not convicted of a crime.

The UK government's plan to bring together the vast amount of medical records that the National Health Service holds, at present scattered among the various doctors' offices, health centers, and hospitals, has been put on hold. The concern is that the data will be sold to health companies and academics to bring about major improvements in health care, but breaches in security may result in patients being identified. It is somewhat ironic that it was a British nurse, Florence Nightingale, famous for her nursing of the sick and wounded in the Crimean War, who pioneered the recording of medical data in the 1850s in order to improve treatments.

Skills Shortage

Handling big data requires special skills. The new kind of scientist—the data scientist—needs to be a combination of statistician, software programmer, and graphics designer. Some knowledge of machine learning, artificial intelligence, and neural networks is required. Furthermore, he or she needs to have an understanding of business goals and have good communication skills. The latter are particularly important because the findings of big-data analysis may have to be put to senior executives who have their own prejudices regarding what action is needed.

Though we can expect to produce sufficient data scientists in the future, there is currently a shortage. This is well illustrated by the experiences of the Institute for Advanced Analytics of North Carolina State University (Burlingame and Nielson, 2012: 60–61). In 2012, there were 38 candidates for the Master of Science in Analytics (MSA). Among them, they had 591 job interviews with 54 employers. One or more offers went to 97% of them, and 47% had three or more offers. Offers covered a range of businesses: banking, finance, consulting, energy, gaming, health care, Internet, pharmaceuticals, research, and software.

A New Concept

The arrival of big data has changed the way we think about statistics. Traditionally, statistics has embodied the principles that correlation should not be taken to imply a causal relationship and that extrapolation is a necessary evil. In the applications of big data analysis, these basic doctrines are not denied, but they are circumvented. The existence of a causal relationship is not considered relevant. If association between variables exists, it can be used to advantage provided that we act quickly, the rapid response minimizing the problem with extrapolation. Some statisticians have reservations about big data on these grounds. Others have noted that with so many conclusions being derived from the sets of data, a proportion will be simply wrong. This point was made in previous chapters when discussing multiple comparisons from the same data.

It has been well recognized in the sciences that the act of observing affects to some extent that which is being observed. Experimental designs and investigative programmers take this into account where possible. When the experiment is of limited range, the consequences of this feedback are of little significance, but the applications of big data can affect large numbers of people. If shoppers appear to prefer Jispo cornflakes, techniques will push the sales even higher. Eventually other brands disappear and everyone eats Jispo. Are we beginning to create a population of puppets, all behaving in identical ways?

The handling and processing of big data is probably the most radical innovation in the practice of statistics that has been seen for a very long time. I can visualize the day when statistics based on modest samples becomes referred to as "traditional statistics" or even "classical statistics."

2214 AD

World Chief Theo 7D9G gazed intently as the 3D screen around him faded. He had witnessed the interviews of two candidates for the position of Deputy World Chief. The interviews, of course, had not been conducted by him, but by PASWRD. The indispensable PASWRD, or, to give it its full name, Processor and Storage of all World Real-time Data, could interview and do many other things better than any human could.

But there was a problem. PASWRD had reported that there was, in the foreseeable future, no difference, economically or socially, whichever of the two candidates were to be appointed. Theo would have to decide, but he did not anticipate the task with enthusiasm—it was rare for him to have to make a decision without assistance.

He thought for a moment, and then his wrinkled face began to show signs of a smile developing. He mentally set PASWRD into forecasting mode and focused on the image of the control panel. He inserted the hypothetical appointment of candidate A and began to steer a precisely defined path moving into the future. Forecasting beyond five years was not permitted, but Theo was able to override the restriction. Eventually satisfied, he stopped the projection. He then repeated the process with the assumption that candidate B was appointed.

When the second projection had been completed, he thought his chair into a relaxing position. He had the answer. Candidate B would be appointed as the new deputy. And Theo would have an extra four-year's life span—plus or minus, of course, the uncertainty, which PASWRD reported as 2.3 years at a 95% confidence level.

APPENDIX A

References and Further Reading

References

Blastland, Michael and Andrew Dilnot. 2007. *The Tiger That Isn't: Seeing through a World of Numbers*. London: Profile Books.

Burlingame, Noreen, and Lars Nielsen. 2012. *A Simple Introduction to Data Science*. Wickford, RI: New Street Communications, LLC.

Croll, Alistair. 2012. "What to Watch for in Big Data." In *Big Data Now: 2012 Edition*. O'Reilly Media, Inc. (Kindle book).

Dumbill, Edd. 2012. "Apache Hadoop." In *Planning for Big Data*. O'Reilly Media, Inc. (Kindle book).

Frank, Eibe. 2009. "Algorithms: The Basic Methods." In *Data Mining: Know It All*, by Chakrabarti, Soumen, et al. Burlington, MA: Morgan Kaufmann.

FT Reporters. 2013. *Decoding Big Data: The Corporate Race to Turn Information into Profit*. London: The Financial Times Ltd. (Kindle book).

Haigh, John. 2003. *Taking Chances: Winning with Probability*. Oxford: Oxford University Press.

Hand, David J. 2008. *Statistics: A Very Short Introduction*. Oxford: Oxford University Press.

Havil, Julian. 2008. *Impossible? Surprising Solutions to Counterintuitive Conundrums*. Princeton: Princeton University Press.

Kahneman, Daniel. 2012. *Thinking Fast and Slow*. London: Penguin.

Mayer-Schönberger, Viktor and Kenneth Cukier. 2013. *Big Data: A Revolution That Will Transform How We Live, Work and Think*. London: John Murray (Publishers).

Seife, Charles. 2010. *Proofiness: The Dark Arts of Mathematical Deception*. New York: Viking Penguin.

Siegel, Eric. 2013. *Predictive Analytics: The Power to Predict Who Will Click, Buy, Lie, or Die*. Hoboken, NJ: John Wiley & Sons.

Smith, Charles O. 1976. *Introduction to Reliability in Design*. Tokyo: McGraw-Hill Kogakusha.

Taverne, Dick. 2005. *The March of Unreason: Science, Democracy, and the New Fundamentalism*. Oxford: Oxford University Press.

Watts, Duncan J. 2011. *Everything Is Obvious: How Common Sense Fails Us*. Crown Business. New York: Crown Publishing Group, Random House Inc.

Wiseman, Richard. 2007. *Quirkology: The Curious Science of Everyday Lives*. London: Macmillan.

Further Reading

Hair, Joseph F., Jr., Rolph E. Anderson, Ronald L. Tatham, and William C. Black. 1998. *Multivariate Data Analysis*. Upper Saddle River, NJ: Prentice-Hall Inc.

Huff, Darrell. 1991. *How to Lie with Statistics*. London: Penguin.

Levin, Richard I. and David S. Rubin. 1998. *Statistics for Management*. Upper Saddle River, NJ: Prentice-Hall, Inc.

Lindley, D.V. and W. F. Scott. 1995. *New Cambridge Statistical Tables, Second Edition*. Cambridge: Cambridge University Press.

McClave, James T., P. George Benson, and Terry Sincich. 1998. *A First Course in Business Statistics*. Upper Saddle River, NJ: Prentice-Hall Inc.

Moroney, M. J. 1953. *Facts from Figures*. Middlesex, UK: Penguin Books.

Porkess, Roger. 2005. *Web-linked Dictionary of Statistics*. Glasgow: Collins.

Reichman, W. J. 1964. *The Use and Abuse of Statistics.* Harmondsworth, UK: Penguin.

Rumsey, Deborah. 2003. *Statistics for Dummies.* Hoboken, NJ: Wiley Publishing Inc.

Sapsford, Roger, and Victor Jupp, eds. 1996. *Data Collection and Analysis.* Thousand Oaks, CA: Sage Publications Ltd.

Taylor, Sonia. 2001. *Business Statistics.* New York: Palgrave Macmillan.

Upton, Graham, and Ian Cook. 2006. *Oxford Dictionary of Statistics.* Oxford: Oxford University Press.

Index

A

Analysis of variance (ANOVA)
    data analysis, 158–159
    F-test, 161
    interactions, 162
    pooling, 162
    ratio test, 161
    residual variance, 159, 161
    significant and non-significant effect, 163–164
    single factor effects, 161
    variability, 160

Applications, big data
    Aircraft, 246
    charities, 245
    disk storage, 245
    fraud detection, 244
    Google and Yahoo, 243
    industrial installations, 245
    medical records, 245
    predictive analytics, 245
    product development, 244
    resource and growth, 244
    retail sales, 243

Autocorrelation
    regression line, 200
    seasonal effect, 200
    simple linear regression analysis, 200
    temperature, 198
    weather and climate, 198

Averages, normal distribution
    central clustering effect, 68
    expectation, 69
    mean value, 68
    median, 69
    mode, 69

B

Bar chart format, 47

Big data
    businesses, 249
    churning, 250
    cloud storage, 251
    communication skills, 253
    computer systems, 243
    economic value, 251
    extrapolation, 254
    health care, 253
    medical insurance, 252
    modules, 249
    monetary value, 251
    nuclear energy, 251
    numerous studies, 252
    organizations, 252
    PASWRD, 255
    PCORI, 253
    players, 246–248
    radical innovation, 254
    real-time data, 249
    statistics, 254
    traditional statistics, 254

Index

Binomial data, 34
Binomial distribution
  description, 186
  population proportion, 186
  probability, 186–189
Boilfast, 21

C

CART. See Classification and regression tree (CART)
Categorical data, 33
Certainty
  common sense, 5
  earthquake, L'Aquila, 3
  fast thinking, 5
  health and safety legislation, 4
  proofs, 4–5
  reasoning/calculation, 5
  seismologists, 3
  traditional British game, conkers, 4
CHAID. See Chi-squared Automatic Interaction Detector (CHAID)
Chi-squared Automatic Interaction Detector (CHAID), 234
Classification and regression tree (CART), 234
Clustering, analytics
  equivalence, 237
  neighbor technique, 238
  optimum grouping, 238
  unsupervised learning, 237
  value of goods, 237
Cluster sampling, 30
Conditional probability
  counterfeit coins, 19
  defender's fallacy, 20
  description, 18
  political debates and advertising, 20
  prosecutor's fallacy, 19
Confidence intervals, 136
  population mean, 85
  population variance, 84
  standard deviation, 84
  standard normal distribution, 85
  Student's-t, 86
  t-distribution, 86
Control charts
  description, 205
  sampling by variable (see Sampling by variable)
  Shewhart charts, 205
Correlation coefficient, 135

D

Data mining, 156
  big data, 222
  cloud computing, 222
  computer storage, 222
  data warehouses (see Data warehouses)
  Hurricane Charley, 227
  Hurricane Frances, 227
  Internet of Things, 225
  monitoring, 225
  Moore's Law, 221
  nanotechnology, 226
  parallel processing, 226
  sale/purchase, 221
  Walmart, 227
Data warehouses
  barcodes, 223
  cubes and hypercubes, 225
  disadvantage, 223
  fact table, 224
  parallel processing, 225
  supplier, 223
  traditional databases, 224
Decision trees, analytics
  CART, 234
  CHAID, 234
  overfitting, 234–235
Defender's fallacy, 20
Descriptive data, 33–34. See also Nominal data
Drugs, 122
Dummy variable, 156
Duplicate ranks, 112–113

E

Electric kettles, 21
Error
  power, 116
  probability, 117
  risk, 118
  Type I error, 115–116
  Type II error, 115–116
Exponential distribution, 191–192
Exponential smoothing
  description, 201
  double, 202
  single, 202
  triple, 202
  weighting factor, 201–202
Extrapolation
  forecasting, 180
  law of supply and demand, 181
  Malthusian Doctrine, 179
  population growth, 179
  satellite circling, Earth, 181
  statistics, 179

F

Female/male staff ratio, 103

G

Geometric distribution
  chance of throwing, 193
  cumulative values, 194
  door-to-door salesman, 193
  exponential, 193
  house calls, 194

H

Hadoop distributed file system (HDFS), 247
HDFS. *See* Hadoop distributed file system (HDFS)

I, J

Index numbers, 34, 42
Irregular relationships
  financial data, 143
  FTSE 100 financial index, 142
  FTSE 100 index, 143
  product-moment correlation coefficient, 144
  profits growth graph, 145
  seasonal variations, 144
  temperature, 146
  time, 146
  to-and-fro variability, 142

K

Kendall rank correlation coefficient, 113

L

Latin and Graeco-Latin squares
  in agricultural experiments, 164–165
  arrangement, 164
  dependent variable, 164
  independent variable, 164
  medical studies, 165
  variances, 164
  Youden square, 166
Levels of significance
  confidence limit, 90
  degrees of freedom, 90
  hypothesis testing, 89
  null hypothesis, 89
  one-tailed/two-tailed, 90
  pedantic convention, 90
  populations, 89
Linear relationships
  confidence intervals, 136
  correlation between two variables, 129–130
  correlation coefficient, 135
  definition, 127
  degree of judgment, 135
  degrees of reliability, 136
  error bar, 136
  independent variable and dependent variable, 133
  linear regression, 131–132
  negative correlation, 128
  non-parametric, 137
  numerical data, 136–137
  one-tail and two-tail test, 136
  positive correlation, 128
  prediction intervals, 136

Index

Linear relationships (cont.)
   product-moment correlation coefficient, 135
   scale changing and origin suppressing, 129
   slope, 131
   straight-line conversion graph, 128
   usefulness of correlation, 135
   vertical error bar, 136
Line graphs, 126

M

Marketing strategy, 132, 146
Mean, numerical data
   F-test, 96
   null hypothesis, 95
   population variance, 97
   production line, 95
   Single Value, 97
   standard deviation, 95
   standard error, 95
   t-distribution, 96
   Z-score, 95, 97
Multidimensional contingency tables
   independent variables, 167
   interaction, 169
   logit analysis, 169
   log-linear, 169
   log odds, 169
   residual variability, 169
   three-way contingency table, 167
Multiple regression
   canonical correlation, 158
   dependent variable, 157
   descriptive variables, 158
   dummy variables, 158
   multiple coefficient of determination, 158
   non-linear relationships, 157
   total population, 158
   t-test, 158
Multivariate analysis of variance (MANOVA)
   Hotelling-Lawley trace, 170
   Pillai-Bartlett trace, 170
   Roy's maximum root, 170
   variance ratio, 170
   Wilks's lambda, 170
Multivariate data
   ANOVA (see Analysis of variance (ANOVA))
   cluster analysis, 175–176
   computer processing, 156
   conjoint analysis, 170–171
   customer evaluation, 175
   data mining, 156
   dependent variable, 156
   dummy variable, 156
   factor analysis, 175
   independent variable, 156
   interdependence methods, 175
   Latin and Graeco-Latin squares (see Latin and Graeco-Latin squares)
   multidimensional contingency tables (see Multidimensional contingency tables)
   multiple discriminant analysis, 176
   multiple regression (see Multiple regression)
   principal components analysis, 175
   proximity maps
      correspondence analysis, 171
      degrees of association, 173
      descriptive variables, 171
      multidimensional scaling, 173
      two-way contingency table, 171–173
   structural equation modeling, 174–175

N

Neural networks
   brain, 238
   hidden nodes, 239
   nodes, 238
   overfitting, 239
   probability, hospital treatment, 240
   weighting factor, 239
Nominal data
   bar chart format, 47
   bar chart, medals won by sports club, 52–53
   categories, 47
   chi-squared test, 150–152
   contingency test, 150
   misleading visual comparison, two factories outputs, 51
   patients, treatment, 149
   pictograms, 50–51

Index

pie chart and bar chart, same data, 49
pie charts and stacked bar chart,
    same data, 49–50
Venn diagrams, 52
visual effects, origin suppressing and
    vertical axis breaking, 47–48
Yule's coefficient of association, 150
Nonlinear relationships
    computer packages, 141
    data transformation, 138–140
    linear relationship and, 141
    polynomial regression, 141
    polynomials, 141
    raw data, 138–140
    re-plotted data, 137
    Titus–Bode law, 140
    trial-and-error procedures, 141
Normal distribution, 184–185
    averages, 68–70
    central clustering, 62, 66
    chi-squared distribution, 67
    chi-squared test, 68
    confidence intervals, 57, 84–86
    construction, grouped data, 60
    continuous curve, 64
    cumulative frequency, 57–58
    data collection, 65
    data sample, 55
    degrees of freedom, 67
    density, frequency, 64
    discrete, 58
    estimated population, 83–84
    frequency and cumulative
        frequency, 60
    Gaussian curve, 62
    goodness-of-fit test, 66
    grouped data
        bands, 75
        bar chart and histogram, 77
        continuous data curves, 77
        frequency density, 77
        relative frequency, 76
    height distributions, 62–63
    histograms, 56
    interquartile, 61
    Kolmogorov-Smirnov test, 68
    measurement repetition, 64
    median, 60

ogive, 59
pooling and weighting (see Pooling and
    weighting, normal distribution)
positive and negative distributions, 61
probability distribution, 55
random fluctuations, 65
relative frequency, 56
spread of data (see Spread of data,
    normal distribution)
standard normal distribution, 64
statistical tests, 68
theoretical distribution, 65
total number, data, 55
uniform distribution, 67
Null hypothesis, 109
    numerical data, 92
    one-tailed and two-tailed test, 92
    standard normal distribution, 92
    statistical significance, 91
    test statistic, 92
Numbers
    negative numbers, 37–38
    prefixes, 35–37
    prefix nano, 36
    standard index form, 35
    superscripts, 36
Numerical data, 34
    ANOVA, 99
    bands, 94
    degrees of freedom, 100
    managing, 94, 101
    mean (see Mean, numerical data)
    normal distribution (see Normal
        distribution)
    null hypothesis, 93, 101
    one-tailed and two-tailed tests, 94
    pooled variance, 100
    population variance, 99
    sample variance, 100
    standard deviations, 94
    Student's-t, 98
    t-values, 98
    variances, 96, 98

O

One-sample runs test, 32
Ordinal data, 149, 152

Index

P

Patient-Centered Outcomes Research Institute (PCORI), 253
PCORI. See Patient-Centered Outcomes Research Institute (PCORI)
Percentages, 40–42
Pictograms, 50–51
Players, big data
    Apache Cassandra, 248
    database management, 247
    HDFS, 247
    MapReduce, 247
    sensor data, 247
Poisson distribution, 189, 191
Pooling and weighting, normal distribution
    food, 82–83
    household index, 79
    Laspeyres index, 79
    overall mean waiting time, 78
    Paasche index, 79
    Retail Price Index, 79
    Simpson's paradox, 80–81
    weighted mean, 78
Prediction intervals, 136
Predictive analytics
    accuracy and coverage, 233, 235
    clustering, 237–238
    database, 235
    decision trees, 233–234
    degree of confidence, 232
    development, rules, 235
    electrical grid inspection, 241
    machine learning algorithms, 241
    neural networks, 238–240
    nonlinear regression, 233
    numerical variables, 229
    One Rule (1R), 230, 237
    overfitting, 233, 240
    PRISM, 233
    probability, 229, 231
    relative probability, 232
    set of combinations, 236
    total column, 231
    training data, 229, 233
Probability
    "and"/"or" rule, 15
    "both", "either" and "neither" events, 16
    coin tossing and dice throwing, 14
    conditional (see Conditional probability)
    definition, 13–14
    failures, 17
    multiplication of, 15
    statistical calculation, law psychologist, 15
    tree diagram, various outcomes, 16–17
Product-moment correlation coefficient, 135
Prosecutor's fallacy, 19

Q

Quota sampling, 30

R

Ranks
    Kruskal-Wallis test, 111
    Mann-Whitney U-test, 109
    nonparametric, 109
    ordinal data, 109
    two-tail test, 110
    value, 110
    Wilcoxon matched-pairs rank-sum test, 111
    Wilcoxon rank-sum test, 109–110
Raw data, 126
    description, 33
    descriptive data, 33–34
    distribution, 34
    format of numbers (see Numbers)
    index numbers, 34, 42
    numerical data, 34
    percentages, 40–42
    rounding, 38–40
Regression, 197–198
Reliability
    alarm bells, 212, 217
    description, 211
    distributions, 216
    practical complications, 217

Index

principles
    chain links, 212
    data, 216
    machines and systems, 211
    probability, wire rope, 211
    reliance, 213
    series and/or parallel, 214–215
    sprinkler system, 213–214

Repeated measurements, sampling, 27

Resampling methods, 31

Rod Craig, Jenson's Switches, 21

Rounding, raw data, 38–40

S

Sampling
    cluster, 30
    databases, 30
    data sequences, 31–32
    problems
        arrangement problems, 26
        hedgehog population, 26
        monthly profits, company, 25
        older respondents, 27
    quota, 30
    repeated measurements, 27
    resampling methods, 31
    sequential, 30
    simple random, 27–28
    stratified random, 29
    systematic, 28

Sampling by attribute, 207–208

Sampling by variable
    cumulative sum or CuSum chart, 208
    diameter, steel tubes, 205
    expressions yield, 207
    warning and action limits, 207

Sequential sampling, 30

Simple random sampling, 27–28

Single proportion
    binary measure, 104
    binomial distribution, 104–106
    null hypothesis, 104
    values of probability, 104
    Z-score, 104

Spearman rank correlation coefficient, 112

Spread of data, normal distribution
    height, 75
    probabilities, 73–74
    quartiles, 70
    standard deviation, 70–71
    total area, curve, 72
    variance, 72

Standard index form, 35

Storks and birth rates
    America, 122
    astrology, 121
    Copenhagen, 122
    drug, 122
    Germany and Netherlands, 122
    medical treatment, 122
    science and technology, 121
    Southern hemisphere, 123
    statistics, 123
    vehicle, 121

Stratified random sampling, 29

Structural equation modeling, 174–175

Systematic sampling, 28

T

Time series
    autocorrelation (see Autocorrelation)
    copper and brass, 203
    exponential smoothing (see Exponential smoothing)
    Lawton plumbing supplies, 203
    regression, 197–198

U

Uncertainty
    6-card sample, 12
    customers, 10
    mathematical procedures, 10
    measurements, 9
    opinion polls, 8
    population, 11
    raw data, 9

Uncertainty (cont.)
   reliability, 8
   science and technology disciplines, 9
   shoppers, 10
   statistical investigations, 7
   US State Department, 8
   Wabash country, 8
   Wikipedia, 9
Uniform distribution, 183

V

Venn diagrams, 52

W, X, Y

Weibull distribution, 195

Z

Z-score, 109

Get the eBook for only $10!

Now you can take the weightless companion with you anywhere, anytime. Your purchase of this book entitles you to 3 electronic versions for only $10.

This Apress title will prove so indispensible that you'll want to carry it with you everywhere, which is why we are offering the eBook in 3 formats for only $10 if you have already purchased the print book.

Convenient and fully searchable, the PDF version enables you to easily find and copy code—or perform examples by quickly toggling between instructions and applications. The MOBI format is ideal for your Kindle, while the ePUB can be utilized on a variety of mobile devices.

Go to www.apress.com/promo/tendollars to purchase your companion eBook.

All Apress eBooks are subject to copyright. All rights are reserved by the Publisher, whether the whole or part of the material is concerned, specifically the rights of translation, reprinting, reuse of illustrations, recitation, broadcasting, reproduction on microfilms or in any other physical way, and transmission or information storage and retrieval, electronic adaptation, computer software, or by similar or dissimilar methodology now known or hereafter developed. Exempted from this legal reservation are brief excerpts in connection with reviews or scholarly analysis or material supplied specifically for the purpose of being entered and executed on a computer system, for exclusive use by the purchaser of the work. Duplication of this publication or parts thereof is permitted only under the provisions of the Copyright Law of the Publisher's location, in its current version, and permission for use must always be obtained from Springer. Permissions for use may be obtained through RightsLink at the Copyright Clearance Center. Violations are liable to prosecution under the respective Copyright Law.

GPSR Compliance
The European Union's (EU) General Product Safety Regulation (GPSR) is a set of rules that requires consumer products to be safe and our obligations to ensure this.

If you have any concerns about our products, you can contact us on

ProductSafety@springernature.com

In case Publisher is established outside the EU, the EU authorized representative is:

Springer Nature Customer Service Center GmbH
Europaplatz 3
69115 Heidelberg, Germany

www.ingramcontent.com/pod-product-compliance
Lightning Source LLC
LaVergne TN
LVHW040734250326
834688LV00031B/285